EARLY MEITEI HISTORY

Religion, Society and the Manipur *Puyas*

EARLY MEITEI HISTORY

Religion, Society and the Manipur *Puyas*

RENA LAISRAM

AKANSHA PUBLISHING HOUSE
NEW DELHI-110002 (INDIA)

AKANSHA PUBLISHING HOUSE
4649-B/21, Ansari Road
Darya Ganj, New Delhi - 110 002
Ph.: 23263193 / 9811582579 / 09435116718
Telefax: 011-23263193
Email: ektabooks@yahoo.com
www.akanshapublishinghouse.com

Early Meitei History: Religion, Society and the Manipur Puyas

First Published 2009
ISBN 978-81-8370-163-1
Reprint - 2020

PRINTED IN INDIA

Published by Akansha Publishing House, New Delhi and Printed at Aryan Enterprises, Delhi.

To

My Parents

Contents

	Preface	ix
	Acknowledgements	xiii
	List of Illustrations	xv
1.	Introduction	1
2.	Social Organization	31
3.	The Meitei Pantheon	66
4.	Rituals and Ritual Specialists	124
5.	*Lai Haraoba* and other Festivals	156
6.	Conclusion	196
	Maps/Illustrations	205
	Appendices	211
	Glossary of Meitei Word(s)/ Term(s)	228
	Bibliography	235
	Index	253

Preface

Histories are powerful instruments which provide memories and perspectives on identities of people. To be able to tell the story of communities, particularly under circumstances where the usual archives do not exist - is how the discipline of History renews and maintains itself. Situated as it is, the erstwhile kingdom of Manipur inevitably formed a link between India and South East Asia, a factor of some importance in understanding its historical developments. To find the kinsmen of the ancestors of the Meiteis, we must look to the present neighbouring tribes many of whom show affinity in areas such as dialect, customs, beliefs and appearances.

An analysis of the traditional religion, religious values and precepts are crucial to understanding most aspects of Meitei history. The chief interest is that they give insights into social relationships, state formation, property and inheritance among others. Clans and lineages played a significant part in the Meitei society thereby forming the basis of the various stages of development of Meitei philosophical thought resulting in the emergence of the cult of ancestor worship. The religion passed through a long process of evolution of the Meitei society and survived even after Vaisnavism was declared the state religion of Manipur in the 18th century A.D. It is important to note that it is the social organization that has sustained the traditional Meitei religion. Therefore, even till today when the Meiteis call themselves Hindus, the cult of ancestor worship runs as a lively undercurrent with a harmonious synthesis of *tulsi* veneration and Sanamahi reverence in every Meitei home.

Beginning the discussion with a background to the study of early Meitei history, *Chapter 1*: **Introduction,** outlines the scope, sources and historiography. Ancestor worship of the Meiteis has attracted much attention but little research. There are some works available but these are in the nature of references in general works on Manipur or part of a history of Meitei religion. One of the reasons for the comparative lack of work on the subject is the unavailability of the *Puyas* for a long time since majority of them have been in the custody of individuals in the aftermath of the '*Puran Meithaba*' (Burning of the *Puyas*) in 1732 A.D. However, these texts, which are roughly comparable to the class of Sanskrit literature called *Puranas*, and are held with great reverence by the people could not be exhumed totally. The result is that what remained in the personal custody of individuals have become the only remnants of the rich tradition. The chapter includes a discussion on the *Puyas* relating to script, dating, classification, preservation etc.

Chapter 2: **Social Organization,** examines the theoretical framework and conceptual foundation that sees the functional role of religion in primitive societies. The principalities that constituted the Meitei confederacy formed the backbone of the social organization in the form of the *salais* (clans) and this system has sustained the cult of ancestor worship in Manipur. *Chapter 3:* deals with the **Pantheon of Gods,** its classsification and the Meitei creation myths. Ancestor worship is often, though incorrectly, subsumed in the more general category of cults of the dead. Without entering into definitional discussions, it is nevertheless important to state that death is dealt with in the framework of ancestor worship, but only at its fringes. **Rituals and Ritual Specialists** ensure the continuance of the relationships between ancestors and descendents at various levels of the family, sub-clan and clan and this is discussed in *Chapter 4*. *Chapter 5*: **Lai Haraoba and Other Festivals**, showcase the living tradition of the Meiteis. Community rituals and the observance of the traditional festivals mirror the entire Meitei world-view. The purpose of the festivals is to integrate the Meitei community and this takes place either actually or through recreating legends and myths. *Chapter 6*: **Conclusion**, reviews the historical processes that shaped the development of ancestor worship in particular and early Meitei history in general. The chapter argues that the social organization, the state and the ancestor cult reinforce one another. In tribal based societies such as that of the Meiteis, religious organization is inseparably connected with the social structure because it arises out of it and justifies it. The continuity of the lineage system has been a successful mechanism for incorporating a diversity of clan groups where each maintained its identity in a relationship of juxtaposition to each other. It also helped in preserving the identity of the Meiteis as an ethnic community.

This book is a concerted attempt towards presenting an objective reconstruction of the religion and society in early Meitei history. The focus is on ancestor worship, the root of Meitei philosophy and life and upon which the society is founded. Studies undertaken so far have been inadequate in terms of handling the mass of manuscripts called *Puyas* which are the only major written source for the study. It may be mentioned here that the floating oral tradition was codified around the 15th century A.D. which coincides with the coming of the *Brahmanas* to Manipur. A study of the *Puyas* encounters the vexing problem of separating the myths from facts and locating the historical in the myriad of legends, traditions, folklore and narratives. Notwithstanding the existence of reliable historical material alongside mythical narrative, the problem has been the treatment of the *Puyas* by majority of scholars as authentic historical records *per se*.

This study attempts at a fresh approach to treatment of the subject. It integrates critical study of the *Puyas*, experiences of the living tradition of the Meiteis, archaeological evidence and secondary data sources to comprehend the subject from a wider perspective. The book will serve its purpose if it contributes towards a meaningful interpretation of the history of the Meiteis. Contemporary Meitei society presents a picture of social restlessness with increasing attention being drawn to questions of identity, ethnicity and nationality. The book is also aimed at contributing towards discourses on the issues affecting Manipur society. It is hoped that the study will provide a more perceptive understanding of the past without which history will have little meaning for the present and the future.

Acknowledgements

Many people have helped me in the course of my work. I take this opportunity to express my appreciation for the same. I owe immense gratitude to Professor J.N. Phukan, formerly Honorary Director, Indian Council of Historical Research, North East Regional Centre, Guwahati and Professor Kunal Chakrabarti, Centre for Historical Studies, Jawaharlal Nehru University, New Delhi, whose valuable suggestions, comments on the subject and experience in related fields have benefited me immensely.

The collection of *Puyas*, the major source for this study was a tedious and arduous experience since majority of them have been in the custody of individuals in the aftermath of the '*Puran Meithaba*' (Burning of the *Puyas*) in 1732 A.D. However, due to revivalism in the recent past, there has been an attempt by both individuals and organizations alike to unearth the *Puyas*. Among the individuals who extended cooperation in collection of data, I would specially like to thank Pandit N. Khelchandra Singh, former Keeper of Records, Manipur State Secretariat Library for giving me access to his personal library, perhaps the single largest collection of *Puyas* by any individual. Dr.Y. Mohendra Singh also made me available some rare *Puyas* for which I am particularly thankful. I owe a special thanks to Huidrom Sunita Devi who taught me the archaic *Meitei Mayek* script which has been of crucial importance in handling the *Puyas*. I express my thanks to the authorities concerned of various libraries for their cooperation in facilitating my use of the same. They include Manipur State Archives, Manipur State Museum Library, Manipur University, Mutua Museum and Manipur State Central Library in Manipur. I also utilized library facilities in New Delhi in Jawaharlal Nehru University, Indian Council of Historical Research, National Museum, Archaeological Survey of India, National Archives, Nehru Memorial Library and Ratan Tata Library at Delhi University.

I will be failing in my duty if I do not acknowledge those who provided me with helpful insights into the history of the Meiteis. I am obliged to K. Mangi Maiba and Pandit N. Ibochouba of *Pandit Loisang*, Oinam Manikchand of Lainingthou Sanamahi Temple Board, Ibomcha Singh, *Pena* singer, J.N. Dance Academy, Imphal, Pandit N. Khelchandra Singh and Dr. Y. Mohendra Singh. There were many other individuals and institutions who contributed towards my deeper understanding of the living traditions of the Meiteis in the course of my field study. Since it will be exhaustive to list them, I shall only keep it in grateful remembrance.

My parents Laisram Gopal Singh and Rajkumari Kadambini Devi have been my greatest strength. As the *Piba* of the Laisram *sagei* and a descendent of the Ningthouja *salai* respectively, I have been fortunate to have had their invaluable support for discussions, helpful criticism and advice.

I record my indebtedness to my husband Jeevan whose constant inspiration has helped me to see this study through. I must also mention my young sons Bani and Kris whose computer skills came to use in some trying times.

And finally, I express my appreciation to Akansha Publishing House, New Delhi for the keen interest evinced towards publication of the book.

RENA LAISRAM

Guwahati, Assam
October 2008

List of Illustrations

MAPS

1. Map of Manipur Showing Clan Principalities 205

2. Map of Manipur Valley Showing Clan Principalities 206

CHARTS

1. Social Structure and Sacred Symbols 207

2. Social Hierarchy 208

3. The Meitei Pantheon as Exemplified in the Creation Myth 209

4. *Salai Apokpas* (Clan Ancestors) 210

1

Introduction

Manipur, situated in the extreme East of India, preserves a religion rich in mythology and colourful in rituals. Manipur, meaning 'the land of the gems' is a Sanskritized name given to the land when the Meiteis i.e., the people of the plains adopted Vaisnavism as a state religion in the 18th century A.D. *Sanamahi Laikan* records the official naming of the land as Manipur during the reign of King Garibniwaz (1709-1748 A.D.).[1] Previous to this, Manipur, the land has been recorded by other names in the *Puyas*.[2] The earliest names by which it was known include Meitei Leipak and Poireinamthak Saron Pung. This land acquired different names in the four human ages of Meitei history viz; Tilli Kokton Ahanba in *Hayi Chak*, Mirai Pongthoklam in *Khunung Chak*, Hana Semba Konna Loiba in *Langba Chak* and Muwapalli in *Konna Chak*.[3]

Located between longitudes 93°6′ E and 94°48′ E and latitudes 23°47′N and 25°41′ N, Manipur formed an important link, culturally and otherwise between India on one side and South-East Asia on the other.

Manipur borders Myanmar (formerly Burma) to its East and South-East. To the North lies Nagaland and to the West lies Assam, while in the South-West it borders Mizoram.

Manipur is called Kathe by the Burmese, a variant of Kase of the Shans, Mekle by the Assamese while according to Col. McCulloch, the Bengali name for the state is Moglai.[4]

The importance of tracing the origin of the Meitei peoples in a study of their religion and society can hardly be overemphasized. To find the kinsmen of the ancestors of the Meiteis, we must look to the present neighbouring tribes many of whom show affinity in areas such as dialect, customs, beliefs and appearances.

The kingdom of Manipur first emerges from obscurity as a neighbour and ally of the Shan kingdom of Pong, which had its capital at Mogaung.[5] The earliest reliable information of the country comes from a Shan account, quoted by Pemberton, dated 777 A.D., describing the visit of Samlong, a brother of the King of Pong.[6]

Attempts have been made in the past to locate the Meitei group of people in the map of the mass of Mongoloid tribes. Grierson tries to seek the relationship of the Meitei language and the language spoken by the hill tribes in the state and beyond it. He suggested that the Meitei language falls into the Tibeto-Burman group but expressed some doubt in placing it in the Kuki-Chin sub-division.[7]

It will be worthwhile to examine some of the theories put forward by various scholars. B.C. Allen suggests that "North West China between the upper waters of the Yang-tse Kiang and the Hoang-Ho was the cradle of the Indo-Chinese race, and that from the starting point successive waves of emigrants entered Assam and India. The first to arrive were the Mon Annam, who are found in Annam and Cambodia, but who have left a colony in Assam in the shape of the Khasis. A second wave of emigration brought the Tibeto-Burmans, the ancestors of the Bodo tribe, who colonized the valley of the Brahmaputra and occupied the Garo, Tippera and a portion of the Naga Hills. Another branch came southwards down the Chindwin, settled in the Chin Hills, and were compelled by the pressure of population to move northwards into Cachar, Manipur and even into the Assam range".[8] The Tai or Siamese branch of the Indo-Chinese peoples, called Shan by the Burmese, according to Max Muller were the first to migrate from their original seat in Central Asia towards the south and to settle along the rivers Mekong, Menam, Irawadi and Brahmaputra.[9]

'It was Samlongpha, the brother of Sinkhampha, the King of Pong who conquered and subdued the surrounding countries of Kachar, Tippera, Manipur and Assam'.[10] For B. H. Hodgson "in the Moitai of Manipur, we have the combined appellations of the Siamese Tai and the Kochin Chinese Moy".[11]

Luce studying the Meitei language notes that the Sak language once spread over the whole of North Burma from Manipur perhaps to Northern Yunnan. Luce further states that this area was possibly the fabled 'kingdom of Pong' of the later Shan and Manipur manuscripts.[12] Phayre believes that the term 'Pong' is not known to the Burmese. It appears, according to him, to be the name by which the country of the Upper Irawadi is still called in Manipur.[13] Dun writes that the 'Shan Kingdom' of Pong was formerly bounded on the North by the range of hills dividing Burma from Assam. It extended to Khampat in the South, Yoma range in the West and Yunnan in the East. This kingdom had its capital at Mogaung and after varying fortunes it was annexed to Burma in 1752 A.D.[14] In another theory establishing link between Manipur and the neighbouring kingdoms then, P. Gogoi quoting W. Shaw states that in the year 707 A.D., the King of Thailand defeated the King of Manipur, Naothingkhong and thereafter Manipur is said to have been ruled by the Thais for ten years.[15] It may be mentioned here that Samlung, the younger brother of Sukhanpha, the King of Pong stayed in Manipur for ten years at Apong Engkhol, a place situated East of the then royal palace.[16]

Since there was no independent Thai kingdom of Thailand in that early period, it is assumed that the reference is apparently Samlung's conquest of Upper Burma and Assam including Manipur in the 8th century A.D.[17] S.K. Chatterjee believes that the Meiteis of Manipur are the most advanced section of the Kuki-Chin people. Linguistically close to the Burmese, Kachin or Singmois, they agree more with Nagas and Bodos. According to him, the Meiteis are known as Kukis in India and Chins in Burma.[18] To quote George Watt, "It is perhaps not far from truth to assume that the present inhabitants of the plains and hills of Manipur have sprung from four great influences: the Kukies in the South, the Nagas in the North, the Shan and Burmese tribes on the East and certain hill tribes on the West more or less related to the great Kachari family now distributed throughout the valley of Assam".[19]

There is another school of thought which attempts to trace the roots of the Meitei peoples to the Aryans. While accepting the fact that the general facial characteristics of the Manipuris are Mongolian, B.C. Allen, E.A. Gait, C.G.H. Allen and H.F. Howard in their work *Gazetteer of Bengal and North East India* observes that there is a great diversity of feature among them some showing a regularity approaching the Aryan type.[20] The Burmese chronicles repeating an ancient tradition assert that the royal *Kshatriya* tribes of Northern India migrated to Upper Irawadi though no cause of the movement is assigned.[21] Manipur, which lies within the basin of the Irawadi lay in the route of the *Kshatriya* princes. To support the theory. the tradition states that the northern part of the Kubo valley, which is the direct route from Manipur towards Burma is still called Mauriya or Maurira, said to be the name of the tribe to which King Asoka belonged.[22] The Manipuris quote the

Mahabharata in support of their statement that they were originally Hindus. Although there is very little evidence saving the mention of Arjun's coming to Manipur, his stay for three years and marrying Chitrangada, a daughter of the Manipuri king Chitrabahan, there is nothing further bearing on the point. The earliest name Manipur appears in the *Adi-parva* of the epic *Mahabharata.*[23] The oldest name was Manlurpur with which name Arjun's visit to the eastern region and his reaching Manipur via Anga and Kalinga is connected. Pravabati understands that the route by which Arjuna came to Manipur was the hill route which connected Manipur valley with Surma or Barak valley. This is believed to be the same route taken by *Brahmanas* and other Aryan immigrants which led to their settlements in large numbers in Manipur in historical times.[24]

There is a popular myth connected with the origin of the land and the naming of the same as Manipur. Claiming Hindu descent, the myth makes us believe that the valley of Manipur remained submerged under water for a very long time. Nine *Laibungthous* (divine youth) and seven *Lainuras* (divine girls) in joint collaboration succeeded in making sixty-four hillocks. Lord Siva is credited with making a hole through the hill with a trident thereby draining out all the water and making the land fit for habitation. To celebrate the happy event, Siva along with a host of gods and goddesses performed a dance, believed to have been the *Lai Haraoba* form still popular in Manipur. Ananta on watching the dance and overwhelmed by it and the beauty of the place brought jewels to the land. Henceforth, the land came to be known as Manipur (*mani* : jewels) or 'The Land of the Jewels'.[25]

The various hypotheses worked out by the scholars show that there are broadly two linkages between the Meiteis and the outside groups of people viz; the Indo-Chinese in general and the Tais in particular and the Aryans' origin. The theory of Aryan origin hold no water due to the lack of evidence to substantiate the proposition. There has not been any conclusive proof that the Manipur of the *Mahabharata* is the same as the present place of the same name. On the other hand, the theory of the Tai origin of the Meiteis which is based among others on language, movement of groups of people in the region and the racial similarities appear more scientific. Grierson and Luce studying the languages of the neighbouring tribes of the then kingdom of Manipur suggests affinity with the Kuki-Chin of Tibeto-Burman group of languages. According to Sagermano, the Tai people and its different branches, is, perhaps the most widely spread of any 'race' in the Indo-Chinese peninsula. Believing that there is a 'racial' connection between the Tais and the Meiteis on facial and language aspects, Sagermano says that these tribes had their home ages ago in Yunnan. He mentions two Shan kingdoms, one in the North of Burma with its capital at Mongmaw on the Sheveli river and another Shan kingdom of Tali which fell under the conquering hands of Kublai Khan in the year 1253 A.D.[26] That the Meiteis, perhaps, are the descendants of the Tai 'race' is also accounted for in sources such as the Burmese and Manipuri chronicles.

The valley of Manipur appears originally to have been occupied by several tribes which came from different directions. Although it is difficult to come to any conclusive statement on the origin of the Meitei people due to lack of enough historical material on the subject, comparative ethnographic studies suggest that it is fairly certain that the Meities might have belonged to the Tai 'race' of the Indo-Chinese group of Mongoloids. Having situated the Meiteis among the larger Chinese group of people, it is tempting to draw a parallel between the ancestor worship prevalent in Manipur and in China where it appears in the highest vigour.

The erstwhile kingdom of Manipur was formed as a result of the amalgamation of independent principalities under Nongda Lairen Pakhangba (33-154 A.D.), who belonged to the Ningthouja *salai* (clan). The confederacy was formed by the union of seven clans viz; Ningthouja, Angom, Khuman, Luwang, Khaba-nganba, Moirang and Sarang-Leishangthem.[27] Gangmumei Kabui states that a *salai* (clan) was originally an ethnic group or tribe speaking a distinct language or dialect, occupying a territory and having an autonomous principality under a ruler who was both a political chieftain and social head of the clan.[28] Pandit N. Khelchandra Singh reveals that the word Meitei which has come to be referred to the people of the Manipur valley was originally applied only to the Ningthoujas. After the formation of the confederacy of the *salais* and the subjugation by the Ningthoujas, the word Meitei became the common nomenclature for all the people of the valley of Manipur.[29]

The people inhabiting the valley of Manipur have been referred to by various names by the scholars dealing on the subject. The Meitheis by T.C. Hodson, Mithais by E.W. Dun and Moitai by B.H. Hodgson is generally considered by local scholars to have been the result of the British writers' inability to correctly pronounce the word. However, the difficulty lies in the debate on whether the word Meetei or Meitei is the correct nomenclature for these group of people. Local scholars have used either of the two words in their works depending on their preference. This present work will refer to the people of the valley as the Meiteis as this is the same used in *Cheitharol Kumbaba*, the royal chronicle, a very important source for the study.

It should be mentioned at the very outset that the terms 'ancient' and 'medieval' in the context of the history of Manipur have different connotation than those of Indian History as such. Manipur remained aloof from the main political trends of the country. We do not have evidence of ancient empires reaching Manipur. Even the Mughals did not conquer Manipur. The change in the mode of relations of productions beginning around the 9th-10th centuries in India, termed feudalism is also not applicable. This accounts for a different treatment for the periodisation of this region. The ancient and medieval periods of Manipur history overlap each other, the ancient merging into the medieval.

The study is an attempt at a reconstruction of the religion and society of early Meitei history, focusing on ancestor worship, the core of Meitei religion and upon which the society is founded. It primarily covers the period from the reign of Nongda Lairen Pakhangba (33-154 A.D.) to the reign of King Kyamba (1457-1508 A.D.) i.e. the period from the reign of the first 'historical' king to the time when the first reliable record of *Brahmana* migration to Manipur is available. The study also includes forms of ancestor worship even after the 16th century A.D. so as to trace the historical link between the earlier period and the contemporary period.

The *Brahmanas* came from Tripura, Assam, West Bengal and even far off places such as Mathura. The learned *Brahmanas* slowly but surely penetrated the age old customs and traditions of the people. However, the fact remains that the ancestor form of worship practiced by the Meiteis from very early times could not be wiped out by the outsiders who by the early part of the 18th century A.D. had settled down and even inter-married with the local people. Therefore, even till today when the Meiteis call themselves Hindus, the cult of ancestor worship runs as a lively undercurrent with a harmonious synthesis of *tulsi* veneration and Sanamahi reverence in every Meitei home. This feature of the religious tradition of the Meiteis have made Ghosh to remark that "the Meiteis are probably the sole exception in the history of the world to follow two religions at the same home".[30] The task is to distinguish and emphasize the ideas that are Meitei, original and divorced from Hindu influence. To accomplish this, therefore, this work is based mainly on the *Puyas*.

To be able to produce written literature, the people must have a certain level of economic, political and cultural development. It has already been mentioned that the people of Manipur were in close contact with a branch of the Shans of Upper Burma called the Pong. It is widely believed that the Meiteis learnt the art of record-keeping from the Pongs, with whom they had a long and close contact over the centuries. S.K. Chatterjee is of the view that among the Tibeto-Burman languages, the most important and in literature certainly much greater importance than the others is the Meitei or Manipuri language. He further states that the Meiteis possessed the art of writing although, a primitive and unsophisticated sort, from some centuries ago which even their kinsmen outside India viz; the Burmese, the Siamese and the Chinese have not produced in such heroic scale in literature.[31]

The reign of King Kyamba is a watershed in the history of Manipur. Although the first reliable recorded *Brahmana* migration began from the 15th century A.D., earlier migration of the *Brahmanas* to Manipur cannot be wholly discarded. If there were any, perhaps, they were absorbed with the indigenous population leaving no trace. But, from the time of Kyamba regular inflow of *Brahmanas* started and along with it inter-marriage with local women, allotting clan names and finally finding a place in the local population. In the political scene, King Ningthoukhomba (1432-1467 A.D.) succeeded the Moirangs into accepting the suzerainty of the Ningthoujas.[32] The constant threat posed by the once independent principalities was now followed by a period of political stability which must have facilitated the development of social and cultural life of the people. By the time of King Khagemba (1597-1652 A.D.), literary culture started to develop. The royal chronicle records the king's endeavour to spread education and that manuscripts came to be produced from the year 1616 A.D.[33]

The Meiteis use two writing systems. Before the 19th century, Manipuri was written in a script called the Meitei *mayek*. When exactly this script came in use has been a subject of controversy. The earliest reference to writing is that recorded in *Ningthourol Lambuba* where King Irengba (984-1074 A.D.) is described as a person who was very fond of reading and writing even in his old age.[34] A study of the epigraphical sources reveal that the Phayeng Copper Plate, written in Meitei *mayek* has been assigned to the year 799 A.D. by W. Yumjao Singh, one of the pioneers in the field of archaeology in Manipur. The plate now available in English translated form refers to three hundred and sixty-three gods, where Siva, Ganesa, Durga and Hari are clearly mentioned.[35] If this date is taken to be correct, the earliest writing of the Meiteis will go back as far as the 8th century A.D. However, scholars like S.N. Parratt have raised strong doubts on the validity of the dating. She takes the date to as late as the first half of the 19th century A.D.[36] The use of the non-Manipuri and Sanskrit words tend to make 8th century A.D. a difficult date to accept for the Phayeng Plate. There is an inscription written in Meitei *mayek* which is assigned to the 15th century A.D. during the reign of King Kyamba. This is the earliest recorded inscription in Meitei *mayek*.[37]

It is possible that the *Brahmanas* who came and settled in Manipur from the 15th century A.D. onwards began writing using their own scripts. Those *Brahmanas* from Nadia and Sylhet must have used Bengali script while those from Gujarat and Kanpur used Devanagiri or some other local script. Keeping in mind the Shans, Tibetans, Burmese and perhaps Chinese influence, it must have created a chaos whereby there arose the need to invent a script acceptable to scholars and common men alike.

Manipuri manuscripts were originally written on small, thin, rectangular boards of the sapwood of a tree called *agaru* or *agar* (*aquilaria agallocha*). The ink used was made of lampblack and gall and the pen was made of small pieces of fully matured and seasoned bamboo.[38] Modern Manipuri is written in Bengali script which was introduced in the wake of Vaisnavism influence as late as the 18th century A.D. The archaic Manipuri and modern Manipuri basically differ in script. One has to admit, however, that there has been a gradual change in the language and therefore there are numerous archaic words and modes of addresses which are still found in ancient manuscripts but no longer in use today. Majority of the manuscripts in archaic Manipuri are now rendered into modern Manipuri.

The sources for the study of ancestor cult of the Meiteis will be the local level texts in vernacular which will be substantiated by field observations. Unlike many North Eastern states, Manipur is fortunate in having a mass of manuscripts called *Puyas*. The main task of manuscript writing was done by learned *Maichous (Pandits)* who were employed by the royal court. Most of the manuscripts were in the possession of the kings and writing was done under their guidance. These manuscripts were preserved sandwiched between wood and sometimes wrapped by a thin piece of cloth, to be tied securely by a string. Manuscripts were also kept inside a *lubak* (a bamboo basket) and kept on a *lap* (a bamboo rack) to prevent exposure to moisture. The *lap* was made high up on the *phungga* (hearth).[39] Therefore, having understood that the Meiteis had the tradition of preserving *Puyas*, the main task lies in choosing, arranging and analysing the data available within the thematic framework of the study.

The *Puyas* may be defined as written records handed down to posterity by the forefathers of the Meiteis. They are a particular kind of old narratives which form a definite class in Manipuri literature. The *Puyas* are in the possession of various individuals and organizations. The State Kala Academy library itself has collected more than a thousand such manuscripts covering various aspects of Manipuri culture.[40] *A Catalogue of Manipuri Manuscripts* published by Manipuri Sahitya Parishad shows that the *Puyas* covered a number of human disciplines.[41] The list is as follows:

Subject	**Number of *Puyas***
Administration	48
Arts and Culture	42
Charms and Mantras	94
Creation Stories	3
Fine Arts	1
Geography	31
Geology	3
Health and Hygiene	6
Genealogy	90
Poetry	40
Prediction	11
Prose	29
Religious Philosophy	72
Scripts	2
Supernatural Stories	8
Yek, salai	42
Miscellaneous	64

It should be mentioned that the *Puyas* are encyclopaedic in nature although many of them have a particular subject as the central theme. A *Puya* with the central theme on creation myths may also contain other subjects like genealogy, charms and *mantras*, religious philosophy etc. Therefore, under such circumstances a source as important as *Cheitharol Kumbaba*, the royal chronicle which is categorized under genealogy is not to be strictly followed in that sense. The *Puyas* are treated as sacred texts and for this reason they were kept at a place in the home where they could be kept untouched, except on auspicious days when they were brought out. Every owner of a *Puya* treats the text with great respect and fear since the *Puyas* themselves mention that an individual who leads a dishonest and sinful life should not even touch a *Puya*. Only a sincere and upright individual after bath, change into fresh clothes and burning of incense lamp can read the *Puyas*. This superstitious belief is one of the reasons why the owners of *Puyas* are not willing to part with the *Puyas*. The result is that the availability of the *Puyas* tends to get restricted. However, the most unfortunate event regarding the *Puya* availability is the infamous '*Puran Meithaba'*. The royal chronicle records as thus: "On the 17th day Sunday, in the year 1654 *saka* (1732 A.D.) at the instigation of the Guru Santidas, King Garibniwaz after sending message on horseback to all the corners of his kingdom, collected the old manuscripts in front of Kangla Uttra of the royal palace and destroyed by burning them".[42] Another reason for the disappearance of the *Puyas* is the consequence of the seven years war fought between 1741 and 1747 *saka* (1819-1825 A.D.). This war with the Burmese resulted in the taking away of many Meitei captives to Burma who were later absorbed into the Burmese community. They took away the *Puyas* which had been worshipped reverently by them.[43] The fear of oppression of the custodians of the *Puyas* by the Meitei kings must have led to keeping these materials in secret places for a very long time.

Manipuri literature prior to 18th century appears as an uncharted thick forest of undated anonymous books. The reason for this is the fact that the *Amaiba Loisang*, the department in charge of the Royal Archives and Record built up and encouraged among the *Amaibas* (scholars) and *Wakmas* (poets) a literary tradition of not disclosing authorship of their works. This tradition was applied to in the case of *Cheitharol Kumbaba* and *Ningthourol Lambuba*, both royal chronicles of the state. There are works whose authorship was dedicated by the writers to their royal patrons. Towards the 17th century A.D., there are particulars of the authors given in the works.[44] While it is true that it is a laborious and difficult task to fix dates of the literature in a chronological order, the problem does not defy solution. The work by R.K. Jhalajit Singh called *A History of Manipuri Literature* in three volumes is a pioneer in the field of dating the mass of anonymous undated manuscripts.[45] The method used to determine the date of the *Puyas* is the language, style of composition and historical allusion to events mentioned in the texts. Ch. Manihar Singh believes that all the manuscripts, a few like those of astrology, medicine and genealogy excepted were meant to be sung or recited.[46] We may, therefore, surmise that the floating mass of oral literature began to be codified from about the 15th century A.D., when initial period of Brahmanical influence is seen. Perhaps, the coming of the institutional religion had a role to play in the codification process.

A study of the *Puyas* at hand encounters the vexing problem of separating the myths from facts and locating the historical in the myriad of legends, traditions, folklore and narratives. Nevertheless, a comparative study of the various *Puyas* helps us in analysing the data objectively and within the historical framework.

Attempts have been made in the past for a study of the Meitei religion. However, ancestor worship, wherever it was dealt with, formed only a part of the general study of the religion of Manipur. The reason for the lack of work on this subject could be largely due to the unavailability of the *Puyas* for a very long time, which has come out of various custodians' hands only in the recent past. The encouragement of revealing the concealed *Puyas* has been due to the revival spirit of the old faith among a large section of the population in the recent past. Many of the *Puyas*, therefore, came to be collected by the State Kala Academy, Manipur State Archives, libraries and related organizations, the publishing of which also added to the opportunity to study the materials. The most important factor for inadequate handling of the *Puyas*, perhaps, was the fact that the initial contributors to Meitei history were the non-Meitei writers who were not in a position to handle the *Puyas*. The anthropological studies conducted by the British writers although significantly enriched the history of Manipur, was the result of second hand information and observation from the view of an outsider to the local setup. Nevertheless, accounts of these British political agents, written in English formed the major source of early Manipur history. Of particular importance are the works of Brown,[47] Dun[48] McCulloch[49] and Pemberton.[50] *The Meitheis* by T.C. Hodson[51] is the first attempt of a full scale ethnography of the Meiteis. However, the book lacks accuracy due to it being based mainly on second hand information.

Local scholars such as Iboongohal,[52] Jhalajit,[53] Sanahal[54] and Yumjao[55] have written in English on the general history of Manipur. Manjusri Chaki-Sircar,[56] studying the women of Manipur has produced in her work an overall picture of the position of Meitei women in the patriarchal society. However, her work is based on field observations and there is no handling of *Puyas* and hence reflects at best the traditional society in the eyes of the modern observer. Gangmumei Kabui[57] in the book *History of Manipur (Pre-Colonial Period)* has tried to work out a systematic account of the political, social and cultural history of Manipur from the earliest times up to the 18th century A.D. M. Kirti Singh's[58] work on the religion and culture of Manipur has limited focus on the traditional religion of Manipur. Research in Manipur University has produced some useful works. Some of them relating to political and cultural history are those of N. Pramodini Devi,[59] P. Pravabati Devi,[60] L. Basanti Devi [61] and L. Sanajaobi Devi.[62] These works deal with ancestor worship only in the periphery and therefore is of not much significance in my study. The thesis on archaeology by L. Kunjeswori Devi [63] has brought to light the fact that this subject is almost absent in 'Pre-Hindu period and that architecture, epigraphs, icons and sculptors emerged in Manipur only about the time when Hindu influence made intrusion in the religious life of the people'. The various aspects dealing with the life of the traditional priestesses (*Maibis*) in the Meitei society can be known from the work of Ng. Ekasini Devi.[64] Saroj N. Arambam Parratt and John Parratt's work entitled *The Pleasing of the Gods: Meitei Lai Haraoba*[65] seeks to examine the festival within the totality of Meitei culture. Some focus on ancestor worship of the Meiteis is given as background to the socio-religious life in Manipur in the 18th century in the thesis worked out by N. Birachandra Singh.[66] A book of some importance is that of L. Bhagyachandra Singh.[67] Although his work relates to the religion of Manipur before the coming of Vaisnavism, it is dealt with as a subject of philosophy and therefore differs much from the historical view point. Perhaps, the most systematic work on the religion of Manipur is that of S.N. Parratt.[68] This book serves as a good base for a study of the traditional religion of Manipur. However, the work covers the entire period upto modern times, a good portion of the book being dedicated to the period of Brahmanical influence in the modern period of Manipur. Further, her handling of the *Puyas* is not adequate and she has relied more on the secondary sources and field study. It leaves much scope in dealing with the mass of information available from *Puyas*.

Local scholars have contributed much to the enrichment of Manipur history by their works in vernacular. R.K. Sanahal

Singh,[69] W. Yumjao Singh[70] and Mutua Jhulan Singh[71] are some of the scholars who were the pioneers in the field of history writing in Manipur. N. Khelchandra Singh's book titled *Ariba Manipuri Sahityagi Itihas* gives an account of the early history of Manipur.[72] The voluminous works of Atombapu Sharma may also be mentioned here. The works are oriented towards finding an Aryan root for the Meiteis. While the author's deep knowledge of Sanskrit and the *Puyas* is much to be appreciated, the parallel he draws at every stage of his hypothesis becomes too far-fetched. Some of his works include *Pakhangba* and *Meitei Meihourol.*[73]

The *Puyas* are the only major source for the study of this aspect of Meitei history. As has been already stated, archaeological sources for the study is almost negligible, as archaeology in Manipur developed at a late stage. The few archaeological material available on the subject may be mentioned here. The epigraphs form the most important section and they are mostly engraved on stones, copper plates and iron plates. Most of them contain few lines and are dedicated to some deity and relate historical events and incidents of war etc.[74] The list of inscriptions are as follows:

1. Phayeng Copper Plate assigned to 8th century A.D.[75]
2. Stone inscription of King Kyamba of 15th century A.D.[76]
3. Konthoujam Lairemma inscriptions No.1 and 2. : These are two records of different dates on the same slab, one of which is of the time of King Khagemba (1597-1652 A.D.) and another of the time of King Charairongba (1697-1709 A.D.). Inscribed in archaic Meitei script, the content is about Konthoujam Lairemma and the Konthoujam clan.[77]
4. Ningel Inscription of Garibniwaz (1709-1748 A.D.) : Inscribed in archaic Meitei script, the king is described here as Simha Nongshakumba. It records the details

> of many high ranking officials, their names along with the village chiefs and their respective villages. The inscription closes with the word Rama, thereby indicating Brahmanical influence at that period of Meitei history.[78]

Nothing definite is known regarding the origin of sculpture in Manipur. O.K. Singh informs us that the earliest available record of casting idols in Manipur is that of Panthoibi and Sanamahi of the early 17th century A.D.[79] The royal chronicle, however, gives the dates for the casting of the idols of the two *lais* as 1621 *saka* (1699 A.D.) and 1622 *saka* (1700 A.D.) respectively.[80]

In Manipur, the concept of temple emerged in the late centuries.[81] It is unfortunate that not a single monument erected before 15th century A.D. have survived. O.K. Singh suggests that, perhaps, early historical monuments in Manipur may have been constructed with wood, bamboo, reed or other like available materials which are easily weathered when exposed to tropical or sub-tropical climate.[82] The art of making brick was probably introduced very late in Manipur. The earliest available record of brick-making in Manipur was during the time of King Khagemba (1597-1652 A.D.).[83] It may be mentioned here that the frequent Burmese invasions to Manipur must have also contributed to the destruction of the early monuments.

The antiquity of coinage in Manipur is not definitely known yet. The ancient coins of Manipur were made of bell metal and were known as *sels*.[84] The material used for minting the coins is believed to have been imported from Burma since bell metal was not locally produced in Manipur.[85] The *Numit Kappa Puya* refers to an inscribed coin called Taret-mayi-maiba which was used for worshipping the sun god.[86] Nongda Lairen Pakhangba (33-154 A.D.) is also said to have introduced coins. Since archaeological evidence so far have not supported these theories, it is difficult to come to any valid conclusion.

The *Puyas* available and referred for the present study may be classified into five groups. In the first category are included the *Puyas* which are written in Meitei *mayek* viz; *Khununglon*.[87] The original *Puyas* in Meitei *mayek* are transliterated in Bengali script and in this category we have *Sanggai Phammang*.[88] The mass of *Puyas* which are translated into the spoken language of today and written in Bengali script form a good section of the sources for study viz; *Leithak Leikharon*.[89] Another group of *Puyas* are the compiled and edited *Puyas* written in Bengali script in transliterated form viz; *Panthoibi Naherol Amasung Aman Sikumlon*[90] and *Sanamahi Puya*.[91] The last group of *Puyas* are those which are extracts of the original *Puyas* written in Bengali script viz; *Parishadki Ariba Manipuri Wareng Lairik*.[92]

The five forms in which the *Puyas* are available to us and the subjects covered have been already dealt with. It is important to briefly analyze the *Puyas* in order to understand the foundation on which the study is based. The ancestor cult of the Meiteis must have necessitated the recording of lineage and descent of each clan. There has been a tradition of recording the pedigree of each *sagei* by the head of the sub-clan. *Langthabalon*[93] and *Sanggai Phammang*[94] are *Puyas* which are classified strictly under the group of genealogy. *Leithak Leikharon*,[95] *Khamlangba Erengba Puwari*[96] and *Pudin*[97] are *Puyas* which deal with creation and cosmology in general as the central theme. It is also a compendium of historical accounts on the origin of clans in Manipur. Since the religious belief of the people are expressed through rituals, Meiteis perform rituals on all occasions when they venerate their ancestors. *Thalloi Nongkhailon*[98] and *Erat Thounirol*[99] deal with various details of rituals. There are a class of *Puyas* which deal exclusively with a particular deity. *Puyas* such as *Sanamahi Puya*[100] and *Pakhangba Laihui*[101] help us to gather information on the parentage, myths associated, names by which the deity is known, rituals to be performed for them, items of food or flowers to be offered etc. *Panthoibi Khongul*[102] is another *Puya* which deals with a particular deity. Here, the life of goddess Panthoibi is narrated, her transformation from a ordinary village girl to the level of a deity by her association with Nongpok after which the two came to be worshipped as Nongpok Panthoibi.

By far the most important source for the study of Meitei history is the royal chronicle called *Cheitharol Kumbaba*. These state chronicles were recorded in Meitei *mayek* in the courts by the learned *Maichous*. *Cheitharol Kumbaba* records the historical events of nearly two thousand years covering the reign of seventy eight kings from Nongda Lairen Pakhangba (33-154 A.D.) to Bodhachandra Singh (1941-1955 A.D.). This chronicle which runs to about eight hundred pages is a voluminous one. When exactly this chronicle began to be recorded has been debated by many scholars. The chronicle itself mentions that it was King Kyamba who introduced the system of *cheithaba* or counting of years in the year 1485 A.D.[103] The accounts before this is sketchy and scholars believe that it must have been constructed out of available source materials. E. Nilakanta quoting the chronicle brings out the event of 1780 A.D. when the king Bhagyachandra is said to have ordered the re-compiling of the lost *Cheitharol*. The incident implies that the chronicle was already in existence before the reign of this king. The language and style of the text has made scholars to conclude that the chronicle must have started the recording of historical events from the 15th century A.D.[104] The contents of the chronicle are varied and almost all embracing. Taking at random, it records the accession of ruler on the throne, military expedition, royal excursion, pleasure trips to lakes and pilgrimage to the abode of deities, major religious and social events, visits of holy men to Manipur, migrations of *Brahmanas* and Muslims to Manipur, religious conversions, natural calamities and a hosts of other information. The significance of *Cheitharol Kumbaba* lies in the fact that this is the only chronicle which record dates, days and year of the historical events. Of particular value to researchers not well versed in Meitei script and language is the translated version of this *Puya* by Saroj Nalini Arambam Parratt[105] entitled *The Court Chronicle of the Kings of Manipur: The Cheitharol Kumpapa*, which also includes the original text and notes.

Ningthourol Lambuba[106] is another chronicle which is a mine of information on various happenings in the kingdom from 1st century to 18th century A.D. Unfortunately, the years in which the recorded events took place are not mentioned. However, the events are recorded according to the reign of each king and therefore, read along-side *Cheitharol Kumbaba* it is possible to find out the time of most of the events. Apart from the accounts of royal tours, *Ningthourol Lambuba* pays special attention to explaining the place names of the military expedition. The narrative and the myth explained helps us to trace the meaning of numerous words and dialects no longer used. R.K. Jhalajit places the writing of this book towards the end of the 17th century.[107] The Meitei philosophy and thoughts are dealt with in the *Sakok Lamlen Ahanba Puya*.[108] It tells the reader about the gods to be worshipped, the ways to worship them, certain myths associated with, the codes to follow in order to attain *mukti* etc. This *Puya* also informs us about the social customs of the early Meiteis.

As already been stated, Manipur history witnessed migrations of various people from different directions from early times. The learned *Maichous* kept accounts of the migration of the people to the Meitei land. *Nongpok Haram*[109] describes the inflow of different people like Burmese, Chinese etc. from the Eastern direction. *Nongchup Haram*[110] deals with the people who migrated from the West. Another *Puya* on migration is that of *Poireiton Khunthokpa.*[111] This book gives an account of the long journey undertaken by Poireiton and a horde of men on their coming to Manipur. The book initially seems more like a mythology. However, there are certain historical facts of people and place names in the book. Further, Nongda Lairen Pakhangba, the first historical king of Manipur is recorded as having married Laisna, the sister of Poireiton. *Poireiton Khunthokpa* is also mentioned in *Cheitharol Kumbaba.*[112] That the *Brahmanas* came and settled in Manipur is known from the *Bamon Khunthoklon Puya.*[113] The *Brahmanas* who came from Tripura, West Bengal, Mathura, Orissa etc. arrived in Manipur at least by the 15th century A.D. They were allotted clan names and some of them married local women and settled down in the valley. The migration of the *Brahmanas* is important in understanding the gradual transformation of the religious history of the Meiteis from ancestor worship to Brahmanical faith.

Apart from the *Puyas* mentioned above there are a mass of other *Puyas* which serve as good source for various aspects of the subject under study. The *Puyas* being encyclopaedic in nature, many of them fall under this group. Taking at random, mention may be made of *Puyas* such as *Thiren Layat,*[114] *Wakok Hilel Thilel Amailon Pukok Puya,*[115] *Khamoi Yamgoi Sekning,*[116] *Sakok Wakok,*[117] *Loiyamba Shinyen,*[118] *Chingoiron,*[119] *Naothingkhong Phambal Kaba*[120] etc.

It is important to note that various organizations have been trying to unearth the numerous *Puyas* which are in the custody of individuals. In an attempt to encourage the study of the past, seminars have been organized and new information is added to the existing knowledge. These seminars help to continue the process of unravelling the mass of *Puyas* still trapped in many homes. The seminar papers made use of in this study include those which have been organized by The Cultural Forum, International Society for Cultural Studies, S.R. Institute of Manipuri Studies, Manipur Folklore Society, Manipur State Kala Academy and Universal Literary Association.

Among the journals which have been made use of in this study are *Umanglai Khunda* and *Journal of Manipuri Sahitya Parishad* in Manipuri. Those in English include *Journal of the Anthropological Institute, Man in India, Transactions of the Folklore Society*, and *Proceedings of the North East India History Association. Encyclopaedia of Religion and Ethics, The Encyclopaedia of Religion, The New Encyclopaedia Britannica: Micropaedia, Knowledge in Depth* and *Encyclopaedia of the Social Sciences* have also been consulted for this study.

The study of *Puyas* has been aided greatly by the dictionaries compiled by N. Dinachandra Singh and N. Khelchandra Singh. Since the archaic words are no longer in use today, *Khununglongi Aartha* and *Ariba Manipuri Longei* which gives the meanings of archaic Manipuri words to modern Manipuri have proved to be very handy. Two other dictionaries which have helped in the writing of this work are *A Vocabulary Manipuri to English Dictionary* and *Standard Dictionary of Folklore, Mythology and Legend.*

Salient aspects of tribal religion such as ancestor worship, role of the priest and magical rituals find parallel in most tribal religions of the world. Anthropologists studied them in detail to find out their significance in the overall religious structure. In many primitive tribal societies, ancestral spirits co-exist with the living influencing and even determining the fortunes of the people. They have also shown that no matter how complicated the socio-economic structure of the tribe is, the everyday affairs of man are still dominated by priesthood and magic. This work will make use of anthropological insights for an understanding of the Meitei ancestor cult. An important difference between the anthropologists and the historians is that they study their material directly in the field while the historians primarily depend on written records. However, many anthropologists and sociologists are becoming sensitive to the need of using what they call local level texts in vernacular which substantiate their field observations. The methodology used is the critical study of the *Puyas* which is supplemented by field survey, observations of the rites and rituals at first hand, information recorded from local scholars and interview of the *Pandits* and other members of the community. The historical approach will be aided by anthropological insights and sociological analysis to understand the subject from a wider perspective.

It must be admitted here that the *Puyas* referred to for the study are only a fragment of the mass of them which are believed to be still remaining in the custody of individuals, families and various organizations. However, the available data throw a flood of light on the traditional religion and society of the Meiteis from the earliest times to the 15th century A.D. when regular migration of *Brahmanas* to Manipur is recorded in the *Puyas*. It is hoped that through an intensive study of the materials at hand a more meaningful understanding of the religion and society prevailing in early Manipur will emerge.

Notes and References

1. O. Bhogeswar Singh (ed.), *Sanamahi Laikan*, 1973, p.50 in Gangmumei Kabui, *History of Manipur (Pre-Colonial Period)*, Vol. I, 1991, p.1.
2. The *Puyas* are a kind of old narratives in Manipuri literature.
3. Y. Bhagya Meitei (ed.), *Sakok Lamlen Ahanba Amasung Meihouron*, 1988, p.8.
4. T.C. Hodson, *The Meitheis*, 1989 (Reprint), p.1.

5. B.C. Allen, et.al, *Gazetteer of Bengal and North East India*, 1979, p.614.
6. *Memoranda on Native States in India*, 1909, pp. 357-358.
7. Dr. G.A. Grierson, *Report on the Linguistic Survey of India*, Vol. III, Pt. III, 1967, (Reprint), p.6.
8. B.C. Allen, *Census of Assam*, 1901, Vol. I (Report), 1984 (Reprint), p. 120.
9. Lt. Gen A.P. Phayre, *History of Burma*, 1967, pp.6-7.
10. *Ibid.*, p.12.
11. T.C. Hodson, *op.cit*, p.10.
12. G.H. Luce, *Phases of Pre-Pagan Burma*, Vol. I, 1985, p.36.
13. Lt. Gen. Sir A.P. Phayre, *op.cit.*, p.12.
14. Captain E.W. Dun, *Gazetteer of Manipur*, 1886, p.188.
15. Parmeswar Gogoi, *The Tai and Tai Kingdoms*, 1968, p.67, fn.1.
16. L. Iboongohal Singh and N. Khelchandra Singh (ed.), *Cheitharol Kumbaba*, 1989, p.6.
17. Parmeswar Gogoi, *op.cit.*, p.67, fn.1.
18. S.K. Chatterjee, *Kirata-Jana-Kriti: The Indo-Mongoloids and their Contribution to the History and Culture of India*, 1974, p.142.
19. George Watt, 'The Aborginal Tribes of Manipur,' *Journal of the Anthropological Institute*, Vol. 16. 1887, in Extract 'Aboriginal Tribes of Manipur', 1991, p.6.
20. B.C. Allen, et al., *op.cit.*, p.614.
21. Lt Gen. Sir A.P. Phayre, *op. cit.*, p.4.
22. *Ibid.*
23. *Mahabharata, Adi-parva*, Ch. 207, sl. 9-12, 13-23; Ch. 209, sl. 23-24., Ch. 213; *'Mahendra Parvatam Dristvatapa Sairupa Sobhitam Samudra Tirena Sanai Manipuram Jagamaha'* quoted in P. Pravabati Devi, *The History of Rise and Growth of Hinduism in Manipur from the Earliest Times to the Beginning of the 19th century A.D.*, 1987, p.17.

24. P. Pravabati Devi, *op. cit.*, p.19.
25. *Ibid.*, pp.16-17.
26. Vincentine Sagermano, *The Burmese Empire*, 1984 (Reprint), p.ix.
27. Konsam Manikchand, "The Evolution of the Meitei State: A Confederacy through the Last Two Millenia", in Naorem Sanajaoba (ed.), *Manipur: Past and Present*, Vol.1, 1988, p.147.
28. Gangmumei Kabui, *op. cit.*, p.10.
29. Information given to me personally by Pandit N. Khelchandra Singh on 17th May 1993.
30. G.K. Ghosh, *Tribals and Their Culture: Manipur and Nagaland*, 1992, p.132.
31. S.K. Chatterjee, *op. cit.*, pp. 157,179.
32. L. Iboongohal Singh and N. Khelchandra Singh (ed.), *Cheitharol Kumbaba*, p.18.
33. *Ibid*, p.36.
34. *Ningthourol Lambuba*, p.73, cited in R.K. Jhalajit Singh, *A History of Manipuri Literature*, 1987, p.9.
35. W. Yumjao Singh, *Report on the Archeological Studies of Manipur*, Bulletin No.1, 1935.
36. S.N. Parratt, *The Religion of Manipur*, 1980, pp.107-109.
37. Mutua Bahadur and P.Gunindra Singh, *Epigraphical Records of Manipur*, 1986, pp.1-3.
38. R.K. Jhalajit Singh, *op.cit.*, p.7.
39. N. Debendra Singh, "Manipuri (Meitei) Manuscripts,"in H. Bilasini Devi (ed.), *The Manipur University Museum Bulletin*, Vol. 2, 1987, p.2.
40. *Exhibition of Old Manipuri Manuscripts and Academi Publications*, 1989.
41. N. Khelchandra Singh (ed.), *A Catalogue of Manipuri Manuscripts*, 1984.

42. L. Iboongohal Singh and N. Khelchandra Singh (ed.), *Cheitharol Kumbaba*, p.93.

43. Y. Gourmani, *Ancient Cult and Culture of Manipur*, n.d., p.6.

44. Kh. Sarojini Devi (ed.), *National Register of Private Records/Manuscripts*, Vol.1,1987, p.(i).

45. R.K. Jhalajit Singh, *op. cit.*

46. Ch. Manihar Singh (ed. and tr.), *Naothingkhong Phambal Kaba*, 1983, p.5.

47. R. Brown, *Selection from the Records of the Government of India*, Foreign Department No. LXXVIII, Annual Report of the Munnipore Political Agency for 1868-69, 1870; *Statstical Account of Manipur*, 1975 (Reprint).

48. E.W. Dun, *op.cit.*

49. W. McCulloch, *An Account of the Valley of Munipoore*, 1980 (Reprint).

50. R.B. Pemberton, *Report on the Eastern Frontier of India*, 1835.

51. T.C. Hodson, *The Meitheis, op. cit.*

52. L. Iboongohal Singh, *Introduction to Manipur*,1963.

53. R.K. Jhalajit Singh, *A Short History of Manipur*, 1965,(Second Edition).

54. R.K. Sanahal Singh, *Glimpses of Manipur*, 1951.

55. W. Yumjao Singh, *An Early History of Manipur*,1966.

56. Manjusri Chaki-Sircar, *Feminism in a Traditional Society: Women of the Manipur Valley*, 1984.

57. Gangmumei Kabui, *op.cit.*

58. M. Kirti Singh, *Religion and Culture of Manipur*, 1988.

59. N. Pramodini Devi, *The Cultural History of Early Manipur*, 1987.

60. P. Pravabati Devi, *The History of Rise and Growth of Hinduism in Manipur from the Earliest Times to the Beginning of the 19th century A.D.*, 1987.

61. L.Basanti Devi, *A Study of Political History of Manipur from Pakhangba to Khagemba. (33 A.D. - 1652 A.D)*, 1988.

62. L. Sanajaobi Devi, *A Study in History and Culture of Manipur (1597 - 1709 A.D.)*, 1988.

63. Laishram Kunjeswori Devi, *A Study of Archaeology in Manipur since Pre-Historic Times*, 1988.

64. Ng. Ekasini Devi, *Meitei Amaibisingi Lai Tingi Oiba Mahei*, 1988.

65. Saroj N. Arambam Parratt and John Parratt, *The Pleasing of the Gods: Meitei Lai Haraoba*, 1997.

66. N. Birachandra Singh, *Socio-religious Life of the Meiteis in the 18th century A.D.*, 1987.

67. L. Bhagyachandra Singh, *A Critical Study of the Religious Philosophy of the Meeteis before the Advent of Vaisnavism in Manipur*, 1991.

68. S.N. Parratt, *op. cit.*

69. R.K. Sanahal Singh, *Manipur Itihas*, 1947.

70. W. Yumjao Singh, *Manipur Itihas*, 1950.

71. Mutua Jhulan Singh, (tr.Y.Khoimacha Singh et al.), *Bejoy Punchalee or History of Manipur*, Pt. I, 1936 (3rd Edition).

72. N. Khelchandra Singh, *Ariba Manipuri Sahityagi Itihas*, 1969.

73. Pt. Atombapu Sharma, *Pakhangba*, 1952; *Meiteigi Meihourol*, 1953.

74. N. Khelchandra Singh, "Sources of the History of Manipur", in S.N. Pandey (ed.), *Sources of the History of Manipur and the Adjoining Areas*, 1985, p.41.

75. W. Yumjao Singh, *Report on the Archaeological Studies of Manipur*, *op. cit.*

76. N. Khelchandra Singh, "*Sources of the History of Manipur*", *op. cit.*, p.42.

77. O.K. Singh, *Archaeology of Manipur*, 1988, p.16.

78. *Ibid.*, p.13.

79. *Ibid.*, p.12.
80. L. Iboongohal Singh N. Khelchandra Singh (ed.), *Cheitharol Kumbaba*, p.63.
81. L. Kunjeswori Devi, *op. cit.*, p.177.
82. O.K. Singh, *op. cit.*, p.17.
83. *Ibid.*, p.18.
84. W. Yumjao Singh, *Archaic Meitei or Early Manipuri Monograph on Archaic Meitei*, 1985, p.25.
85. O.K. Singh, *op. cit.*, p.10.
86. N. Khelchandra Singh, *Ariba Manipuri Sahityagi Itihas*, 1969, p.35.
87. *Khununglon*, custodian, N. Ibochouba.
88. *Sanggai Phammang*, custodian, Y. Mohendra Singh.
89. Bhagya Singh Yenkhoiba (ed.) *Leithak Leikharon*, 1988.
90. Naorem Amuyaima Singh (ed.), *Panthoibi Naherol Amasung Aman Sikumlon*, 1986.
91. B. Kullachandra (ed.), *Sanamahi Puya*, 1989.
92. N. Khelchandra Singh, *Parishadki Ariba Manipuri Wareng Lairik*, 1972.
93. *Langthabalon*, custodian, Y. Mohendra Singh.
94. *Sanggai Phammang*, custodian, Y. Mohendra Singh.
95. Bhagya Singh Yenkhoiba (ed.), *Leithak Leikharon*, *op. cit.*
96. Athokpam Yaima Langdum (ed.), *Khamlangba Erengba Puwari Neinarol*, 1993.
97. *Pudin*, (Handwritten copy), custodian Y. Mohendra Singh.
98. Yumnamcha Buddhachandra)ed.), *Thalloi Nongkhailon*, 1986.
99. Mayanglambam Gourachandra (ed.), *Erat Thounirol*, 1988.
100. B. Kullachandra (ed.), *Sanamahi Puya*, *op.cit.*
101. *Pakhangba Laihui*, custodian L. Suresh Singh.

102. M. Chandra Singh (ed.), *Panthoibi Khongul*, 1987 (3rd Edition).

103. L Iboongohal Singh and N. Khelchandra Singh (ed.), *Cheitharol Kumbaba*, p.20.

104. *Ibid.*, p. (iii).

105. Saroj Nalini Arambam Parratt (tr.), *The Court Chronicle of the Kings of Manipur: The Cheitharol Kumpapa*, 2005.

106. O. Bhogeswar Singh (ed.), *Ningthourol Lambuba*, 1967.

107. R.K. Jhalajit Singh, *op. cit.*, p.140.

108. Y. Bhagya Meitei (ed.), *Sakok Lamlen Ahanba Amasung Meihouron*, 1988.

109. *Nongpok Haram*, custodian N. Khelchandra Singh.

110. *Nongchup Haram*, custodian N. Khelchandra Singh.

111. Kh. Yaima Singh (ed.), *Poireiton Khunthokpa*, 1971.

112. L. Iboongohal Singh N. Khelchandra Singh (ed.), *Cheitharol Kumbaba*, p.1.

113. *Bamon Khunthoklon*, (anon.), n.d.

114. N. Ibochouba (ed.), *Thiren Layat*, 1981.

115. M. Laimit and L. Iboyaima (ed.), *Wakok Hilel Thilel Amailon Pukok Puya*, 1972.

116. Malem Yaiphasang (ed.), *Kamoi Yangoi Sekning*, 1974.

117. *Sakok Wakok*, (unpublished *Puya*), custodian Y. Mohindro Singh.

118. Kh. Chandrashekhar Singh (ed.) *Loiyamba Shinyen*, 1975.

119. N. Khelchandra Singh (ed.), *Chingoiron*, 1982.

120. Ch. Manihar Singh (ed. and tr.), *Naothingkhong Phambal Kaba*, *op. cit.*

2

Social Organization

Sociologists tend to treat religion primarily as a social product. The functionalist school argue that in primitive societies religious organization is inseparably connected with social structure, because it arises out of it and justifies it. The functional approach is basically an attempt to understand social phenomena in terms of their relationship to some system. Functionalists see religion as an integrative force, maintaining status quo, legitimizing the normative order and enforcing social control through value consensus.

Among those sociologists of the functionalist school of thought, an influential tradition on religion is derived from the writings of the classical sociologist Emile Durkheim.[1] Durkheim suggested that society was the origin and essence of religion: 'Men did not begin by imagining gods; it is not because they conceived of them in a given fashion that they became bound to them by social feelings. They began by linking themselves to the things they made use of, or which they suffered from, in the same way as they linked each to the other—without reflection, without the least kind of speculation'.[2] Thus: 'Religious society is only human stretched ideally to beyond the stars; the gods were not conceived of as members of the tribe, but formed one, or rather several societies located in separate regions, some of which were friendly, others hostile, and with which men have entered into relationships of an international character'.[3] Further, according to Durkheim, society favours rise of beliefs because individuals, brought together, living in communion with one another, are able in the exaltation of festivals to create the divine.[4] While asserting the central point that the first ideas of men were representations of religious reality, Durkheim brings out the dual concepts of the real and ideal societies. While the real society is that which is and act before our eyes, the ideal society reflects the real society and hence is a natural product of social life. This 'ideal society is not outside the real society; it is a part of it'.[5] Durkheim perceives the cosmic archetype as a generalized projection of the specifically social institution.[6] This understanding of religion has been further developed by other sociologists. It has been observed through empirical studies that primitive religions are on the whole oriented to a single cosmos: they know nothing of a wholly different world relative to which the actual world is utterly devoid of value.[7] Not only is every clan and local group defined in terms of the ancestral progenitors and the mythical events of settlement but, virtually every mountain, rock and tree is explained in terms of the actions of the mythical beings.[8]

Peter Berger who shares this understanding, looks on religion primarily as a system of legitimation of this real world. 'Religion has been the historically most widespread and effective instrumentality of legitimation'.[9] According to him, a meaningful order or nomos appear as a microscopic reflection of the world of men as expressing meaning inherent in the universe as such. Legitimation cannot be discussed apart from the universe that is being legitimated.[10] The universe which is a socially constituted reality is explained and justified by legitimation. Berger emphasizes the point that legitimation implies a status of objectivity and is not merely a body of ideas existing in the society. The socially constructed world legitimates itself by virtue of its objective facticity.[11] Legitimation of the social order may occur on a variety of levels viz; proverbs, moral maxims, traditional wisdom, myths, legends or folk tales.[12] The essential purpose of all forms of legitimation may be described as reality-maintenance, both on the objective and the subjective levels. There exist a nexus between the nomos and the cosmos: everything 'here below' has its analogue 'up above'. The social institutional order reflects directly the divine cosmos. Human sexuality reflects divine creativity, kinship relation of men are extensions of the kinship relations of the gods at a higher level and the political authority is ideally a divine incarnation.[13] Religion possesses the unique capacity to legitimate social institutions by locating the human phenomena within a sacred and cosmic frame of reference. The humanly constructed *nomoi* is thus given the semblance of the ultimate security and permanence.

The cosmic significance attached to social institutions permits the individual to have an ultimate sense of rightness in the roles he is expected to play in society. All social roles are representations of large complexes of the objectivated meanings. The specific roles of individuals are understood as mimetic reiterations of the cosmic realities for which they are supposed to stand.[14] Berger explaining this cites the example of the role of father who represents a wide variety of meanings ascribed to the institution of the family, and more generally to the institutionalization of sexuality and interpersonal relationships. The role of fatherhood 'here below' becomes mimesis of the sacred prototypes 'up above'. When the role of the father in the actions of creation, sovereignty or love is legitimated in mimetic terms, the representative character becomes endowed with a quality of immortality. 'The role of fatherhood is ultimately untouchable not only by his own conceivable transgressions against it but also by all the conceivable vicissitudes of history'.[15] Having formulated that worlds are socially constructed and socially maintained, Berger goes on to say that each world required a social base for its continuing existence as a world that is real to actual human being.[16] This base which he calls the plausibility structure is a prerequisite for all religious traditions. The firmer the plausibility structure is, the firmer will be the world based upon it. Yet, the less firm the plausibility structure, the more active will be the need for world maintaining legitimation. However, Berger clarifies that while maintaining the notion that society and religion are both the products of human activity, the religious system is not simply the reflection of the social process only. 'The implication of the rootage of religion in human activity is not that religion is always a dependent variable on the history of a society, but rather it derives its objective and subjective reality from human beings who produce and reproduce it in their ongoing lives'.[17]

The functionalist theory has been criticized as speculative and intestable as a deductive system.[18] This approach has been accused of neglecting the individual and of inadequate treatment of the relationship between the individual and the society.[19] The critics of Durkheim argue that he has overemphasized the role of collective behaviour in a society. Durkheim has been criticized for his notion of the society as being real and ideal at the same time. Raymond Aron thus states: "To suggest that the object of the religious feelings is society transfigured is not to save but to denegrade that human reality which sociology seeks to understand".[20]

Whatever be the shortcomings of the functionalists, their contribution to the understanding of primitive religions cannot be underestimated. The symbolic relationship between man and the other world is crucial to the sociological analysis of religion.

This is the starting point of our analysis, because it seems possible to work out a correspondence between the kinship organization of the Meitei society, contained in the various origin myths, clan and lineage systems, recorded in the indigenous *Puyas* and the tradition of ancestor worship among them. This is not suggest a direct correlation between the two spheres. However it is reasonable to begin with the hypothesis that one reflects and reinforces the other. Religious speculation spread over a long period of time and secondary legitimation have created a pantheon which do not exactly mirror the Meitei kinship organization. Also codification of the *Puyas* in different stages of Manipur history has introduced inconsistencies which further complicate the effort to match the details in these two spheres. But it is difficult to get away from the study of the Meitei social structure for a proper understanding of their religion.

The early Meitei society was an amalgamation of several different but closely knit and allied principalities once settled in different parts of Manipur. Each principality had its own chief and fixed territory. They were, however, not states but independent tribal chieftainships who constantly fought with each other for supremacy.[21]

The principalities that constituted the Meitei confederacy formed the backbone of the social organization in the form of the *salais* (clans). Each *salai* consists of a number of *sageis* (sub-clans). The Meiteis use two terms of significance rather frequently in their social introduction among themselves: *yek*, the name of the *salai* and *yumnak*, the name of the *sagei*. A *phungga* (hearth) represents a family and is the smallest social unit.

The Meiteis had the tradition of maintaining genealogical records of each *sagei*. It was the responsibility of the *sagei-piba* i.e., the head of each *sagei*, to maintain such records. Therefore, the Meitei community has today many *Puyas* dealing with the pedigree of all the *salais*. There are three types of such *Puyas*. The first group include the family tree of each *sagei* viz; *Thokchomlon*,[22] *Khumukchamlon*[23] etc. The second group of *Puyas* are those which record the *yek* tree of each *salai* viz; *Khumanlon*[24] etc. The third group includes those *Puyas* which record the genealogical tree of all the *salais* viz; *Sanggai Phammang*,[25] *Langthaballon* [26] etc.

The local chronicles trace the existence of *salais* from the beginning of Meitei history. However, the date of origin, number of *salais* and the chronology of events leading to diversion or amalgamation of one with another is open to question. Myths and legends attempted to explain the origin and interconnection of the *salais*. Although there are slight variations in the number of clans listed, all the *Puyas* agree that the *salais* descended from *Sidaba Mapu* or *Sidaba Salailel*, the Divine Ancestor of Ancestors.[27] The *Thiren Layat Puya* asserts that all the *sageis* descended from one family, being born of the same *lai* (god).[28]

The Meitei community of today has seven clans. They are Ningthouja, Angom, Chengloi, Nganba or Khabanganba, Looang, Khoomon and Moirang.[29] The *Puyas* are not uniform in the recording of the number and names of the *salais*. The diversity of traditions indicates the independent status of the principalities. The *Puyas* which are codifications of the oral traditions must have been recorded from such independent sources. With the emergences of the Ningthouja *salai* as the unifier of the principalities, there arose the need for a common social order. The tradition as recorded in the *Puyas* shows a clear attempt at systematization of the different tribal units. By the process of alignments and re-alignments, the various *salais* were reduced to seven. The *Sakok Lamlen Ahanba Puya* gives the names of the eight *salais* that constitute the Meitei society. These are Khaba-Nganba, Luwang, Khuman, Haorok Konthou, Sarang-Leisang, Angom, Moirang and Ningthouja.[30] Haorok Konthou seems to have existed as a separate *salai* at some point of time.[31] The *Leithak Leikharon Puya* also gives the names of the eight *salai* which are Ningthouja, Angom, Leishangthem, Moirang, Khaba, Nganba, Khuman and Luwang.[32] It also refers to the clan of Lapubi Heloi, the name of a goddess.[33] This is the same as the Chenglei clan.[34] However, *Wakoklon Hilel Thilel Amailon Pukok Puya* mentions the names of only six *salais*; viz; Luwang,Khuman, Angom, Moirang, Khaba-Nganba and Sarang-Leishangthem.[35] Yet another list found in *Khamoi Yangoi Sekning*, records the name of seven *salais* viz; Mangang, Luwang, Khuman, Moirang, Angom, Khaba-Nganba and Leishangthem.[36] Of these Khaba and Nganba plainly made up the Khabanganba while the three *salais* of Haorok Konthou, Sarangthem and Leishangthem are subsumed as *sageis* under the Chenglei *salai* indicating amalgamation of clans at a certain stage of their evolution, Mangang is dropped, although the cumulative evidence of the *Puyas* suggest that they are identical with Ningthouja.

It appears that before the first century A.D. a struggle started for supremacy among the various independent principalities for the occupation of the valley. Several of these tried to establish their strongholds in different parts of Manipur before the accession of Nongda Lairen Pakhangba (33-154 A.D.) to the throne of Kangla, the historic capital of Manipur.[37] Konsam Manikchand suggests that Angom, Moirang, Khaba-Nganba and Chenglei were in existence much before the Christian era while Khuman, Luwang and Ningthouja emerged only around the beginning of the Christian era.[38] E.W. Dun in the *Gazetteer of Manipur* writes: "The Manipuris are supposed to be descendants of four old tribes, called Kumal, Luang, Moirang and Maithai ...."[39] N. Birachandra attempts to present a systematic account of the emergence of the various *salais* on the basis of *Puyas*. The first ever king of the Meiteis was one Poirei-Leishangthem-Hanba-Khunung-Nganba-Mapu of the Nganba clan. The

Sarang Leisangthems was the next to emerge under one king Srang. A later king Tari, of the same clan shifted his capital from Thanutwa to Moirang where they settled permanently and became a section of the Moirang clan.[40] The rule of the Angoms were followed by the Khumans who replaced them.[41] The Mangangs seem to have emerged next and ruled for a considerable long time till it was brought to an end by a great war.[42] The Khaba clan established its stronghold for sometime till it was replaced by Nongda Lairen Pakhangba of the Ningthoujas.[43] Therefore, going by this account the probable sequence of emergence of the various *salais* till the 1st century A.D. is Nganba, Sarang Leishangthem, Moirang, Luwang, Angom, Khuman, Mangang, Khaba and finally the Ningthouja.

The popular tradition regarding the formation of the *salais* is that the Meitei confederacy consisted of nine territorial divisions which was later reduced to seven. When exactly these units emerged is difficult to ascertain. The *Sakok Lamlen Ahanba Puya* records the beginning of the seven *salais* of Kangla under Ko-Sana Pakhangba. This event took place in *Konna Chak,* the last of the four human ages in Meitei tradition.[44] The Ningthoujas, under the first 'historical' king emerged victorious in the struggle for power among the various principalities. The seven territorial divisions had each a king and a capital. The *Wakoklon Hilel Thilel Amailon Pukok Puya* records that the Mangangs had their capital at Sanggai, Luwangs at Langon later at Luwangkhong and still later at Lamphel. The Khumans ruled over Yairipok, Umukhong and later at Pumlel. The Angoms had their capital at Kontha, Okshanthong and later over areas surrounding Kongba river. The Moirangs ruled over Leikoipung and Loktak, Khabanganba over Kangpokpi, later at Langlon, Luwangching and areas surrounding Takna Thana. The Leishangthems had their capital at Leisang Hiten and later at Nungseng.[45]

The Mangangs, had their capital at Sanggai i.e., Kangla, the very seat of the Ningthoujas. From this we may assume that the Mangangs were perhaps subsumed under the Ningthouja clan at some point of time. The Khaba *salai* and Nganba *salai* trace their origin to Leichik Ningthou Chanu, showing that the principle of amalgamations was on the basis of common ancestry.[46] Thus, it is quite certain now that the separate twelve *salais* mentioned earlier existed at different periods of Meitei history and that common ancestry or political alignments must have led to the final reduction of the *salais* to seven. However, the *Cheitharol Kumbaba* indicates that the Meitei confederacy was threatened by instability due to rebellions by some chiefs of the *salais* till about the eleventh century A.D., although these were successfully put down by the kings. The Angoms rebelled against King Sameirang (518-568 A.D.) and the Moirangs and Khumans against King Irengba (984-1074 A.D.).[47]

Having established that every Meitei belong to one or the other of the seven *salais*, attempts were made by the *Puyas* to attribute divine origin to each *salai*. In trying to explain the relation between gods and men, the local learned men created the myths which are contained in these *Puyas*. Traditions in the *Puyas* dealing with the *salais* show that there is an inseparable link between the living and the ancestral deities.

The *Meihouron Thiren Puya* classifies the seven *salais* according to the particular *Piba* with which it is associated. *Piba* ordinarily means the head of a social group such as a *salai* or a *sagei*. However, in this context it means the ruling deities of the *salais*, because the names of the *Pibas* do not figure in the genealogical tree found in the *Puyas*. The *Pibas* and the corresponding clans are as follows: Nongpok Ariba-Ningthouja, Soraren Namungba-Angom, Koubru-Luwang, Chingkhei Marjing-Khabanganba, Thangjing-Moirang, Nongchup Ariba-Sarang Leishangthem and Khana Chaoba-

Khuman.[48] Later these ruling deities were adopted as guardians of different directions. The *Meihouron Pukok* traces the origin of six *salais* from five kings, viz; Tari, Kangba, Sakuppa, Kanghal and Kaksu Tonkonba. Tari had two wives. His union with Huihu Leima begot Nunai Emthangba, the progenitor of Sarang Leishangthem *salai* and with Leima Kanghal begot Purang and Pureiromba. Pureiromba was the head of the Angom clan. The union of Kangba with Tanu begot Kangkhujam Toriya. He was the progenitor of the Mangang clan Sakuppa and Leinung Keibi Tera had two sons, Nganghunthok and Ngangningsing. They became the progenitors of the Moirang Anouba and Moirang Ariba clans, in general the Moirang clan. Kaksu Tongonba and Leima Urum Kongjon begot two sons, Luwang Nongtamlon and Khuman Nongdamlon Akhuba. As the name suggests, the former was the head of the Luwangs and the later of the Khumans. The last king Khangkhal must have established the beginning of the Khabanganba clan.[49]

The ancestors of the eight *salais* as recorded in *Leithak Leikharon* are the following: (Khui) Pakhangba for the Ningthoujas, Pureiromba for the Angoms, Khum Khum for the Leishangthems, Yucheng for the Moirangs, Poireiton for the Khumans, Taoren Khaba for the Khabas, Nganba Leichik for the Nganbas and Luwang Punshiba for the Luwangs.[50] The same *Puya* gives a list of the goddesses from whom descended the seven *salais.* Similarly, Layibi was for the Angoms, Lapubi for the Chengleis, Mangwaibi for the Khumans, Tuwainu for the Luwangs, Sachibi for Moirangs and Tangkappi for the Nganbas.[51] It is significant to note here the discrepancy in the information given by the same *Puya.* The reduction of the number of the *salais* from eight to seven only reinforces the point that there was a definite attempt at systemization of the existing social order. *Pudin* is another *Puya* which follows the same line as *Leithak*

Leikharon.[52] The genealogical tree tracing the ancestor of the eight *salais* and the list of ancestresses of the seven *salais* mentioned above are the same in both the *Puyas*. The *Pakhangba Phambal* records the same list of the ancestresses of the *salais*.[53]

The names of the ancestresses of the seven *salais* as recorded in *Puyas* such as *Leithak Leikharon, Pudin* and *Pakhangba Phambal* are each associated with an animal or an object. Leikak Leiyaren, the ancestress of the Ningthouja *salai* is associated with Pakhangba.[54] Pakhangba is generally believed to manifest in the form of a snake. According to a popular myth, Pakhangba assumed the form of a snake by day and man by night.[55] The snake called *paphal*, being the extensions (*phal*) of Pakhangba (*pa*) were regarded as symbolic diagrams of the incarnations of Pakhangba.[56] The names of the other ancestresses along with their respective clans and the animal or object associated with it are as follows: Laiyibi (Angom) - *nonglum* or divine egg, Laipubi (Chenglei)-goat, Mangwaibi (Khuman) - elephant, Tuwainu (Luwang)-buffalo, Sachibi (Moirang) - deer and Langkappi (Nganba)-tiger.[57] This indicates that the Meitei social groups recognized some type of relationship between themselves and some object in nature, either animate or inanimate. This phenomenon commonly called 'totemism' is a familiar feature with many primitive societies. However, totemism may be surrounded by very different sets of beliefs and practices having quite different roles in specific cultures. In spite of these differences in various primitive cultures all over the world, ethnographers have suggested some universal features. They include the following; totemism is the most primitive form of religion, it is always associated with marriage regulations, members of totemic groups have reverential attitude towards the totem object, all clans are totemic, members of totemic groups are forbidden to eat the totem object.[58] Although the *Puyas* do not furnish us with more information on the origin, nature etc., of totems among the Meiteis, this isolated single reference suggests that the notion of totem was not unknown to the Meiteis. Totemism in primitive societies have been understood to be essentially concerned with the matriarchal stage culture (mother right), though it passes over to the patriarchal stage (father right).[59] It may be mentioned here that this type of connection existing between the totems and the ancestresses of the *salais* brings forward the question of the prevalence of matriarchal type of society in the early Meitei history. The recording of the genealogical tree of the *salais* in matrilineal descent upto the founders of the *salais* perhaps indicate that the early Meiteis existed as totemic groups before passing over to the patriarchal system.

J. Shakespear has noted the names of seven ancestresses of seven *salais*.[60] Although he mentioned the source of this list as "*Pundit's* books" without any specification, a similar list of the names given in *Pakhangba Phambal Puya* makes us believe that the source is perhaps the same.[61] Lei-khak-bi-ya-rel was the ancestress of the Ningthouja clan. She also gave birth to Singsing-yai-nu, from whom sprang all trees, grasses etc. Thursday is her birthday. Lai-i-bi-him-nu was the ancestress of the Angoms. She was the mother of Ireimas-thou-thangnu and from her came water and cotton. Her birthday is on Monday. Thung-woibi-Thoiyinu, the ancestress of the Luwang clan had two daughters. Priprinu produced gold and silver and Noinu Thumleima was the goddess of salt wells. Thung-woibi-Thoiyinu was born on Friday. Mangwoibi Thongthangnu, ancestress of the Khumals and mother of Lemlei-nga-na-na-woibi produced iron and all fishes. She has her birthday on Tuesday. Chitnu Leima was the ancestress of the Nganba clan and mother of Piyainu Pisamnu. Born on Saturday, the production of fire is attributed to her. The ancestress of the Khaba clan was Theirei-longbam-chanu. Credited with the bringing forth of winds, she is the mother of Laimon-phau-woibi, the goddess of rice. Theirei-longbam-chanu has her birthday on Sunday. Lai-phubi Laimanu, the ancestress of the Chenglei clan is the mother of earth. She was born on Wednesday on which day no land is sold.

The learned scholars in trying to bring about a uniform social order and universalization of the different groups of people devised various methods to achieve the end. The *salais* were made identifiable with known units of time. The seven *Pibas* of the seven *salais* were identified with seven directions whereas the seven ancestresses of the seven *salais* were identified with the seven days of the week.

The *Meihouron Lathup Puya* gives the names of the *salais* and the progenitors of each of them. Emiraba brings forth Luwang, Engouraba brings forth Khuman, Asunba brings forth Sarang-Leishangthem, Aranba brings forth Moirang, Khemanba brings forth Kha-Nganba, Memanba brings forth Angom and Anganba brings forth Ningthem. L. Birachandra believes that these names indicate ethnic groups.[62]

A well known popular theory about Pakhangba runs as thus:[63] Atiya Guru Sidaba wanted to test which of his sons Sanamahi and Pakhangba recognize him not only as their father but also as their *guru*. He therefore took the form of a dead cow and floated down the Bijaya river. Sanamahi showed his dislike for the carcass but Pakhangba wondered how the tail of a dead cow could move. He realized that it may be god in disguise. Atiya Guru Sidaba had moved his tail to give his sons intimation of his own identity, wishing to reveal himself. Sanamahi and Pakhangba, in accordance with the latter's wish dragged the carcass out of the water. Atiya Guru Sidaba was pleased and resuming his original form said to Pakhangba, "You know your father, the *guru* and so let your name be Pakhangba" (*pa*: father, *khangba*: to know). The story goes on to say that the carcass of the dead cow was cut into seven pieces and distributed among the founders of the seven *salais* as follows:[64] The significance attached to the cow may indicate an attempt to reinforce the totem idea, though no definite conclusion can be drawn.

Founder	*Salai*	*Parts of the Carcass*
Kuptreng (Sanamahi)	Angom	Neck
Sentreng (Pakhangba)	Ningthouja	Eyes
Pammaringba	Luwang	Head
Leisatao	Khuman	Knee
Konsouren	Moirang	One stripped belly
Asangba	Khaba	Left side of head
Tuma Nganba	Nganba	Red heart

Two more versions of the same myth are noticed. One version states that Angom sprang from brain of the sage, Luwang from between his eyes, Khaba-Nganba from his eyes, Moirangs from his nostrils, Chenglei from his nose, Khuman from his liver and Ningthouja from his spleen. The other version has the Ningthoujas born from the left eye of the sage, Angoms from his right eye, Chengleis from his right ear, Khaba-Nganba from his left ear, Luwang from his right nostrils, Khumans from his left nostril and Moirangs from his teeth.[65]

Another myth associated with Pakhangba makes him the ultimate head of all the *salais*. His union with seven *Lainuras* (divine girls) produced seven sons, who became the founding head of each *salai*. The seven *Lainuras* and their respective sons are: Laikik Huimulei Puksikombi-Mangnang, Huimuleima-Luwang, Loikhumbi Mawai Thongailelpi-Khuman, Leiyek Pithetleima-Angom, Ulum Khaichou Tonpi-Moirang, Leitham Taileima-Khanganba and Nonghainu Lila Leima-Sarang Leishangthem. Each of these seven sons was born at seven different auspicious periods of the day.[66] Once again we find in this reference another attempt of the learned scholars of early Meitei history to identify the seven *salais* in terms of known units of time. Further, each of the seven sons was allotted a specific room in the ancestral house. The sequence of the occupation of rooms were; Mangang, Luwang, Khuman, Angom, Moirang, Kha-nganba and Sarang Leishangthem.[67] Perhaps the principle of the allotment of rooms was according to the notion of seniority. It may also indicate the stages of clan formation. Hsu, while studying the social organization in West Town China, in which the figure of the ancestral head has an overwhelming presence, suggests that the distribution of living quarters or homes provides one with useful clues to understanding the relationship in a family home. According to him, the rules of room distribution emphasize the importance of generation, sex and seniority on the one hand and of lineage on the other.[68]

It is now clear that the local chronicles attempted to trace the origin of the Meiteis to divine ancestry. In doing so various myths have been created. Both gods and goddesses have their role in the formation of the social organization of the community. Thus the seven schools of thought discussed above may be reduced to the following five groups:

1. Divine (from gods), 2. Divine (from goddesses), 3. Ethnic group theory, 4. *Piba* theory, 5. Origin traced from the divine kings.

Therefore from the bewildering mass of contradictory details in the origin myths, it seems possible to arrive at this general agreement that the *Puyas* place Atingkok at the top of all ancestral genealogy, divine and human, of each *yek* of the Meiteis. Atingkok is the primal expression of the Ultimate Reality.[69] Along with Atiya and Atinga, they form the triad manifestations of Taibangpanba Mapu, the Ancestor of Ancestors.[70] It is Atingkok's union with Taoroinai which brought forth the first heads of the *yeks* of the Meitei confederacy.[71] According to *Meihourol Sakok*, Taoroinai is Leimarel Sidabi, who was brought forth by Atiya Sidaba, the Supreme Father, from his left side.[72]

The *Loiyumba Shinyen* (1110 A.D.) which attempted to organize the Meiteis on the basis of occupational groups, territorial divisions etc., and, therefore, generally referred to as 'the constitution' records the list of *yumnaks* of each of the seven *salais* as follows : Ningthouja - 131, Angom -74, Khuman -111, Khaba Nganba -23, Sarang Leishangthem - 50, Luwang - 69 and Moirang - 80.[73] The *Meihouron Sakok Puya* has given the list of four hundred and sixty-one *yumnaks* of the Meitei community.[74] A more detailed list is found in *Meihouron Puya*.[75] The *Census 1901* gives the list as follows: Ningthouja -115, Angom -50, Chengloi -41, Nganba -17, Looang - 56, Khoomon -103 and Moirang - 66.[76]

Genealogical ties serve the social purpose of establishing relationships between individuals. It is on genealogical basis that organizational divisions have evolved among the Meiteis, demarcating the larger Meitei society into *salai-yek, sagei-yumnak* and finally the individual. In many societies, especially those which lack any kind of specialized political authority, the principle of unilineal descent may play a fundamental part in social organization.[77] Living within a small social radius, the people maintain a close link with their affinate and cosanguinal kin groups.[78] The study of the Meitei ancient religion, traditions and customs thus cannot be fully understood without a proper insight into the genealogical ties that binds the community together.

W.H.R. Rivers studied the customs and beliefs of the Todas of South India based on material derived from genealogies. He draws attention to the importance of wide use of genealogies in anthropological investigation. Rivers also emphasized that the genealogical method of anthropological enquiry helps one to understand more precisely the rituals, ceremonies and customs of tribal communities. This method is essentially a mode of eliciting, recording and cross-checking the relationships of kinship and marriage of all members of a small community.[79] Kin groups are bound by social obligations. In a tribal religion, participation, subscription to and efficacy of the rites and beliefs is limited to membership of each group.[80] Rivers writes "..... it has been found that very definite function in ceremonies are assigned to people who stand in certain relationships either to the performer of the ceremony or to the person on whose behalf it is being carried out .... and duties or privileges or kin discovered in the manner can be much more clearly defined.[81]

The kinship system among the Meiteis is a vast network, stretching in every direction to embrace all members of the community. This means that everybody is related to everybody else. There are many kinship terms which express the precise kind of relationship between two individuals. In the Meitei society terms vary according to age, generational rank, sex of the person in relation to whom relationship is determined and sex of the kinsmen.[82]

There is a custom among the members of some African societies such as the Bushmanoids and the Pygmoids. "When two strangers meet in a village, one of the first duties is to sort out how they may be related to each other and after discovering the kinship, they behave to each other according to the accepted behaviour set down by society. If for example, they discover, then, they will treat each other as equals, or as an older or younger brother".[83] This runs parallel to the Meitei custom. Thus it is possible that once the relationship is established, Meiteis will refer to each other by the kinship term of, for instance, brother (*tada*), sister (*iche*), uncle (*khura*), mother (*ima*) with or without their proper names. This being the case, a person may have hundreds of fathers, mothers, uncles, sons and daughters.

Marriage, death and birth rituals allocate specific roles for an individual in the Meitei kin groups. Right from the day a baby is born, the Meiteis observe a number of rituals. As the baby is born, the woman's natal family sends special gifts through a procession of women. This is known as *'potyengba'*. The shooting of arrows in four directions to ward off evil spirits for the new born is the prerogative of the maternal uncle of the child. On the occasion of Meitei marriage, it is the bride's maternal uncle who is responsible for making her wedding bed in the bridal chamber. The Meiteis even allocate roles for such relations as sons-in-law and sister's husbands. They are expected to help in general supervision of feasts, cleaning the utensils and making arrangement of the left-over after the feast.

The basis of Meitei kinship is patriliny. It is difficult to ascertain when exactly the Meiteis began to adopt this pattern. It is, however, certain that this was not the earliest form of family. *Puyas* such as *Chada Laihui*,[84] which record the genealogy of Meitei kings from the mother's side, make us believe that women were definitely given a high position in Manipur history at least till the crystallization of the *salais*, after which patriarchal elements became more pronounced. Yet although the genealogy of the *salais* are maintained in matrilineal form till the arrival of the heads of each *salais*, there is no enough evidence to suggest that the Meitei society was a matrilineal one. It should be noted that the royal chronicle *Cheitharol Kumbaba*, a very important text for our purpose records the list of kings from the paternal side. Unlike typical matrilineal societies such as the Khasis, the Meitei society does not follow the matrilineal rules of marriage or inheritance of property. Rather the system of the Meiteis is akin to the Chinese pattern of kinship relations. The Chinese system based on patriliny places the relationship of the father and son above everything else.[85] All other relationships are regarded as extensions of the father-son relationship or supplementary to it. The desire for male descendants among the Meitei is intense. There are two ways of acquiring male descendants: natural son through marriage or by adoption. Parents without a son usually have an adopted son-in-law. This is known as *ya-ong-inba*. He assumes the responsibility of the son for all practical purposes, though he does not have legal or ritual rights.

The male superiority in the Meitei society is best exemplified by the role that he plays in family rituals. It is the son who performs the main ritual in the funeral rites of the parents, annual ancestor worship etc. The position of the *Piba* or head of the *sagei* is automatically taken over by the eldest son of the *Piba*, after his demise. He conducts the rituals performed in honour of the respective *sagei*. In case he is conversed with the intricacies involved in the worship, he acts as the priest. Otherwise the specialized priests or *Maibas* would officiate in such rites. Significant as the office of the *Piba* is, the *Pandit Loisang* (College of Priests) attached to the royal palace scrutinizes the eligibility for a being a *Piba* in accordance with the prescribed rules. A person cannot occupy the status of a *Piba* if happens to be the son of a widow or a divorcee or if he marries a divorcee or a widow. The person will also be disqualified from occupying the position if he marries any individual outside the *salai* system eg., the *Lois* who are considered to be of low status in society.

In a patrilineal social setup, Meitei women stand as a collective body, and act as a moral backing to men.[86] The analysis of traditional rituals reveal that inter-sex relationships among the Meiteis are based on mutual dependence, respect and co-operation.[87]

The role of a Meitei women as direct participant in the economic activities and the ritual status of the priestess in the core of the religious system are two unusual features in a primarily male oriented society. The two most dominant economic occupation of the Meiteis are agriculture and weaving. While agriculture is an occupation adopted by both the sexes, weaving is entirely on the hands of women. The *Lai Haraoba* ritual presents the traditional priestesses as the principal functionary who run the entire celebration. This ritual represents women not only in terms of their reproductive power, but also in their roles as daughter, wife and mother.[88] The priority of place assigned to women in a traditional social structure is that of the wife and the daughter-in-law, after the superior position of the husband and the father. A Meitei woman, upon marriage, relinquishes her jural and ritual rights on her parental home. However, it is significant that the widowed, unmarried and divorced daughters and sisters retain the right of residence in the natal home.[89] This offers a strong security to women in a patrilineal society.

Marriage is an integral part of the system of kinship.[90] Marriage is called *Lu-Hongba* (*lu*: head, bone; *hongba*: solemnize, change). *Kujaba* is an intrinsic aspect of Meitei marriage. It consists of four elements, the earth, the food grains, the cloth and the accessories which the Meitei groom must carry along with him to his bride's family and offer them to the ancestral deity. *Kujaba* ensures that the bride retains her *sagei* or sub-clan identity while she is transferred to the groom's *salai*.[91]

The Meiteis are as a whole an endogenous group. But the seven inter-marrying clans have rigid rules about *yek* exogamy. It is *namungba* or taboo for men and women of the same *salai* to marry each other. Even if they belong to different *sageis* within a *salai*, they are not allowed to marry. Four kinds of prohibitions are imposed on marriage in kinship terms which are called *Mungnaba, Pendinnaba, Shairik-Tinnaba* and *Pee-Tinnaba*.[92] *Mungnaba* forbids those persons who have a common maternal grandfather of the fifth degree and those persons who have a common maternal grandfather of three degrees to marry within each other. *Pendinnaba* taboo pertains to those group of persons belonging to different *yek salais* but having a common maternal grandfather. Such a relationship is caused by a woman having issues from more than one husband. Marriage between descendants of uterine brothers born of the great grandmother by more than one husband are said to fall within the prohibited degree called *Leinung Pendinnaba*. Another group among whom marriage are prohibited is *Pee-Tinnaba* i.e. persons having a common maternal ancestor. In the *Shairuk-Tinnaba* category are included those individuals whom belong to the same common ancestor although they now belong to separate *salais*. Khuman and Luwang *salais* for example, are descended from Poireiton and hence observe this rule of marriage prohibition.[93] The Ningthouja *salai* does not marry into two *sageis* of the Moirang *salai* viz; Mungyangjam and Loirenjam, as they are also descendants of Pakhangba.[94] Any deviation from the prescribed rules of marriage laid down by the society led to ostracization of the persons involved.[95] The couple who married within the same *salai* was sent to a *Loi* village in the West, called Haujaupan. For other breaches of exogamic rules, for example, marrying a mother's sister or her children, the offender was sent to the Yaithibi group of *Loi*.

The Meiteis attach great importance to leaving an issue before departing from this world. The issueless couples are considered bad omens. When they die, there shall always be a special rite of *Chupsaba* performed at the time of cremation. The belief is that such people die thrice.[96] The *yek-salai* exogamy has lost some of its rigidity due to the prevalence of the institution of marriage by elopement. In the past such unions resulted in the deprivation of social privileges. Women who adopted this form of marriage were not allowed to carry ceremonial articles on auspicious occasions such as marriage. Further, the husband of the woman was not permitted to cook food for lineage deities at the time of ancestor worship.[97]

Sanabam Raghumani has listed four forms of marriage viz; *Hainaba* or engagement, *Chenba* or elopement based on love and consent, *Chingba* or capture and *Loukhatpa* or recognition of unsolemnized elopement. *Hainaba* is the purest form of marriage, whereas *Chenba* is commonly practiced. This is one way of circumventing the procedures and the restrictions of the marriage rules.[98] Hodson states that the usual marriage ceremony is that known as *Prajapati* or Brahma. However, other forms of marriage were also practiced viz; *Sampati, Rajbibaha, Rakshasa* and *Gandharva*, the latter being, of course constituted by simple cohabitation.[99]

Marriage by elopement can be traced back to early period of Manipur history. The text *Panthoibi Khongul* (In Quest of Panthoibi) depicts the romantic story of the divine couple Panthoibi and Nongpok Ningthou.[100] The lovers, according to the text, eloped and later were united as man and wife at the Nongmaijing hill, which was the abode of Nongpok Ningthou. The date of the book, as mentioned in the text, is as early as the 8th century A.D.[101] R.K. Jhalajit, however, opines that the text is not earlier than the second half of the 17th century A.D.[102]

Perhaps the *pana* system is also related in some way with the marriage system in Manipur. The royal chronicle records that the original *panas*, which were essentially territorial divisions of the kingdom, introduced during the reign of King Loiyumba (1074-1112 A.D.), were six in number. They were Luplenlup, Thouchalup, Kongchalup, Lupkhubalup, Chingchalup and Khaicharup.[103] By the time of King Garibniwaz in 1729 A.D., the whole kingdom came to be divided into four units viz; Laipham, Ahallup, Khabam and Naharup. However, these divisions also had bearing on the economic and social life of the people.[104] The *Piba* or lineage head had the responsibility to report to the king's court any instances of violation of the marriage rules of the society. If the king found that *Piba* concealed a fact of marriage within the prohibited degrees, he was even liable to be prosecuted or banished. All the members of the *pana* were required turn by turn to attend the royal palace and offer services to the king. This system was known as *Lallup Kaba* (*lallup*: forced labour; *kaba*: to attend). Each member was assigned tasks to do depending partly on specialization of the individual in a particular skill, and partly and more importantly on the grounds of social status acquired through marriage by the individual concerned and his parents. With the increase in population and the scattered nature of Meitei lineage organization, it became increasingly difficult for the *Piba* to record the activities of their respective descent groups. As a result people ceased to be very particular about the social stigma attached to violation of the social norms set by the king in particular or the society in general.

When a marriage is dissolved, a woman may return to her natal home but she remains affiliated to her divorced husband's *salai* until she remarries. She may remarry a person belonging to any *salai* following the usual norm of marriage regulation. This shows that a woman is transferred to her husband's *salai* only temporarily as long as the marriage remains valid, and she retains the right to transfer into another *salai* when the occasion arise.[105] Therefore, marriage in a Meitei society is not just a concern primarily between the two individuals involved, and the state which legalizes the union, but a concern shared by the kin groups of the parties involved in the marriage and its continuance. Widows may remarry, but not with their deceased husband's brothers. There is no ceremony for the remarriage of widows.[106]

There is a leniency in the rule of patrilineage in favour of women. The absence of veil and segregation of sexes, the privilege to initiate *khainaba* (divorce), the right of residence of widowed, unmarried and divorced daughters and sisters in her natal home, the retaining of *sagei* identity by a bride while she is transferred to the groom's side, right of widows to remarry, the privilege to choose a marriage partner by the method of *Chenba* (elopement) and the high ritual status accorded to the *Maibis* (priestesses) are some of the distinct features of the traditional Meitei society. All these show that even though the Meitei women belong to a patriarchal social set up, they enjoy considerable freedom and social protection. This is not unusual in a social group which evolved out of and retained several tribal features. However, when they came under Vaisnavism, they began to subsume not only religious elements but also aspects of social organization, for example, the rules of commensality, pollution taboos on food and water, vegetarianism etc.[107]

The *Brahmanas* who came to Manipur made numerous attempts to introduce Hindu codes such as prohibition of divorce, prohibition of widow remarriage and encouragement of pre-puberty marriage.[108] Under the influence of Hinduism, the custom of *sati* also came to be practiced in some circles. The first recorded instance occurred in 1726 A.D. when 'in the month of *Inga* (May-June), on the 25th day, Thursday, Sanahal Murari died. He was cremated and two of his wives leaped into the fire and died.[109] S.N. Parratt opines that since *sati* was certainly not a usual custom followed in Manipur and that the royal chronicle having singled out these acts may indicate that the practice was uncommon.[110] Nevertheless, the *Brahmanas* did manage to influence a section of the people even into following such acts indicating that the Meitei society absorbed at least some of the socio-religious features of the Brahmanical faith.

In spite of the introduction of Hindu codes of conduct, religious rituals etc., Hinduisation did not submerge the folk religion, rather it had to accommodate itself within the strongly established Meitei religious and social framework. Therefore, although the Meitei women met with some attempts to curb their freedom by the process of

Brahmanisation, they have in general maintained their potential autonomy both socially and economically. Chaki-Sircar observes "Meitei women's economic role has proved to be too valuable and pervasive to be replaced through any of the processes of historical change that the society experienced".[111] All these suggests that before the formal classification of the Meitei society under the initiative of the kings as they moved towards a state structure, the womenfolk perhaps enjoyed almost comparable privileges along with the males. The *Maibis* and ancestral goddesses give evidence to that. Even after Hinduisation this social organization has not witnessed much change.

In a patrilineal society such as the Meiteis, the concept of sonship is important in that it determines the rightful status of a male individual in matters concerning inheritance and the role he has to play in the various rituals. There are ten forms of sonship recognized by the Meitei law.[112] They are *pokchaba-macha* (legitimate son), *ayokpa- macha* (adopted son), *ayaba-macha* (accepted son), *chellakpa-macha* (brought son), *lannaba-macha* (son begotten by another), *mapa-mashak- khangdaba- macha* (son of unknown father), *meerolakpa-macha* (son of pregnant bride), *lonnaba- macha* (son of a concubine), *poktaba-macha* (step son) and *aronba-macha* (secret son). The son is treated as legitimate one, if the son belonging to any of these categories is accepted by the father with due recognition by the society.

Land belonged to the king and a person held land at the will of the king. The father of the household was the dominant authority looking after the property. He was the absolute owner of all the property in his possession, whether ancestral or self acquired, movable or immovable. The ancestral *inkhol* (homestead) is distributed among the sons in a traditional way with the eldest son getting the southernmost portion of the land, the next son getting the portion of the land next to it till the youngest son is given the northernmost portion of the *inkhol*. Women's property might be either *ningol-maral* or *nupi-maral*, that is property over which she has absolute right.[113] As regards movable property, the general practice seems to be to provide for the sons during the lifetime of the father and to regard the youngest son as the heir general if at the time of the father's death he is still living in the ancestral home. If he had separated and was living apart from his father, the property should be equally distributed among the sons.[114]

With the division of the society into unit such as *salai, sagei* and *phungga*, the notion of descent groups and their rights of inheritance at different levels also emerged. According to the law of primogenitor, the eldest son of the eldest wife stands as the legal heir in preference to the son of the other wife or co-wives. But this law was confined to royal families. The adopted sons and step sons were also recognized in case the deceased did not have any *pokchaba- macha*. In the case of adopted son, the male line of the deceased husband of the widow was established through the male descendants of the adopted son. Although the son and daughter of a couple are regarded to have been equally born of their parents, for the purpose of inheritance the later was always considered secondary to the former.[115]

Concern with the family as a unit of production, reproduction, distribution and consumption was, and for that matter still is, a valid emphasis in studies of family and kinship. The smallest unit of the family in a Meitei community is the *phungga* or the hearth. The members of a *phungga* of a deceased male include his wife, sons, daughters, father, mother, brother, adopted sons or daughters having a separate *phungga* and the maids and servants of any category. A *phungga* may sometimes be very small, consisting of only one or two members such as the deceased alone or with his wife.

There was no notion of caste in pre-Hindu Manipur.[116] In the traditional society, nobody was ever considered high or low. The only exception was the presence of the outcaste *Lois* i.e. those who were punished by the king for violation of marital customs. Exile to *Loi* villages, either temporarily or permanently, was a traditional punishment for Manipuris.[117] The *Lois* are believed to be one of the earliest bands of settlers in Manipur but were subdued by the Meiteis.[118] Even after their subjugation, they were not directly admitted into the Meitei society and till today preserve a separate identity. They resisted conversion into the fold of Vaisnavism and remained satisfied with following the age old religion and customs. Anybody could follow any type of profession or occupation. Goldsmiths, carpenters, weavers etc. existed as a unit of endogamous inter-marrying families and not in the sense of a caste as found in other Indian villages.[119] After the conversion of the Meiteis into the fold of Hinduism, the society came to be grouped into three categories viz; the *Brahmanas*, the *Kshetriyas* and the outcastes. The *Brahmanas*, a minority group, immigrated into Manipur from about the middle of the 15th century A.D.[120] A majority of the immigrant *Brahmanas* arrived in Manipur as bachelors and married Meitei women. These *Brahmanas* who came from such places as Assam, Tripura, Nadia in West Bengal and Mathura etc., settled down in Manipur and were also allotted *yumnaks* and *sagei* titles.[121] They came to enjoy the highest ritual status in the Meitei society. The Meiteis along with the king were assigned the *Kshetriya* caste after their conversion to Hinduism.[122]

The *Sakok Lamlen Ahanba Amasung Meihouron Puya* records that each of the seven *salais* of the Meiteis came to be identified with a particular *gotra*. However, the *Puya* gives the list of only five of the *salais* at first viz; Ningthouja-Shandilya, Angom-Kaushik, Khuman- Madhukalya, Moirang-Batsya and Sarang Leishangthem-Bhadwaj.[123]

Luwang *salai* is identified with Kashap *gotra*.[124] The same *Puya* which records the genealogy of all the *salais* including the Khabanganbas do not mention the *gotra* assigned to this *salai*. It is difficult to come to any definite conclusion regarding the initial negligence shown to the Khabanganba *salai*. Perhaps the first five *salais* which were assigned the *gotras* were those which were politically and economically superior than the other two *salais*. "The Ningthoujas had special regard for the Angoms. The Khumans and Moirangs had internecine feuds with the Ningthoujas. There is, however, no evidence of such strained relations between the Ningthoujas and the Luwangs. The Khabanganbas first went out of existence at the advent of the Christian era".[125] The Chengleis also must have made their presence felt even though there seem to have been no strained relation between them and the Ningthoujas after their integration with the Ningthoujas by the first century A.D. The Khabanganbas were, however, assigned a *gotra* at some period of Manipur history. T.C. Hodson gives the list which was prepared for the *Census of 1901*. The Khabanganba *salai* is identified with Noimisha *gotra*.[126] The list of the other *salais* is the same as that found in *Sakok Lamlen Ahanba Amasung Meihouron Puya* except for the Moirang *salai* which is identified here with Atreya *gotra*.[127] It should be mentioned here that although the royal clan (Ningthoujas) came under the fold of the *Kshetriya* caste, the king, however, was above the priests. By virtue of his position, he maintained his status as the head of the new religion as much as he was, as the head of the old religion. The Meitei *Kshetriyas* except the king have an egalitarian relationship. The outcastes in Manipur included the *Lois*, the hill tribes and the non-Hindus in general. The Meiteis and the *Brahmanas* do not accept cooked food and water from these people. There is no stratified caste system in a Meitei village. The absence of occupational caste (except for the *Brahmanas*) has helped the Meiteis to develop a community life based on co-operative labour. Inspite of the prevalence of the above mentioned three castes in the Meitei society, there is no system of caste exploitation as found in the high-caste dominated-communities in India.[128] The Meiteis which form the major group of the population maintain their caste identity as an endogamous and commensal unit without any ritual prohibition of contact among themselves. The outcastes live in their villages without any ritual or social tie to the Meiteis or *Brahmanas.*[129]

Scrupulous fidelity to tradition is everywhere a characteristic of tribal religion.[130] The Meiteis attached prime importance to the sanctity of communal life amounting to adoration of blood kinship and observance of social rules. In every respect clans and lineage played a significant part in the Meitei society, thereby forming the basis of the various stages of development of Meitei philosophical thoughts, resulting in the emergence of the cult of ancestor worship. The lineage is a significant entity in considerations of purity and pollution at birth initiation, marriage, death and many other occasions in life.[131] In a largely agricultural community, the traditional religion drew its support from such institutions as the family of related household or the village as an organizational unit. A single household cannot satisfy all the demands of life. To cope with these demands, families band together in various ways. The *sageis* united by ties of blood, marriage, adoption etc.,and possessing an awareness of relationship to a common forebear, had given rise to the *salai* system, the ultimate family. Each member of the *salai* group is drawn together for co-operative observance of ancestral rituals. This gives the members of the *yek-salai* group a sense of emotional security and also reinforce the internal solidarity of the group themselves.

Notes and References

1. Emile Durkheim,(tr. Joseph Ward Swain), *The Elementary Forms of the Religious Life*, 1965.

2. Anthony Giddens (ed.), *Emile Durkheim: Selected Writings*, 1985 (Reprint), p.219.
3. *Ibid.*, p.220.
4. Raymond Aron, (tr.R.Howard and H.Weaver), *Main Currents in Sociological Thought*, Vol.2, 1982 (Reprint), p.61.
5. Emile Durkheim, *op. cit.*, p.470.
6. E. Dominick La Capra, *Emile Durkheim: Sociologist and Philosopher*, 1972, p.290.
7. R.N. Bellah, 'Religious Evolution', in Roland Robertson (ed.), *Sociology of Religion: Selected Readings*, 1971 (Reprint), p.265.
8. *Ibid.*, p.270.
9. Peter L.Berger, *The Social Reality of Religion*, 1967, p.41.
10. Peter L.Berger and T. Luckmann, *'Sociology of Religion and Sociology of Knowledge'*, in Roland Robertson (ed.), *op. cit.*, p.68
11. Peter L.Berger, *op. cit.*, p.39.
12. *Ibid.*, p.40.
13. *Ibid.*, p.43.
14. *Ibid.*, pp. 46-47.
15. *Ibid.*, p.47.
16. *Ibid.*, p.54.
17. *Ibid.*, p.56.
18. M. Francis Abraham, *Modern Sociological Theory*, 1988, p.94.
19. *Ibid.*, p.100.
20. Raymond Aron, *op. cit.*, p.68.
21. M. Ibohal, "The Outlines of Constitutional History of Manipur", in Naorem Sanajaoba (ed.), *Manipur: Past and Present*, Vol. I, 1988, p.293.
22. *Thockchomlon* (Unpublished *Puya*), custodian, Oinam Bhogeswar Singh.
23. *Khumukchamlon* (Unpublished *Puya*), custodian, Oinam Bhogeswar Singh.
24. *Khumanlon* (Unpublished *Puya*), custodian, N. Khelchandra Singh.

25. *Sanggai Phammang* (Unpublished *Puya*), custodian, Y. Mohendra Singh.
26. *Langthaballon* (Unpublished *Puya*), custodian, Y. Mohendra Singh.
27. M. Laimit and L. Iboyaima (ed.), *Wakolol Hilel Thilel Amailon Pukok Puya*, p.49.
28. N. Ibochouba (ed.), *Thiren Layat*, p.32.
29. List prepared in connection with *Census 1901*; in T.C. Hodson, *The Meitheis*, 1989, (Reprint), p.182.
30. Y. Bhagya Meitei (ed.), *Sakok Lamlen Ahanba Amasung Meihouron*, 1988, p.37.
31. *Ibid.*, p.160.
32. Bhagya Singh Yengkhoiba (ed.), *Leithak Leikharon*, pp. 79-82.
33. *Ibid.*, p.113.
34. L. Ashokumar Singh, "Khuman-Salai", *Seminar on Ancient History of Manipur*, 1987, p.1.
35. M. Laimit and Y. Iboyaima (ed.), *Wakoklon Hilel Thilel Amailon Pukok Puya*, p.52.
36. Malem Yaiphasang (ed.), *Khamoi Yangoi Sekning*, 1971, p.15.
37. Konsam Manikchand, "*The Evolution of the Meitei State - A Confederacy Through the Last Millenia*", in Naorem Sanajaoba (ed.) *op. cit.*, p.149.
38. *Ibid.*, p.149.
39. E.W. Dun, *Gazetteer of Manipur*, 1992 (Reprint), p.13.
40. *Langdai Lunghei* (Unpublished manuscript), pp. 28-29, cited in N. Birachandra "Kings and Emperors who Reigned in Manipur before the Christian Era", *Seminar on Cultural History of Manipur before 33 A.D.*, 1990, pp.6-8.
41. *Lai Khunda* (Unpublished manuscript) cited in N. Birachandra, *op. cit., p.8.*
42. *Khundarol* (Unpublished manuscript) cited in N. Birachandra, *op. cit., p.8.*
43. *Singkak* (Unpublished manuscript) cited in N. Birachandra, *op.cit., p.8.*
44. Y. Bhagya Meitei (ed.), *Sakok Lamlen Ahanba Amasung Meihouron*, , p.5.

45. M. Laimit and Y. Iboyaima (ed.), *Wakok Hilel Thilel Amailon Pukok Puya,* pp. 54-55.
46. Y. Bhagya Meitei (ed.), *Sakok Lamlen Ahanba Amasung Meihouron,* pp. 163, 167.
47. L. Iboongohal Singh and N. Khelchandra Singh (ed.), *Cheitharol Kumbaba,* pp. 4,8.
48. *Meihouron Thiren,* cited in L. Birachandra, *op. cit.,* p.2.
49. *Meihouron Pukok,* p.5., cited in L. Birachandra, *op. cit.,* p.3.
50. Bhagya Singh Yengkhoiba (ed.) *Leithak Leikharon,* pp. 79-82.
51. *Ibid.,* p.113.
52. *Pudin* (Handwritten copy of the published *Puya*), custodian, N. Khelchandra Singh.
53. Kh. Yaima Singh (ed.) *Pakhangba Phambal,* 1964, p.35.
54. Bhagya Singh Yengkhoiba (ed.), *Leithak Leikharon,* p.113.
55. *Ibid.,* p.90.
56. P.Gunindra Singh(ed.), *Catalogue of Manuscripts and Manucript Paintings of Manipur,* 1987, Introduction.
57. Bhagya Singh Yengkhoiba (ed.), *Leithak Leikharon,* p.113.
58. William A. Lessa and Evon Z. Vogt, "Totemism: Introduction", in William A. Lessa and Evon Z. Vogt (ed.), *Reader in Comparative Religion: An Anthropological Approach,* 1958, p.221.
59. Alexander Goldenwiser, "*Totemism*", in William A. Lessa and Evon Z. Vogt (ed.), *op.cit.,* p.223.
60. J. Shakespear, "The Religion of Manipur", *Transactions of the Folklore Society,* 1913, pp. 425-426.
61. Kh. Yaima Singh (ed.), *Pakhangba Phambal,* p.35.
62. *Meihouron Lathup,* cited in L. Birachandra, *op. cit.,* p.3.
63. Mutua Jhulan Singh,(tr.Y. Khoimacha Singh et al.), *Bejoy Punchalee or History of Manipur,* (Pt. I), 1936, p.3.
64. Pandit Raj Atombapu Sharma, *Pakhangba,* 1950, p.2.
65. T.C. Hodson, *op. cit.,* p.100.
66. M. Laimit and Y. Iboyaima (ed.), *Wakoklon Hilel Thilel Amailon Pukok Puya,* pp.49-51.

67. *Ibid.*, p.52.
68. Francis L.K. Hsu, *Under the Ancestors' Shadow*, 1971, p.51.
69. Bhagya Singh Yengkhoiba (ed.), *Leithak Leikharon*, p.4.
70. Y. Bhagya Meitei (ed.), *Sakok Lamlen Ahanba Amasung Meihouron*, p.27.
71. Bhagya Singh Yengkhoiba (ed.), *Leithak Leikharon*, pp. 79-82.
72. Kh. Chandrashekhar Singh (ed.), *Sakok Lamlen Ahanba Amasung Meihourol Sakok*, 1992, p.5.
73. Gangumei Kabui, "A Note on Loiyumba Shinyen (1110 A.D.): the first Written Constitution of Manipur", in Naorem Sanajaoba (ed.), *op. cit.*, p.308.
74. Kh.Chandrashekhar Singh(ed.), *Sakok Lamlen Ahanba Amasung Meihourol Sakok*, p.5.
75. Y. Bhagya Meitei (ed.), *Sakok Lamlen Ahanba Amasung Meihouron, p.27*
76. T.C. Hodson, *op. cit.*, pp. 182-187.
77. John Beattie, *Other Cultures*, 1964, p.103.
78. Manjusri. Chaki-Sircar, *Feminism in a Traditional Society: Women of the Manipur Valley*, 1984, p.65.
79. W.H.R. Rivers, *The Todas*, Vol. II, 1986, pp. 465-467.
80. Paul Bohannan, *Social Anthropology*, 1963, p.328.
81. Patricia Uberoi, "Introduction", in Patricia Uberoi (ed.) *Family, Kinship and Marriage in India*, 1993, p.17.
82. Manjusri, Chaki-Sircar, *op. cit.*, p.64.
83. John S. Mbiti, *African Religions and Philosophy*, 1971 (Reprint), p.105.
84. N. Khelchandra Singh (ed.), *Chada Laihui*, 1966.
85. Francis L.K. Hsu, *op. cit.*, pp. 56-57.
86. Manjusri, Chaki-Sircar, *op. cit.*, p.63.
87. *Ibid.*, p. 185.
88. *Ibid.*, p.211.
89. *Ibid.*, p.203.
90. Leela Dube, "Sociology of Kinship: A Trend Report", in M.N. Srinivas et al.(ed.), *A Survey of Research in Sociology and Social Anthropology*, Vol.II, 1974, p.270.

91. Sanabam Raghumani, "Meitei Personal Law", in Naorem Sanajaoba (ed.), *op. cit.*, p.331.
92. Sanabam Mangang, *Meitei Law and Hindu Law: Compared and Contrasted,*1991, p.105.
93. Kalachand Singh, *Sagei Salailon,* 1965, pp. 142-143.
94. Konsam Manikchand, *op. cit.*, p.147.
95. Manjusri Chaki-Sircar *op. cit.*, p.58.
96. Sanabam Raghumani, *op. cit.*, p.331.
97. N. R. Singh, "Marriage by Elopement Among the Meiteis of Manipur", *Man in India*, Vol. 53, 1973, p.138.
98. Sanabam Raghumani, *op. cit.*, p.330.
99. T.C. Hodson, *op. cit.*, p.113.
100. M. Chandra Singh (ed.), *Panthoibi Khongul,* 1987, pp. 94-95.
101. *Ibid.*, p.(i).
102. R. K. Jhalajit Singh, *A History of Manipuri Literature,* 1987, p.149.
103. L. Iboongohal Singh and N. Khelchandra Singh (ed.), *Cheitharol Kumbaba,* 1989, p.9.
104. *Ibid.,* p.89.
105. N. R. Singh, *op. cit.*, p.143
106. T.C. Hodson, *op. cit.,* p.77.
107. Manjusri Chaki-Sircar, *op. cit.*, p.186.
108. *Ibid.*, p.188.
109. L. Iboongohal Singh and N. Khelchandra Singh (ed.) *Cheitharol Kumbaba,* p.85.
110. S. N. Parratt, *The Religion Of Manipur,*1980, p.147.
111. Manjusri Chaki-Sircar, *op. cit.*, p.188.
112. Sanabam Raghumani, *op. cit.,* pp. 334-335.
113. *Ibid.*, pp. 338-341.
114. T.C. Hodson, *op. cit.*, p.77.
115. Sanabam Raghumani, *op. cit.,* pp. 342-343.
116. K. B. Singh, "Social Stratification and Mobility in Manipur", in S.M. Dubey (ed.), *North-East India: A Sociological Study,* 1978, p.62.

117. S. N. Parratt, *op. cit.*, p.4.
118. Konsam Manikchand, *op. cit.*, p.23.
119. K. B. Singh, *op. cit.*, p.63.
120. *Bamon Khunthoklon* (anon.), (n.d), p.1.
121. *Ibid*, pp. 1-9.
122. Y. Bhagya Meitei (ed.) *Sakok Lamlen Ahanba Amasung Meihouron*, p.62.
123. *Ibid.*, p.62.
124. *Ibid.*, p.171.
125. Ch. Manihar Singh (ed. and tr.), *Naothingkhong Phambal Kaba*, 1983, p.13.
126. T.C. Hodson, *op. cit.*, p.184.
127. *Ibid.*, p.186.
128. Manjusri Chaki-Sircar, *op. cit.*, p.24.
129. *Ibid.*
130. Masahasu Ansaki, *History of Japanese Religion*, 1928, p.36.
131. A.M. Shah, "Lineage and Change in a Gujarat Village", in Patricia Uberoi (ed.), *op. cit.*, p.145.

3

The Meitei Pantheon

The core of the ancient religion of the Meitei people of Manipur is the cult of ancestor. In fact it is the basis of the entire religious system and as such ancestor worship is at the root of the Meitei philosophy of life, and upon which the Meitei society is founded. The ancient religion passed through a long process of evolution of the Meitei society and survived even after Vaisnavism was declared the state religion of Manipur in the 18th century A.D.

Scholars widely differ in their views on the term 'ancestor'. Ronald Berndt has characterized ancestors as "mythical beings who are believed to have been responsible for creating the natural species which included man ....", and also to "have established an aboriginal way of life ... " as "deities", and added that some of them "are ancestral, credited with having created the progenitors of contemporary men".[1] To Fortes: "an ancestor is a named dead forbear who has living descendants of a designed genealogical class representing his continued structural relevance. In ancestor worship, such an ancestor received ritual service and tendance directed specifically to him by the proper class of his descendants. Being identified by name means that he is invested with attributes distinctive of a kind of person.[2] Robert Smith in his study of the memorial tablets of Japan observed: "....the memorialized dead are everywhere referred to as *senzo* (ancestors)...."[3]

Ancestor worship anywhere thus comprises of customary beliefs and practices and are directed towards veneration of dead predecessors. In the religious system of the Meiteis death is considered as a certain determined and indispensable condition for attaining ancestorhood. A person after his death becomes an ancestor when he dies, not simply because he is dead, but that he leaves behind him a legitimate successor. Thus death without successor is not a sufficient condition for becoming an ancestor entitled to receive worship. Far from severing the relationship of the dead to the living, death merely promotes the relationship to a plane technically different but theoretically similar to that which existed before the event.

The relationship of the living to the dead is maintained by prayers as in many African and Asiatic societies. Prayer, whatever its intent, whether to solicit help, offer thanks, tender apologies, admit guilt or promise of reform, brings the ancestors into direct communication with the worshippers.[4]

I

Since the Meitei ancestor worship is inextricably associated with the legend of creation, we may briefly recount it. The *Leishemlon* (The Meitei Creation Myth) shows two great time orders: the *Hangko* followed by the *Chak*. The *Leishemlon Ariba Puya*[5] divides the *Hangko* age into four major sub-periods viz; *Ko-Hangko, Thoi-Hangko, Tayo-Hangko* and *Poi-Hangko*. Each period was ruled by Chinggu Mapuren Sidaba, Pakhangba, Kourouhanba and Koubaren respectively. However, the *Pakhangba Laihui Puya*[6] differs in the names of the rulers of *Thoi-Hangko* and *Tayo-Hangko* sub-periods. These four sub-periods cover 19,55,88,945 years, 16,29,906 years, 57,845 years and 11,79,900 years respectively bringing a total of 19,84,56,596 years according to the Meitei calendar. According to the *Pakhangba Laihui Puya* during the *Hangko* age the universe was enveloped in total darkness. It was during the age of *Poi-Hangko* (the fourth sub-period) that the creation of earth was done. The land of the Meiteis was then known by the name of Poirei Namthak Saronpung. In the three earlier periods (*Hangkos*) of *Ka*, *Thoi* and *Tayo* interaction among primal elements such as vapour, gas, water and fire occured.

The *Hangko* age was followed by the *Chaks*. The *Leithak Leikharon Puya* gives four human sub-periods of the *Chaks* viz; *Hayi, Haya, Langba* and *Konna*.[7] *The Sakok Lamlen Ahanba Puya* repeats these names in a similar order.[8] However, it also refers to *Haya Chak* as *Khunung Chak* in the subsequent pages.[9] The *Thiren Layat Puya* refers to *Khunung Chak* as the second *Chak*.[10] Since both *Haya Chak* and *Khunung Chak* are mentioned interchangeably, we may assume that they refer to the same age. This tradition is recorded in the *Leishemlon Ariba Puya* as well.[11] The *Hayi, Haya* or *Khunung, Langba* and *Konna*, are time cycles which replace each other from the legendary period up to the present day in the history of the universe created by Taibangpanba Mapu (Ancestor of Ancestors).

The myth of creation is an attempt by a particular community to understand the apparently mysterious beginning of the universe. All significant temporal events are articulated in the language of the cosmogonic myth, for only by placing them in this primordial model will they have significance. The recollection and recounting of the creation myth enables the community to comprehend and participate in the fundamentally real time, space and mode of orientation that enable them to define their cultural life in a specific manner.[12] The cosmic evolution as visualized by the ancient Meiteis was preserved orally in their traditions which was written down in the historical time. These traditions are recorded in many *Puyas*, such as *Leithak Leikharon*,[13] *Pudin*,[14] *Wakoklon Hilel Thilel Amailon Pukok Puya*,[15] *Khamlangba Erengba Puwari: Neinarol*[16] etc. The *Leithak Leikharon Puya* version of the myth is narrated below. This is the most elaborate version which takes care of the varied accounts of the myths recorded in other *Puyas* mentioned above.

Leithak Leikharon literally means 'Of heaven (*leithak*) and the netherworld (*leikha*)'. The *Puya* claims to have been initially written during the time of the first 'historical' king Nongda Lairen Pakhangba (33-154 A.D.). It was edited with minor additions by the great literary *guru* Khongnang Thaba during the reign of King Khagemba (1597-1652 A.D.).[17]

The narration begins with the condition that prevailed in the end of *Langba Chak* and the beginning of *Konna Chak*, the last of the four human sub-periods mentioned above. It states how all things and creatures, including the gods, perished, and how the Ultimate Lord created the world anew with the commencement of new cycles of another *Chak* age. While everything was consumed by the devastating fire at the end of the *Langba Chak*, only three deities, survived. They were Taibangpanba Mapu, Atingkok and Amamba.[18] The nine layers of heaven and the nine layers of earth which the Lord had created were also subjected to decadence and eventually vanished. Taibangpanba Mapu then decided to create the universe afresh. The Lord uttered the primal sound '*hung*'. He then uttered, "*Here Make Nahe Kare, Hanu Mihe Hasi Nare Mare Hasi, Hasi, Kare, Nare, Mahe, Maru Kare, Haere, Tiuite Miking Mihingsang Chingtete Ching Thete Naphu, Siring Kiring Kethureng Nou, Saha Ani Kangpiru Kalapun Saha. Kiring Siring Sannuringkhai Nongta Kangpiru, Nungchiren Purin Hiring Saha Ueitei Nungtarengpi Sangthupnu Angka Siring Kiring Nongta*".[19] Once these unintelligible words were uttered, there appeared a halo which was the seed of the universe. The halo now developed seven colours like a rainbow. Taibangpanba Mapu broke it into two parts. The one on the right hand side became the king of the gods and the one on the left became the queen of the gods. Then began the germination. Atingkok, as the point of germination, became *sunnaching* or the divine mount. Amamba was placed below the divine mount. Taibangpanba Mapu covered the entire area like a protective sheath. He was present in both the spheres and for this reason acquired the title of Lord of the Universe.[20]

Taibangpanba Mapu brought forth from himself Atiya Guru Sidaba, and Atingkok was instructed to entrust Atiya with the work of creation. Atiya thus came to be known by the name of Asiba (from *siba* i.e., to be on an errand).[21]

Now, Atiya Sidaba, having been given the responsibility to create the earth, decided to seek the help and advice of the supreme god Atingkok, the manifestation of Taibangpanba Mapu.[22] On hearing this Atingkok opened his mouth and Atiya saw the whole universe resting within him. Atiya saw the sun, the moon, the pole star, air and much more. He then begged of Atingkok to bring these out of himself. Atiya sang the *Hoiru* song: "*Ahei He Hoiru Hoiru Hoiru Nakase*", and Atingkok opened his mouth generously to allow the elements to come out. This act was accompanied by another happy song: *Ha Hoi Ha Ha Ha, Hoi Ha Ha Ha Hirin Linla Herinla, Herinla Hayute Khulaite Heiyase Heiyase, Ashibu Thoina Haraoba Leibane. Tahou Hou He Hou Haya Nakate.*[23] It is significant that while enacting the creation myth during the *Lai Haraoba* festival the *Maibis* still utter this unintelligible cry.

Among the many insects and animals which came into being in the course of the creation of the earth was a tortoise. It was on the back of this tortoise floating in the water, that the earth was first created. As the earth was initially very small in size, it could not survive and turned into cloud. The floating broken pieces of earth were collected by Atiya and he created an eel out of them. On the advice of the Supreme Lord another earth was created. It was destroyed again and this time the earth turned into snow. Then Atiya created a black beetle which was sent to the Supreme Lord for further instruction. With his advice, the earth was finally created.[24]

The destructive force was also a god by the name of Haraba. When Haraba was planning for the destruction of the earth for the third time, Atiya, the Immortal Guru realized his evil design and decided to distract him. Therefore, the goddess Nongthangleima, daughter of Guru Sidaba and Leimaren Sidabi was created as a beautiful girl to enamour Haraba.[25] Meanwhile, the creation of the earth was undertaken vigorously and with great care. The four cardinal points of the earth were now guarded by four deities viz; Kara (East), Pisatau (West), Nongtam Khuba (North) and Kari (South).[26] The creation of Nongthangleima and the guardian of the four directions helped in preventing Haraba from destroying the newly created earth. The earth assumed its final shape at the end of this long process of construction, destruction and reconstruction.[27] The untiring efforts of Taibangpanba Mapu, Atingkok, Atiya Sidaba and Asiba was therefore proved fruitful.

After completing the creation of *leithak* and *leikha*, Atiya, along with Apanba, created human beings in the shape of the shadow of Taibangpanba Mapu, the Immortal Lord. Mankind was then given five principles of life, each located in a specific part of the body. The five gods who represented the five principles are Pongthanglen, Koubaren Apanba, Thangjing, Marjing and Kouparu.[28] The *Leithak Leikharon Puya* mentions that many gods and goddesses helped Guru Sidaba in the task of creation and these deities were brought forth from the body of Taibangpanba Mapu.[29]

The cosmogonic myths prevalent in primitive societies as mentioned in *The New Encyclopaedia Britannica* have been categorised into five types.[30] The primal myth of creation, as narrated in the *Leithak Leikharon Puya*, confirms to the first type. According to this notion discovered by Andrew Lang,[31] the creation of the world is credited to a supreme being. Such myths are said to be found in the cultures of Africa, the Ainu of the Northern Japanese island, the Central Australians and in several other parts of the globe. Although the precise nature and characteristics of the supreme deity may differ from one culture to another, some common characteristics may be discerned. The supreme deity is all powerful and wise. The world comes into being because of this power. The deity existed alone prior to the creation of the world and there was void before him. The mode of creation is deliberate, conscious and orderly. The supreme creator deity is often a sky god and the deity in this form is an instance of the expression of the symbolism of the sky. The presence of a destructive force is also a common feature.

II

Like majority of the primitive religions all over the world, the Meiteis also personified the forces of nature. However, the *Puyas* reveal that ancestor worship lay at the base of all Meitei religious beliefs. It is important to remember that the Meiteis had a tradition of conferring many names for a single deity or an individual, perhaps a new name on the occasion of every significant ritual. This creates confusion to one who is not associated with ancient religious rituals. *Puyas* such as the *Lainingthou Sanamahi Mingkheiron* and the *Sanamahi Ming*, for example, furnish lists of forty-five names and one hundred and sixty-eight names, respectively of the deity popularly called Sanamahi.[32] However, a comparative study of the names mentioned in the many *Puyas* helps in the identification of these deities.

In the Meitei pantheon Taibangpanba Mapu occupies the highest place of all ancestors. This 'Immortal Lord of the

Universe', is also known as Taibang Mapu Sidaba,[33] Atinga Sidaba,[34] Ipung Loinapa Apakpa,[35] Lainingthou Asuppa,[36] Hei Ha Mapu Sidaba,[37] etc. He is omnipresent, omnipotent and omniscient. The majority of the *Puyas* begin with an obeisance to this Immortal Lord. The royal chronicle *Cheitharol Kumbaba* also begins with an obeisance to Taibangpanba Mapu.[38] Taibangpanba Mapu is believed to manifest in the forms of Atingkok as air, Atiya as the *Guru* and Atinga as the father.[39] *Leithak Leikharon* adds that Amamba or the Infinite Darkness is another immortal manifestation of the Supreme One.[40]

The *Puyas* attach significance to the nine *Laibungthous* (divine youths) and the seven *Lainuras* (divine girls) whom Taibangpanba Mapu had brought forth from within himself in order to help him in the creation of the universe. They are credited with the task of levelling the uneven earth which was thus made habitable. The nine *Laibungthous* are Laininghanba, Khamlangba, Mongba Hanba, Chakhaba, Naokan, Muwa Ningthou, Luwang Punshiba, Marjing and Koubru.[41] The seven *Lainuras* are Leishangthem Lairemma, Sarangthem Lairemma, Phouiobi, Thoomleima, Panthoibi, Nongthangleima and Ngaleima.[42] The nine divine youths emanated from the nine orifices of *Kuru* (or *Guru*) *Sidaba's* body.[43] Laininghanba sprang from the right eye, Muwa Ningthou from the left eye, Mingba Hanba from the right ear, Naokon from the left ear, Chakhaba from the right nostril, Koubaren alias Koubru from the left nostril, Khamlangba from the mouth, Luwang Punshiba from *eshingthong* (urinary tract) and Marjing from *penthong* (anus).[44] The seven *Lainuras* are the manifestation of Leimaren Sidabi or the Ultimate Mother.[45]

There are eight gods who are distinguished from the rest by the title of *Maigei Ngakpas* i.e., guardians of directions.[46] They are Soraren (North), Khana Chaoba (South), Nongpok Ningthou (East), Nongchup Ariba (West), Koubru (North-

West), Wangbren (South-East), Thangching (South-West) and Chingkhei Ningthou (North-East).[47] A slightly different version of the names of the gods and the directions are given by R.K. Sanahal Singh, which is as follows: Nongpok Ningthou (East), Irum Ningthou (South-East), Wangbren (South), Thangjing (South-West), Khorifaba (West), Loiyarakpa (North-West), Marjing (North) and Chingkhei (North-East).[48] In every religious ceremony, four gods are invoked by the *Maibas* and *Maibis* to protect the ritual from evil spirits. These four deities, are regarded as four incarnations of the guardians of four directions. They are Thangjing (South-West), Marjing (North-East), Wangbren (South-East) and Koubru (North-West).[49]

The progenitors of the seven clans that make up the entire Meitei people are collectively known by the name of *Salai Apokpas* or clan ancestors. The *Salai Apokpas* are the ancestors who are worshipped by the concerned clans. But Taibangpanba Mapu, the nine *Laibungthous*, the seven *Lainuras* and the *Maigei Ngakpa lais* are ancestors for all the Meiteis and are evoked at various public rituals, although they may also be worshipped along with the *Salai Apokpas* at home. This is different from the worship of the *Salai Apokpas* who can be evoked exclusively by the descendant of a particular *apokpa* .

The *lais* which the Meiteis worship are nearly four hundred in number. All of them can be characterized as ancestor *lais* who encompass the entire Meitei pantheon. For the Meiteis, there is no god greater than Taibangpanba Mapu or Taibangmapu Sidaba. All the families trace their roots from this Immortal Father.

The ancestral spirits, both divine and human, are designated as *Umanglais*. There are various interpretations of the term *Umanglai*. *Umanglai* literally means presiding deity of the grove (*umang*: grove, *lai*: god). J. Shakespear calls them forest deities.[50] They are believed to dwell in groves which are so thick that they came to be known as *Umanglais*. S.N. Parratt[51] observes that while the etymology of the term may suggest association of the *Umanglais* with groves, they were never regarded as limited to the forest. Kh. Chandrashekhar,[52] on the other hand, argues that *Umanglai* is a corrupted form of the word *Uramba-lai* (from *uba*: to see). He claims that the *Puyas* indicate that there was a time when the gods and men lived together, and therefore the gods were visible to men. Then the gods retired from the earth. This view seems too farfetched, but there are references in the *Puyas* that till the time of the second human sub-period or the *Haya Chak*, the gods co-existed with men.[53] It seems possible to believe that the *Umanglais* were originally worshipped in sacred groves.

In Manipur, the concept of the temple emerged much later. Archaeological findings do not support the assertion of the *Puyas* that temples were in existence from the time of Nongda Lairen Pakhangba in the first century A.D.[54] The *Cheitharol Kumbaba* records the construction of the first temple in 1617 A.D. during the reign of King Khagemba.[55] However, *Umanglais* are worshipped at home as well. But as the anthropologists[56] argue that community worship precedes family worship it is possible to assume that the Meiteis, in the absence of temples, tried to venerate the *Umanglais* in the sacred groves. There are numerous references in the royal chronicle which show that reverence of trees was very common during the pre-Khagemba period. During the reign of Meidingu Mungyamba and Khagemba (1569 to 1665 A.D.) there are no fewer than twelve references to *u-hongba* in the royal chronicle.[57] *U:* tree was fit for *hongba:* initiation, inauguration. However, there are no explanations as to why the tree was revered and whether the trees were dedicated to the *lais*, or any particular *lai* was associated with any particular tree. There is not enough evidence to come to any definite conclusion regarding these *u-hongba* rituals. It might have had originated as a kind of formal thanksgiving to the trees for the benefits they rendered to the people. It has also been speculated that since the trees existed from 'time immemorial' certain supernatural qualities were attributed to them, which accounts for their veneration.[58] However, in the absence of any convincing connection between *u-hongba* and *Umanglais*, the study of *Umanglais* will be treated as separate from the tree-cult in Manipur in this study.

One can perhaps draw a parallel between the Meitei *Umanglais* and the Japanese *Kami*. Bunce observes that the term *Kami* denotes a variety of meanings and it is difficult to find a truly accurate definition of the term. He says that the term was applied to the deities of heaven and earth, to those spirits which dwell in shrines and to beasts, birds, plants, seas, mountains and to such natural phenomena as storms, winds and echoes.[59] Ono defines *Kami* as thus: "Fundamentally, the term *Kami* is an honorific for noble sacred spirits, which implies a sense of adoration for their virtues and authority. All beings have such spirits, so in a sense all beings can be called *Kami* or be regarded as potential *Kami*. However, because the term is an honorific, it is not customary to apply it to ordinary individuals".[60] Earhart further explains, ".... any being whosoever which possess some eminent quality out of the ordinary and is awe-inspiring is called *Kami*. Perhaps the best general term for understanding *Kami* is the notion of the sacred".[61] Although the *Umanglais* are essentially ancestral spirits they are almost equally difficult to define, and have as large and varied associations as the *Kami*. The similarity also consists in both being ubiquitous, powerful, and sacred.

III

The *Umanglais* were originally nine in number. Now, the

list has expanded to include as many as three hundred and seventy-eight.[62] The first nine *Umanglais* were the nine *Laibungthous* (divine youths) who assisted the Supreme Lord in levelling the newly created earth and making it habitable. With the increase in the number of lineages, other *Umanglais* emerged. The *Lai Khunta Lon Puya* states that it was *Lairen Taoroinai* who extracted the nine *Umanglais* from a place called Linwaikhong identified in Kangpokpi in the present Senapati district. The *Puya* does not give details as to why, or how this extraction incident took place or the significance of Linwaikhong. The names of the *Umanglais* according to this *Puya* are Muwa Ningthou Apanba, Laithou Ahanba, Chakhaba, Koubaren, Khamlangba, Luwang Ningthou, Marjing, Wangbren and Thangjing. The *Puya* goes on to say that these deities guard the corners of the earth and that they should be propitiated with annual offerings of fish, certain animals, wine and human flesh. It specifically mentions that the *lais* accept non-vegetarian items, unlike Atingkok who accepts only vegetarian food.[63] The *Nunglon Puya* records that the nine *Umanglais* should be worshipped with offerings of cow's meat. The names of the nine *Umanglais* given in this *Puya* i.e., Muwakon, Chakhakon, Naokhangkon, Tinsikon, Yumoikon, Taothingkon, Yoiheikon, Leitolkon and Mongbakon, are somewhat different from that of *Lai Khunta Lon*.[64] The difference in the names of the *Umanglais* can be understood in the context of different people writing *Puyas* at different periods. Each clan might have had different lists which were preserved and got mixed up with other names. However, despite such differences, the original number of the *Umanglais* is always mentioned as nine and that they are invariably described as the manifestations of the Ultimate Father.

The *Umanglais* are ancestral deities.[65] According to W. Lukhoi Singh, the Meiteis today venerate as many as three hundred and seventy-eight *Umanglais*.[66] Pandit Ng.

Kullachandra of *Pandit Loisang*, Royal Palace has prepared a list of three hundred and sixty-two *Umanglais*.[67] A comparative study of these lists indicates that a number of *Umanglais* were incorporated into the Meitei pantheon during various stages of the history of Manipur. For example, it is quite obvious that with the beginning of the Hindu influence in Manipur from around the 17th -18th centuries a large number of new *lais* were added to the Meitei pantheon. Although the name *Laphupat Kalika* suggests that she is a Hindu goddess of the place Laphupat, Kalika is definitely not a traditional Meitei *lai*. Similarly, the influence of Vaisnavism can be seen in the inclusion of such names as Thinungei Ramji Ningthou.[68] This is not unusual in view of the fact that Vaisnavism has always accommodated tribal features as a carrier of the Brahmanical faith in the peripheral areas. Surajit Sinha[69] studying the influence of Vaisnavism on the Bhumij tribe, an eastern offshoot of the Mundas of Ranci observes that the Vaisnava *gurus* were not concerned with replacing the traditional rituals of the Bhumij. Rather, the *gurus* were more interested in increasing the number of his clientele. With a view to achieving this end, they were mainly interested in superimposing a few rituals of their own to make their presence as rituals specialists essential on the life of the Bhumij. The Bhumij on their part did not look upon their contact with the Vaisnavas as displacing their own rituals. The association with the Vaisnavas and accepting their ritual traits were, instead,considered by the Bhumij as conveying an element of respectability. This identification with the local faith proved to be highly effective in influencing the attitude of the people towards an alien cult. The point made is that the number of *Umanglais* worshipped nowadays reflect the religious history of the Meitei people, in its various stages of development.

In order to bring about an elementary order among the vast number of *Umanglais* they may be classified under five broad heads:

(1) Divine Family of Taibangpanba Mapu viz; Taibangpanba Mapu, Leimaren Sidabi, Atiya Sidaba, Asiba or Sanamahi and Konchin Tingthokpa (Pakhangba). Nongshaba, a manifestation of Atiya, and Imoinu Ahongbi, a manifestation of Leimarel Sidabi are included in this group. Nongthangleima, the daughter of Taibangpanba Mapu, and Leimarel Sidabi should also be considered as members of this group.

(2) *Maigei Ngakpas* (Guardians of Directions) viz; Marjing, Wangbren, Nongpok Ningthou, Loiyarakpa, Chingkhei, Irum Ningthou, Koubru and Thangjing.

(3) Clan Ancestors (Head of *Salais*) viz; Pureiromba, Poireiton etc.

(4) Human Beings Worshipped as Deities - due to the possession of supernatural qualities as exemplified in myths viz; Pitanga, Konthoujam Lairembi.

(5) Deified Kings - due to their benevolent characteristics and popularity viz; Naothingkhong, Khagemba .

1) **Divine family of Taibangpanba Mapu**

Taibangpanba had three sons from his consort Leimarel Sidabi viz; Atiya, Asiba (Sanamahi) and Konchin Tingthokpa (Pakhangba). The *Leithak Leikharon Puya* mentions Nongthangleima as the daughter of the Ultimate Parents.[70] Two other *lais* included in this group are Nongshaba, described in some *Puyas* as the manifestation of Atiya, and Imoinu Ahongbi, a manifestation of Leimarel Sidabi.

Leimarel Sidabi, as the first manifestation of the Supreme Lord, acquires great significance in that she represents the highest female form. All goddesses are either incarnations of herself or her daughters. As Taoroinai, her union with Atingkok gave the Meiteis their pedigree, classifying them into seven *salais*.[71] She resides in the seven layers of *leikharon* (earth). Leimaren is a *yumlai* (household deity). Her place is near the northern wall in the middle chamber of every Meitei home. She is represented by a sacred earthen pot which is filled with water. The pot is wrapped in a thin piece of cloth and is covered with a lid. She is compared to *malem* (earth)[72] Thus for the Meiteis, Leimaren Sidabi is the mother goddess. The water which is contained in the pot and her association with the earth are symbols of life and fertility.

A rather unusual incident is associated with Leimaren Sidabi. It has already been mentioned that Leimaren gave birth to three sons, Atiya, Asiba (Sanamahi) and Pakhangba. Yet another tradition makes Leimaren the spouse of Sanamahi. The story runs as thus: When Supreme Father decided to retire and hand over the seat power to his sons, he gave his sons a test. He declared that the one who reaches the Guru first after circumambulating the world seven times would be crowned as the king. Sanamahi and Atiya set forth for the journey. However, Pakhangba, on the advice of his mother Leimaren Sidabi, circumambulated the throne of his father seven times. The Guru placed Pakhangba on the throne because the seat of the Supreme Father represented the whole earth. When Sanamahi returned after the journey, he found his brother Pakhangba already seated on the throne. He learnt that Pakhangba had merely taken rounds of his father's throne, and became furious. He then declared that in case his brother's advisor was a man, he would kill him, and if she was a woman, he would marry her. In order to fulfill his vow Sanamahi married his mother Leimaren under these strange circumstances.[73] On every *Cheiraoba* (the commencement of a new year) Sanamahi is venerated along with his spouse mother Leimaren.

Leimaren manifests herself as a number of deities, such as Lul Leima (goddess of wealth), Phoi-oibi (goddess of granary), Ngareima (goddess of fish), Ireima (goddess of water), Lan Leima (goddess of industries and crafts). She is also Heepokpi, Yaipokpi, Heeleima, Yaileima, Heekubi, Yaikubi and Yaisna.[74]

Atiya is depicted in the *Leithak Leikharon Puya* as one of the three sons of Guru Sidaba, the Ultimate Father and Leimaren Sidabi, the Ultimate Mother.[75] Popular myths, however, mention only Sanamahi and Pakhangba as the two sons of the divine couple. The same *Puya*, narrating the story of how Pakhangba became the temporal king, goes on to say that the Supreme Father, in trying to pacify his two other sons, made Sanamahi the Lord of all households, while Atiya was made to replace the Supreme Father. The *Sakok Lamlen Ahanba Puya* informs us how Atiya saved the traditional faith of the Meitei people from the influence of a *Pangal* (*pangal*: a corrupt form of Bengal) *guru*, who came to the land of the Meiteis during the reign of King Naophangba (428-518 A.D.).[76] The *guru* tried to change the traditional customs of the people by first persuading the king to order his subjects to practice burial in place of the prevailing custom of cremation of the dead. He also declared that eating beef was a taboo. At this critical juncture, Atiya incarnated himself in the form of a man and appeared on earth as Laiba. He lived on earth for thirteen years to set the order right, and advised the king not to follow the instructions of the *Pangal guru*. At the instance of the *Pangal guru* a palace was to be constructed at Kangla, the royal capital of the Meitei kings. This sacred spot is associated with the belief that Pakhangba in its coiled snake form lies at the base of Kangla. Therefore, any construction or repair at the site of Kangla requires consultation of renowned priests and performance of appropriate rituals. Whenever a hole is to be dug at the site, great care is taken not to disturb the coiled Pakhangba.

The Meiteis believe that if the body of Pakhangba is hurt, blood oozes out of the hole and this signifies death of the king and destruction of his subjects and the land. Hence Atiya convinced the king of the ill-effects that would follow if the *Pangal guru's* advice was carried out, and thus averted a great disaster for the Meiteis.

Atiya Sidaba is said to be identical with Taibangpanba Mapu in many *Puyas*.[77] The place of Atiya is taken by Nongshaba in *Nongshaba Laihui*.[78] The Meiteis worship him as the bestower of prosperity and happiness. The places Wangu, Clothe and Moirang became prosperous due to their dedicated worship of Nongshaba. A story recounts that when Nongshaba became identified with the prosperity of Moirang, two fisherman, Mungyang Ngairangba and Yumnam Tonba, bought the idol of the *lai* to King Khagemba. The king then built a fine temple in honour of Nongshaba and worshipped him.[79] The cult of Nongshaba was introduced during the reign of Khagemba.[80] Nongshaba is also known for punishing the wrong-doers. A temple of Nongshaba was built at the royal palace and on every Wednesday food is offered to the deity. He is served by the Laithangbam *sagei* only. Of the three groups of *Maibis*, only the Phura group of *Maibis* are allowed to serve Nongshaba.[81] The reason for only one *sagei* and one group of *Maibis* serving Nongshaba could be perhaps that Nongshaba is their ancestral deity. The royal chronicle records the name of Soibam Chanu as the wife of Nongshaba.[82]

Nongmoinu Ahongbi, popularly known as Imoinu Ahongbi, is a manifestation of Leimaren Sidabi.[83] *Phungga Lairu*, the seat of Imoinu Ahongbi, is one of the three places the Meiteis consider sacred in a typical Meitei home. The *phungga* is a hearth situated in the centre of the main chamber of the house. According to L. Iboongohal, the *Phungga Lairu* is a small hole with a mouth above it, dug just to the West of and close to the said *phungga*. Older generation bowed down everyday in front of the *lairu* and kept their valuables in this hole. The hole was so much respected and feared that even a thief did not dare to touch it. The hollow was covered with a clay roof, in the centre of which was a small hole. Offerings were dropped through this hole into the pot.[84] It is difficult to ascertain the exact relationship of Imoinu Ahongbi with fire, although the sacred place allotted to her is close to the hearth. Imoinu is the goddess of wealth and prosperity. That the *lairu* was associated with Imoinu is also known from the *Leimarel Sekning Puya* where the *lairu* is called Imoinu Tillisang.[85] The goddess is worshipped on the 12th of *Wakching* (December-January).[86] In Manipur, harvesting generally takes place in the month of *Poinu* (November-December). *Wakching* is considered a sacred month and so no commercial transaction of paddy is conducted during this month.

There is a myth associated with the beginning of Imoinu worship, which is of comparatively late origin. A certain Khuman king is said to have brought to his palace an old lady whose antecedents were unknown. She stayed in the palace for many years and looked after the royal household. Ever since she came to the palace, the Khuman kingdom became extremely prosperous. At Kanglei, the contemporary Meitei King Chalamba (1545-1562 A.D.) was told by his mother that the old lady with the Khuman king was none other than an incarnation of Imoinu Ahongbi. She advised her to bring the lady to the Meitei kingdom. Later, during the reign of Chalamba's successor King Khunjao (1562-1666 A.D.), Imoinu Ahongbi became a popular goddess. Till today, this goddess of prosperity and sustenance is venerated every year.[87]

Nongthangleima is mentioned in the *Leithak Leikharon Puya* and the *Pudin Puya* as the daughter of Guru Sidaba and Leimaren Sidabi.[88] She is one of the seven *Lainuras* (divine girls) who assisted the divine father in the creation of the universe.[89] *Sanamahi Laihui* mentions one

Nongthangleima as the wife of Sanamahi.[90] Apart from this, nothing much known about this goddess.

The two sons of the divine couple are Sanamahi and Pakhangba. These two deities will be dealt with in detail later, as they eventually emerged as the presiding deities of the Meitei pantheon. Pakhangba, as the ancestor of the Ningthouja *salai* became the temporal head, while Sanamahi came to be recognized as the household deity of every Meitei family. It will be worthwhile to study why only these two deities stood out among the hundreds of Meitei *lais*. It may be mentioned here that the Supreme Father is said to have revealed his true self through these two *lais*. According to the Manipur *Puyas*, Pakhangba as the first historical king initiated the long line of Ningthouja *salai* which ruled Manipur for many centuries. Sanamahi as Asiba is credited with the creation of the universe.

2) *Maigei Ngakpas* (Guardians of Directions)

The next category of *lais* include the guardians of the directions. The creation of the world was made possible by them. These *lais* guarded the strategic points of the earth from the hostile intentions of the evil spirits.

Marjing guards the North, His abode is at Heingang, a place located to the North of Imphal.[91] He is one of the nine *Laibungthous* (divine youths) whom Guru Sidaba brought forth to assist him in the creation of the world.[92] Apart from being the guardian of the North, Marjing is also one of the five souls seated in the human body. He is also known by the name of Wangkoibe in this form.[93] Marjing is also associated with the game of *Sagol Kangjei* (a variant of modern polo). He is believed to have emerged from the intestines of Atiya Sidaba, to catch hold of the divine horse (*sagol*) which emanated from the foot of Asiba.[94] The gods are said to have first played this game. To remind the Meitei people of the original game, a *Maibi* always enacts the game in the *Lai*

Haraoba festival. It is due to this association of *Sagol Kangjei* with Marjing that any offering made to this *lai* has to include a *kangdroom* (a ball made of bamboo root) and a *kangjei* (a kind of stick). *Cheitharol Kumbaba* lays down that the *lai* should be venerated with meat offerings. In 1618 A.D., Marjing was worshipped with the offering of wild boar, dog, duck, hen, pigeon and other living creatures.[95] This text mentions that Chingjaraobi married Marjing in 1734 A.D.[96] Since no more details are available, the identity of this Chingjaraobi is not clear. However, Chingjaraobi is still worshipped in the locality of Khurai Konsam Leikai, 6 kms. from Imphal.[97]

Wangbren, who is also known as Khana Chaoba is the guardian of the South.[98] He too is also one of the nine *Laibungthous* (divine youths).[99] Wangbren is the god of water.[100] His mother was Wangu Leima Khongchom Phabichak and his father was Chinggu Koubarel Ahanba.[101] *Ningthourol Lambuba* mentions a place called Loibi Lamngang which was invaded by King Chingkhong Lamgaingamba (1512-1523 A.D.). It is believed that Wangbren Khana Chaoba resided in this place in the houses of his four wives. The names of his four wives are given as Anal Khunthak Chanu, Maraipung, Khundol Chanu, Loibi Thaku Chanu and Marem Thayai Chanu.[102] Anal is one of the hill tribes of Manipur. It is stated that a stone still stands in Anal Khullem village, South-East Manipur to commemorate the marriage of the Anal girl to Wangbren.[103] The *Chingoiron Puya* records that the abode of this *lai* is located at the Wangbren hill. The stone seat of Wangbren is found in a temple, built on the peak of this hill. Lokningthou, considered to be another guardian of directions, is the son of Khana Chaoba.[104]

Nongpok Ningthou literally means the 'King of the East'. A popular legend has it that Nongpok fell in love with Panthoibi, who was already married to Tarang Khoinucha.

They were finally united at Nongmaiching, the abode of Nongpok. Nongmaiching is believed to be the first ever created hill with divine attributes. From the account of *Panthoibi Khongul* (In Quest of Panthoibi) it seems that Nongpok and Panthoibi were superior to many other *lais* in the Meitei pantheon.[105] The text says that Wangbren, Thangjing, Koubarel, Koubru Asuppa, Khoriphaba, Ekeirel, the gods of wind and fire, and hundreds of other gods and goddess climbed up the abode of Nongpok and Panthoibi to pay respect to the divine couple. Nongpok is also known by the names of Nongpok Ningthou Yoiremba[106] and Nongpok Malung Haomoiba.[107] According to one tradition, Nongpok was a *Maiba* (traditional physician) who cured the illness of Panthoibi.[108] Later Nongpok has been identified with Siva and Panthoibi with Parvati.[109] This explains his dress of tiger-skin, matted hair and a snake round his neck for a garland. This also explains his riding a bull and holding a trident for his weapon. He has three eyes and is the lord of animals.

Nongpok Ningthou and his divine consort Panthoibi are taken to be indispensable. The Meiteis generally worship them as Nongpok-Panthoibi. Panthoibi, the daughter of Taoroinai and Lainamung Namungba, is described as a great goddess of mankind.[110] She is the daughter of the fire god, a benevolent goddess who grants wealth and long life to her devotees. Her many names include Thoomleima, Wangamloi, Tampha, Yumjao Leima, and Chinglai Leima.[111] Panthoibi is also one of the seven *Lainuras* (divine girls) brought forth by Taibangpanba Mapu.[112] She had seven brothers. Her other name Mangang Panthoibi indicates that she belonged to Mangang *salai*.[113] Panthoibi was also a chief *Maibi* and played an important role in social and religious activities.[114] After comparing the accounts contained in *Thiren Layat* and *Panthoibi Khongul*, N. Khelchandra concluded that King Sapaiba, who was the first to ask for the hand of Panthoibi, lived in the *Langba* age.[115] Panthoibi was married off to

Tarang Khoinucha, the son of Khaba Sokchrongba, the chief of the Kangleis.[116] Khaba Sokchrongba and Tarang Khoinucha are human personalities mentioned in *Cheitharol Kumbaba*[117] Throughout the early part of *Panthoibi Khongul Puya,* Panthoibi is depicted as a typical married woman, respecting and obeying the instructions of her parents-in-law. Only at a later stage she joins Nongpok and finally comes to live at Nongmaijing hill when she assumes divine status. In *Thiren Layat Puya* she is described as the wife of Pakhangba.[118] This makes Pakhangba identical with Nongpok Ningthou. However, this is rarely mentioned in the other *Puyas*. Scholars have debated on whether Panthoibi was a human being or a divine personality. It may be concluded from the above discussion that Panthoibi was a human personality to begin with and was later raised to the status of divinity. As she is depicted as killing a tiger in the same *Puya*, she is compared to Durga and is also known as a war goddess.[119]

The earliest reference to Panthoibi is found in the *Numit Kappa Puya.*[120] Here her role is of an errand girl who was sent as messenger of the gods to the Sun God to persuade him to come out of hiding. From the errand girl in *Numit Kappa* she matured into a major goddess mounted on a tiger in *Panthoibi Khongul*. R.K. Jhalajit[121] argues that Panthoibi was not a mother goddess. Barring the solitary occasion where it is mentioned that she would respond irrespective of whether she is addressed to as father or mother, there is a total absence of reference to her motherhood. In *Panthoibi Khongul* there is not even the slightest trace of her being the mother of a god or a goddess.

The royal chronicle records that the first idol of Panthoibi was made in 1699 A.D. A temple was built for her in 1700 A.D. It was inaugurated on Wednesday, the 16th of *Enga* (May-June), of the same year.[122] She came to be served by the *Brahmanas* during the reign of King Garibniwaz. On

Friday, in the month of *Hiyangei* (October-November) in 1723 A.D., the king allowed the *Brahmanas* to take over from the traditional priests the duty of worshipping Panthoibi.[123]

Loiyarakpa is the guardian of the Western corner of the earth. Legend has it that in the battle between the gods and the *sarois* (evil spirit), Loiyarakpa showed great courage and destroyed the *sarois*. More popularly known as Loiya Lakpa Pangganba or Loiya Lakpa (the brave), this deity is worshipped mainly by the people of Chakpa village.[124]

There is not much information about Chingkhei and Irum Ningthou, apart from the fact that these deities are guardians of the North-East and South-East directions respectively.

Koubru watches the North-East. He is one of the nine *Laibungthous* (divine youths).[125] Koubru is also known by the name of Mihinglen Mipokpa.[126] This *lai* has his abode in the Koubru hill. A temple is constructed of stone on this peak where Koubru is worshipped.[127] The royal chronicle records that this deity was worshipped in 1631 A.D. during the reign of Khagemba. The occasion was the inauguration of Kangla, the historic capital. It further states that Koubru was worshipped under a sacred canopy along with other deities. This event took place at Kuchu and the item offered included hundred each of buffaloes, goats, lambs, cows, swans, ducks, pigeons, hens, pigs, dogs, fruits and flowers.[128] The Meiteis consider Koubru to be the greatest god of the *Langba Chak*.[129] He is one of the five souls of an individual.[130]

Thangjing, the son of Chingu Ningthou Soraren Awang Palchang Yoiremba is the ruling deity of Moirang, a place situated on the South-West of the valley of Manipur. The temple of Thangjing Koiren Ningthou is situated on the Thangjing hill.[131] There are three sacred stones and also a number of sacred spots on this hill.[132] He is one of the five *lais* who entered the body of man as one of the five souls.[133] He is addressed to as Thangjing Koilel Lai Sitapa, and is one of the nine *Laibungthous* (divine youths).[134] A story recounts that a bull, caught by the brave Khamba was offered to Thangjing, which implies animal sacrifice was made to this *lai*.[135] At Moirang, the *Lai Haraoba* festival is celebrated to propitiate Lord Thangjing. Thangjing had two wives viz; Thangjing Koiran Leima and Laiwa Leima.[136] He has been described as a historical figure in many *Puyas*. The royal chronicle records that Kapaw Nungoitongba Chanu was given in marriage to Thangjing.[137] The *Sanamahi Laihui Puya* states that as one of the *Laibungthous* (divine youths), Thangjing was the master of Tripura (Takel Lakchin Phamba), Cachar (Mayang Saken Tongba) and Bengal (Pangantampak Koiba).[138]

3) Clan Ancestors (Heads of *Salais*)

The progenitors of the *salais*, popularly known as *Salai Apokpas*, are venerated by the descendants of the different clans on appropriate occasions. The *apokpas* of Angom, Khuman and Luwang clans are dealt here to represent this category of ancestral *lais* in the Meitei pantheon. Only these three *salais* are taken up for study since there are *Puyas* dealing exclusively on them. Pureiromba is the progenitor of the Angom *salai*. The *Leithak Leikharon Puya* states three versions of the parentage of Pureiromba. The first one states that Erik Ekongset Heitam Heiba, in union with Kangkhan, begot Pureiromba.[139] The second one mentions Ningthou Tari as Pureiromba's mother.[140] Yet, the genealogical tables of all the *salais* record that Khakpa Ningthou Chanu and Kuptreng begot Pureiromba.[141]

Poireiton established the lines of Khumans and Luwangs. A contemporary of Nongda Lairen Pakhangba, Poireiton is believed to have been a contender for the throne of Kangla. In the struggle that took place, Pakhangba emerged victorious and Laisna or Laisra, the sister of Poireiton, was given in marriage to Pakhangba. Poireiton married Leima

Leinaotabi and had a son called Singtanpung Tapung Singmunnaba. Singtanpung married Santhong Pamingnaba. Aarong is Khuman-pokpa while Pamingnaba is Luwang-pokpa.[142] The story of Poireiton is narrated in detail in the *Poireiton Khunthok Puya* (Immigration of Poireiton). It is said that he, along with a of group of people, travelled many places in search of men free of disease and death. They finally reached the small village of the Chakpas. Chingkhong Poireiton, as he is otherwise known, is said to have been the first to introduce fire and cooked food to the Meiteis. Tolong Lampak is believed to be the place where these people left the utensils they used for cooking.[143]

4) **Human Beings Worshipped as Deities**

There are many human personalities whom Meiteis worship till today, because of some extraordinary qualities which they are supposed to possess. Pitanga and Konthoujam Lairembi are studied here as representatives of this category of ancestral *lais* due to the popularity associated with the story of deification of these two human personalities.

The story of Pitanga who was later raised to the status of Yumjao Lairembi (household goddess), is beautifully narrated in the *Naothingkhong Phambal Kaba Puya* (The Coronation of Naothingkhong). Hongnem Yoi Khunjao, a prince of the Ningthouja kingdom, married Pitanga Liklu Louthibi and began to live in her house at the golden Selloi-Langmai hills.[144] When hostilities suddenly broke out between the Selloi-Langmais and the Ningthoujas, the infuriated people of Selloi-Langmai gathered at the courtyard of Pitanga's house and threatened to kill him. Pitanga persuaded her people to give her sometime to boil some arum roots for her husband to eat before he departed for the other world.[145] Believing her, the people agreed but continued to guard the front gate to prevent his escape. Pitanga was actually boiling pebbles to gain time while the prince escaped through a hole made in the back wall of the hut. As advised by his wife, the prince fled to the Khuman kingdom where he was granted asylum. He later married the princess of this principality.[146] Khunjao then visited the principality of Moirang, where the king gave his daughter in marriage to Khunjao.[147] When Hongnem Yoi Khunjao's father died and the throne of the Ningthoujas fell vacant, the prince was invited to come and ascend the throne. The news of his accession reached Pitanga. Hoping for a happy reunion she set out in her best clothes for the capital of the Ningthouja kingdom.

Hongnem Yoi Khunjao ascended the throne in 663 A.D. and assumed the name Naothingkhong. Pitanga reached Naothingkhong's palace and entered the hall where she found that her beloved was seated with Keirum Hangbi, the Khuman princess. The king greeted Pitanga and directed her to sit on his right. Pitanga was shocked that her beloved had betrayed her love and that he had married another woman. Unable to bear the pain, she suddenly inflicted a heavy blow on her head and took her life which filled the king with remorse. The story has it that in an instant Pitanga's soul forsook the mortal casement and turned divine. Pitanga Liklu Louthibi, in her eternal form, turned towards the foot of the Langmai hills and made her eternal abode in a forest near the Chinggoi stream. Every year at the onset of spring, when the hill is aflame with *chingthrao* flowers and the air is charged with jubilant spirit, the Meitei king with his people used to march to that spot for a holy dip in the water of the Chinggoi stream.[148] Pitanga was thus raised to the status of a goddess and came to be popularly known as *Yumjao Lairembi* (household goddess).

Konthoujam Lairemma is another human personality who came to be worshipped by the Meiteis because of the supernatural feats she performed during her lifetime. Konthoujam Lairemma was the wife of Soraren, the god of rain and thunder.[149] The story of the transformation of this mortal woman into an immortal divine figure is told in the text *Konthoujam Nongaren* (The Ascent of the Konthou Girl). It says that Huimu Leima of the Konthou clan had a beautiful daughter. Unlike her friends, the girl did not work in the rice field to pick up vegetables. One day her mother asked her to go to the field to pick up vegetables. Soraren saw her there and was enamoured by the beauty of the young girl. He made himself invisible and told the girl to tell her mother that after five days he would come to visit her. Struck with wonder, the girl returned home and narrated the event to her mother. As promised, Soraren visited her on the fifth day and married her. At the time of returning with his bride to the abode of the Lord in the clouds, Soraren gave a boon to the people of the Konthous that henceforth no one belonging to the clan would ever die.

One day, when a hunting dog died of snake bite the Konthous decided to give it a funeral as if a man had died. They beat drums and cymbals and pretended to wail. The sound was heard in the heavenly kingdom and his wife asked Soraren if she could go down to see what was happening on earth. Soraren knew that it was only a mock funeral and cautioned her not to take food and drinks when on earth. He told her that if she violated this instruction, she would not be allowed to come back to heaven. When she reached the earth, her mother insisted on her taking at least one meal with her. The girl remembered the god's warning and refused. At this, her mother fixed a thick canopy of cloth and offered her daughter food and wine underneath the curtain, believing that Soraren would not be able to see her. However, Soraren saw everything and just as the feast was about to begin he spat down on them. Struck with terror the girl got up, for she knew that the god was angry. When still in air, she cursed her people that they would once more be subject to disease and death, as Soraren had withdrawn the boon. When she reached Soraren's kingdom, she was refused entry by her husband. At least, the wind god testified that the girl had not eaten anything on earth. Soraren and his wife were then reconciled and the girl was granted immortality by Soraren.

A slightly different ending of the story is given in another version, in the text *Langol*. The Konthou girl, known by the name of Tampha in this version, is said to have believed that one of the relatives died and went down to earth using a golden ladder. Soraren did not allow her to take their suckling infant with her. When Soraren found that his wife was about to take food cooked by human beings, he pulled up the golden ladder. Tampha was left helpless and she suffered the pangs of separation from her husband and the infant son. It was then that Soraren's mother came down to earth and assured her daughter-in-law of the well being of both Soraren and the child. Tampha was relieved to hear this, but she took an oath to live alone for the rest of her life. Soraren's mother instructed the people of Konthoujam to offer her food and pray so that no one else suffers her tragic fate. From this time, Tampha came to be worshipped as Konthoujam Lairembi or Konthoujam Lairemma.[150]

5) Deified Kings

Among the many kings in Meitei history, only a few have risen to the status of ancestral *lais*. Two of such defied kings are Naothingkhong (663-763 A.D.) and Khagemba (1597-1652 A.D.).

Naothingkhong is one of the *Umanglais* worshipped by the Meiteis. His abode is at Taoba Umang near Patsoi village.[151] An annual *Lai Haraoba* festival is held in honour of Patsoi Taomang, by which name Naothingkhong is venerated here. He is also worshipped at Thangmeiband as Kangkhujam Naothingkhong.[152] The *Sakok Lamlen Ahanba Puya* records that it was during the reign of Naothingkhong that the three wise *gurus* i.e., Mangang, Luwang and Khuman, manifested themselves as human beings to reveal to the king and his subjects the path of righteousness. The king was told that the only way to attain righteousness was to follow *Areppa Laining* (*areppa*: truth; *laining*: way of god). *Areppa Laining* is essentially the ability to discover the truth and accept one's faults committed in everyday life. The *Puya* also records that Sanamahi (Yoirenba) incarnated as the son of Naothingkhong to help the king to follow the right path.[153] These two instances seem to suggest that the king was repenting for some past misdeeds as he was in desperate need to make amends for it. It maybe recalled that Naothingkhong was the husband of Pitanga, the mortal form of goddess Yumjao Lairemma, who killed herself when she learnt that the person whose life she saved did not give her what she deserved.[154] Perhaps this is the reason why Naothingkhong is also credited with the innovation of the coronation costumes of the Meitei kings, such as *phirel phurit* (a long and loose shirt), *kumshang phanek* (a dark coloured skirt) etc. The costumes came to be known as Naothingkhong *phijet* (the coronation costumes of Naothingkhong). *Tharaochi* (a bugle-like pipe, made of copper) became an inseparable object for the performance of the religious rites of the Meitei royal family. It is said that Naothingkhong recovered this object from among the spoils of war with the Mangangs. Naothingkhong is also known to have been profoundly conversant with *ningsa* (a yogic breathing technique).[155]

The reign of Khagemba marks a watershed in the history of the Meiteis for a number of reasons. Perhaps the most important contribution of Khagemba was that he initiated the codification of the *Puyas* and encouraged writing in the Meitei *mayek* (*mayek:* script). As a result, by the year 1616 A.D., a number of *Puyas* written in the Meitei *mayek* came to be circulated among the people.[156] Besides, the texts claim that the three *lai-gurus* (wise men) viz; Langon Lukhoi, Yumnam Tonaba and Khaidem Tenba revealed to Khagemba that the highest *lai* in the last of the human ages was Pakhangba and that there was no other god higher than him.[157] Although the deity Sanamahi was known to the Meiteis for a long time, it is generally believed that it was Khagemba who popularised Sanamahi worship among the people. The *Khagemba Langjei Puya* narrates that Sanamahi was born as Khagemba's son in order to reveal to the Meiteis His greatness. According to the story, when the child was eight years of age, he expressed his wish to accompany his father to the royal court. Khagemba persuaded his dearest child to stay back, as no child was permitted to attend the court. The child was so disappointed that he decided to end his earthly existence. One day a lady by the name of Khongul Phangbi went to the river and noticed that the clothes and ornaments of the child were hanging from a tree top. When her attempts to find the missing child failed she reported the matter to his parents. It was then that Leimaren appeared before the bereaved parents in the guise of an old woman and revealed to them that their lost son was none other than the divine Sanamahi, and that he had returned to godhood.[158] The *Sakok Lamlen Ahanba Amasung Meihouron Puya* also records that Khagemba and Nongthilchaibi had a son called Taibangkhaiba, who became a *lai* (god).[159] Taibangkhaiba is identical with Sanamahi.[160]

The names of the king given in the list of *Umanglais* are Kyamgei Khagemba and Sagoltongba Surairem Khagemba.[161] Khagemba is also credited with the introduction of the divine game of *Sagol Kangjei*, the precursor of the modern polo, in Manipur. The practice of addressing the king as *Lainingthou* (*lai*: god; *ningthou*: king) was started by him in the year 1608 A.D.[162] and he initiated the festival of *Hiyang Tannaba* (boat race) in which the king and the god were made to sit in the same boat.[163]

One can detect a common theme in the lives of the two kings Naothingkhong and Khagemba. The advice given by the three wise men, and the fact that Sanamahi manifested himself as the son of both the kings is significant. Tradition records the arrival of the *Pangal Guru* during the reign of Naothingkhong, which had been a source of threat to the existing religious system of the Meiteis. Khagemba's reign is well known for the beginning of the Brahmanical influence in Manipur. Therefore, it seems possible that in order to remind the kings of the importance of the traditional *lais* in particular and the Meitei belief system in general, that these myths were constructed. The divine association also helped to elevate the status of the kings.

IV

We now turn to the two most important divine personalities in the Meitei pantheon viz; Sanamahi and Pakhangba. The religious system of the Meiteis may be said to have revolved around these two *lais*. Sanamahi is a more approachable *lai* who is venerated in every Meitei home. Pakhangba is the temporal *lai* and was therefore evoked mainly at the state rituals. Both the *lais* have their benevolent and destructive forms and are respected and worshipped equally by the Meiteis on appropriate occasions. The myths which recount how Sanamahi became the presiding deity of every home and how Pakhangba came to acquire the status of the ruling deity of the kingdom have already been discussed. In order to understand the significance attached to these two *lais* we will now discuss their defining characteristics.

(a) Sanamahi

Sanamahi is the most popular and widely worshipped *lai* in the Meitei pantheon. Being the presiding *lai* of every home, he is venerated by the entire community. As Asiba, he created the sky with all its cosmic and celestial bodies and the earth with all the animate and inanimate objects.[164] As ordered by his father, the Immortal Guru, Asiba also created mankind.[165]

The greatness of Sanamahi lies in the fact that he is creator of the world and mankind.

The South-West corner of a typical Meitei home is reserved for Sanamahi. This corner, known by the name of Sanamahi Kachin is the abode of the *lai*. There is no image of Sanamahi. Originally there used to be a mat and a bamboo stick in the Sanamahi Kachin.[166] Nowadays, a *sel* (coin) represents the deity. The *Sanamahi Phankhong Puya* informs us that this *lai* exists in round form[167] which may explain why a coin stands for Sanamahi. Alongside the *sel* is placed an earthen pot filled with water. This pot represents Leimaren, the mother of Sanamahi, who became his spouse through a strange set of circumstances, mentioned above. Sanamahi is believed to keep watch over the whole house. For this reason, he resides at the gate, the front and the back courtyards, the *phungga* (hearth) and the northern verandah of each home.[168]

There are a number of *Puyas* which deal with various aspects of Sanamahi. As Asiba he is generally known as the son of Atingkok and Taobilonai.[169] But according to a lesser known version his mother was the divine Leimaren, while his father was a human personality by the name Sile.[170] Sanamahi married Langmai Sana Chingjaoroibi, also called Nongthangleima.[171] They have a son by the name of Leishang Khekwaiba.[172]

Sanamahi is also known by as many as two hundred and seventeen names.[173] When he dwells in the sky, he is called Hum Pit Pit, when he is the king, he is called Sameiren; when he comes out of the left nostril of Atiya Sidaba, he is called Sora Mahi Sana; and when he resides in the northern verandah of a Meitei home, he is called Hikpha.[174] Some of the names which are more commonly used while addressing the *lai* are Asiba, Onthi, Ungset, Soraren Amamba, Achiba Kanglei Ningthou Apanba, Thongaren, Kourouhanba, Sana Mahirel, Pisatau, Pongthanglen and Sanamahi.[175]

Every Meitei prays to Sanamahi to protect his house from danger and bless him with long life free from illnesses, and shower them with prosperity and happiness. Sanamahi is believed to reside near those who pray to him.[176] The various types of rites to be performed for *Sanathong Lai* (*sanathong*: South-West direction; *lai*: god) are recorded in *Sanathong Laigi Thouni Lairik*. The items to be offered, the specific days which are auspicious for the rituals, the manner in which the rituals should be included and the proper location for the performance of the rituals are mentioned. All offerings made should be of raw items,[177] which may include banana, grains of rice, the husk of which is peeled by hand, plantain leaves, betel-nut and leaves, flowers etc.[178] Flour, white sugar, and milk are some other items which may also be offered to the *lai*.[179] The *Puya* assures the devotee that if the rituals are performed in accordance with the prescribed norms, he would be able to hear the voice of the *lai*.[180] Some of the rituals are also said to enable the devotees to see the *lai* in human form or in the form of a bright light covering the entire sky.[181] Sanamahi, as the *Sakok Lamlen Ahanba Puya* records, was the reigning *lai* of *Hayi Chak*, the first of the four human ages. The earliest period of Meitei history was a time when the people ate raw or uncooked food, used leaves to cover their bodies and the proper method of disposal of the dead was unknown. King Kangba Kangkhan, the son of Silpi Leima Leitang Chanu, who reigned during the *Hayi Chak* is credited with the introduction of Sanamahi worship to the people.[182]

It is significant that while the *Puyas* trace the beginning of Sanamahi worship from *Hayi Chak*, the *Cheitharol Kumbaba* refers to him although in other names apart from Sanamahi, for the first time as late as the reign of King Paikhomba (1666-1697 A.D.). From this time onwards, we find frequent mention of this deity. The royal chronicle mentions that a temple of Laiwa-Khaiba was burnt down in

1685 A.D.[183] which suggests that temples of the deity were already in existence. During the reign of Charairongba (1697-1709 A.D.) temples were built in honour of the *lai* in the years 1702, 1704 and 1709 A.D.[184] An idol of Sanamahi was made in the year 1700 A.D.[185] and in the year 1710 A.D., King Garibniwaz (1709-1748 A.D.) had a stone erected in honour of this *lai* at Leishangkhong.[186] The chronicle records further that a pond was dedicated to this *lai* at the same place in 1715 A.D.[187] There are also references to the construction of shrines for Sanamahi in the years 1718, 1721, 1729 and 1732 A.D.[188]

The study of Sanamahi will not be complete without a discussion on the worship of the Sanamahi idol, housed at the Sanamahi temple at Haying Tolong Yumphum in the premises of the present 1st Battalion Manipur Rifles at Imphal. Although the beginning of the worship of Sanamahi at this shrine is traced back to a period as recent as 1891 A.D.,[189] it is difficult to ascertain the exact date of making of the idol, the king associated with its making, and the previous site where the *lai* was venerated before his idol was finally installed at the Tolong Yumphum etc. The myth that Sanamahi incarnated himself as the son of King Khagemba and queen Nongthil Chaibi is fairly well known. This is, however, not supported by the royal chronicle. Yet, Khagemba is credited with the introduction of the worship of Sanamahi in his iconic from.[190] Although there are references to the temples built in honour of Sanamahi by 1685 A.D., we come across the earliest recorded reference to the making of Sanamahi idol in the year 1700 A.D., during the reign of Paikhomba.[191] The next reference to Sanamahi in the chronicle is in connection with the destruction of the idol of Lai-wa-haiba on the 23rd day of *Engen* (June-July) in 1726 A.D.,[192] during the reign of Garibniwaz. Following the destruction of the Sanamahi idol the royal family was struck with one disaster after another. A princess died and the prince

Tolentomba Shatrughan Sai fell seriously ill. When the king began to suspect that the sufferings inflicted upon him was the result of his attitude towards Sanamahi, a learned *guru* by the name Moirang Lalhamba Maichou advised him to re-construct the idol of the *lai*,[193] which began in the year 1729 A.D. and was completed on Monday the first of *Thawan* (July-August) in 1733 A.D.[194] During the reign of Chingthangkhomba (1759-1761 A.D.) Manipur was invaded by the Burmese, and the idol of Sanamahi was taken away by the invaders.[195] Chingthangkhomba ordered the making of another idol of Sanamahi on Monday, the 9th of *Kalen* (April-May), 1778 A.D., and in the following year the idol was inaugurated and kept at Wanggoi.[196] After the reign of Marjit, (1813-1819 A.D.) Manipur once again suffered an invasion by the neighbouring Burmese. During the next seven years, known as *Chahi Taret Khuntakpa* or 'The Seven Years of Desertion', the Sanamahi idol was taken away for the second time[197] by the Burmese. *Cheitharol Kumbaba* records that the idol was recovered from Burma by one Sagolsem Soipai from Chengang village on Thursday, the 2nd of *Phairen* (January-February), in the year 1822 A.D.[198] Finally it was during the reign of Kullachandra (1890-1891 A.D.) that a temple was built in 1891 A.D. for Laibungthou Sanamahi at the present site of Haying Khongbal Tolong Yumpham, and the idol of the *lai* placed there for worship.[199] It should be noted that the name of Sanamahi is mentioned in *Cheitharol Kumbaba* for the first time in 1778 A.D. during the reign of Chingthangkhomba.[200] Lai-wa-haiba, Taibangkhomba and Phalloukhomba were the names for him in the earlier accounts.

At the present temple of Sanamahi at Tolong Yumpham, there are two images of Sanamahi and Leimaren. It has already been mentioned that Sanamahi is always worshipped with his spouse Leimaren. Both the idols are in a sitting position. Mitchi Sana Leiyolang Tanouba, as

Sanamahi is referred to in this temple, represents the father of mankind and he faces the East, while Mitchi Sana Leiyanglong Tanoubi represents the mother and she faces the South. The seated image of Sanamahi has both his palms facing downwards whereas that of Leimaren has the right palm turned upwards and the left palm turned downwards. Oinam Manikchand, Mapari Thougal Langba (the term used for the head priest of the temple), interprets the position of the hands of Sanamahi as signifying the protection of all beings on earth and of Leimaren as that of the control of both the heaven and earth.[201] Every morning, the *lais* are awakened by a *pena* (one stringed fiddle) player who sings *Yakeiron* or the awakening hymn and raw fruits and vegetables are offered to them.

Sanamahi is worshipped as a household deity by the Meiteis. The biggest festival in honour of Sanamahi, when the whole community venerates him, is organized on Cheiraoba or the beginning of a new year in Manipur. This festival falls on the month of *Sajibu* (March-April).

The *Sakok Lamlen Ahanba Puya,*[202] as well as popular myths, credit Sanamahi with the creation of the world and mankind.[203] That this deity held a high position in the pantheon of Meitei *lais* is known from the references available from various *Puyas*. The *Sanamahi Laihui Puya* states that a number of important *lais* such as Wangbren, Thangjing, Chingu Loiyarakpa Khongphen Thouba, Thongnang Yaibi Ariba Koubaren Ahanba and Koubru Asuppa are subordinated to him in the hierarchy of the Meitei pantheon.[204] So pervasive is his influence that the pre-Hindu Meitei religion has come to be known by the term Sanamahism.[205] It is significant to mention here that the main reason why Sanamahi assumed such importance is because he is the protector and guardian of every Meitei household. He is the *lai* who looks after the well-being of the family, the smallest as well as the most fundamental of Meitei social organization. As a result, he cuts across specific clan loyalties and becomes acceptable for the entire community. The royal patronage offered to him is perhaps the consequence of this realization so that from 17th century A.D., he is consistently projected as the most important deity repeatedly mentioned in the *Cheitharol Kumbaba*. That Sanamahi came to occupy the central position in the Meitei pantheon is also indicated by the fact that the Burmese invaders as mentioned earlier on two occasions had taken away the idol of Sanamahi after invading Manipur.

(b) Pakhangba

Pakhangba is the ancestral deity of the royal family of the Meiteis.

Being patronized by the Ningthoujas, Pakhangba emerged as a significant *lai* in the pantheon in the *Konna Chak*, the last of the four human ages.[206]

It should be made clear at the outset that Pakhangba is not the name of any particular *lai* but a title conferred to a *lai*. Pakhangba literally translates as 'one who knows the father'. The *Leishemlon Ariba Puya* gives the names of Pakhangbas who ruled over a *Chak*. The ruler of *Thoi Hangko* or the second divine sub-period is mentioned simply as Pakhangba. The other Pakhangbas who ruled over the human sub-periods, are mentioned by their names, such as Lila Pakhangba (*Hayi Chak*), Lonja Pakhangba (*Khunung Chak*). Lolong Pakhangba (*Langba Chak*) and Nongda Lairen Pakhangba (*Konna Chak*).[207] N. Khelchandra suggests that Nongda Lairen Pakhangba is the incarnation of the earlier three Pakhangbas.[208]

The Pakhangba who belonged to the divine sub-period, is identified with Konchin Tingthokpa (also mentioned as Tuthokpa). He was the son of Guru Sidaba, the Ultimate Father. As the son who knew the secrets of his father,

Konchin Tingthokpa was nominated the king of the universe, when Guru Sidaba decided to retire to Thingrum hill. Konchin Tingthokpa became king by going round the throne of his father seven times, unlike his brother who followed the order of their father literally, and circumambulated the world seven times. It was also Konchin Tingthokpa who identified the carcass as his father in the test by Atiya Guru Sidaba as to which of his sons knew his father.[209] For these reasons, he earned the title of Pakhangba, i.e., on who understands the secrets of his father. According to the *Wakoklon Hilel Thilel Amailon Pukok Puya*, Konchin Tingthokpa provides the crucial link between the divine and the human, as he is both the last of the gods and the first of the mankind.[210] The sources are more or less silent on the other Pakhangba (Lila, Lonja and Lolong), except that all of them are considered to be the manifestations of the original Pakhangba.

The most popular and well known Pakhangba, with whom the *Puyas* deal exclusively, is Nongda Lairen Pakhangba, supposedly the first historical king of Manipur.[211] *Cheitharol Kumbaba* records that Nongda Lairen revealed to his wife Laisna that he descended from the heavens and therefore possessed the ability to assume the form of man as well as that of god. Nongda Lairen, a semi-divine personality, ascended the Meitei throne assuming the title of Pakhangba and ruled the kingdom for one hundred and twenty years (33-154 A.D.).[212]

Pakhangba is also referred to by various other names. They include Laitingthou Apanba, Leinung Lonja Pakhangba, Ningthem, Sana and Leinung Lonja Ariba etc.[213] *Cheitharol Kumbaba* records Meidingu Pakhangba (*meidingu* : king) as the 'first historical king' although in the list of the Meitei kings and the periods of their rule in the same chronicle he is referred to as Meidingu Nongda Lairen Pakhangba.[214]

There is some confusion over the parentage of Pakhangba. Some of the *Puyas* such as *Sakok Lamlen Ahanba*, regarded Yaibirok as the mother of Pakhangba. The story of the mysterious origin of Nongda Lairen as contained in this *Puya* is as follows: The creation of earth and mankind was completed by the three deities viz; Atiya Sidaba, Apanba and Asiba. After this, Atiya and Apanba ordered Taoroinai (a personification of Asiba) to go to the sun and bring down Apanba on the centre of the earth where Atiya's shadow was to cast. As ordered, Apanba was brought in the form of a cloud egg (*nonglum*) in Asiba's mouth and handed over to Atiya. Atiya descended on earth and nourished it in the disguise of Apanba's mother and thus acquired the name Yaibirok or lady sustainer.[215] However, according to the *Leithak Leikharon Puya*, Leinung Yabi Yakha Chanu is the mother of Pakhangba.[216] Mahindra and Birachandra conclude that Yaibirok was his foster mother, while the actual mother of Pakhangba was Linung Yabi Yakha Chanu.[217]

The *Puyas* do not mention the name of Pakhangba's father, although according to the story in the *Sakok Lamlen Ahanba Puya* the sun god should be considered as his father. Taoroinai had brought the divine egg in his mouth to give it to the lady sustainer. He stammered while handing over the egg to her, for which he was called stammering progenitor or *Puleiromba* (*pu*: progenitor; *lei*: tongue; *romba*: stammer), and later Pureiromba. The story of the divine egg is found in a number of *Puyas*, with slight variations.[218] In keeping with the story of Atiya Sidaba and King Apanba going to the sun, *Thiren Meiram Liba* says that Pureiromba and Luwang Lungmaiba went up to the sky, and later Sana (Pakhangba) was born. Mahindra and Birachandra suggest that Pureiromba was the foster father, while the actual father of Pakhangba was Luwang Lungmaiba.[219] It may be mentioned that the royal chronicle is silent about the parentage of Pakhangba.

Mahindra and Birachandra argue that these stories point to a struggle for succession among the rival brothers before Pakhangba's accession to the Meitei throne. Pakhangba became a fugitive and took shelter in various places when he was protected and looked after by five goddesses. These goddesses came to be considered as Pakhangba's foster mothers. He later emerged victorious and became the first king to occupy the Meitei throne at Kangla.[220] It has been mentioned earlier that Pakhangba is credited with the unification of the Meitei people. It was under his rule that seven clans which formed the Meitei confederacy came under the control of the Ningthouja *salai*. He is, therefore, the first ancestor of the Meitei kings. Pakhangba married Laisna and had a son by the name of Khuiyoi Tompok who succeeds his father to the throne.[221] Laisna was the sister of Poireiton, a migrant to the Manipur valley.

It is obvious that the *Puyas* attempt to endow Pakhangba with divine attributes. His descent from the sun, his birth from a divine egg, and his direct association with Taibangpanba Mapu and Atiya Sidaba, all point to this. However, it seems quite likely that Nongda Lairen Pakhangba was a human being, who is mentioned in the royal chronicle as the first king of Manipur, although this text also claims that he was a semi-divine figure. Perhaps the fact that so little is actually known about him has led to the mythification of one who possibly was a historical personage. Moreover, he married a migrant to Manipur which also sounds factual. It was natural on the part of the *Puyas* to shroud the obscure origin of the first king of Manipur in mystery and thus secure divine status for him.

The ruling deity of the Ningthoujas is represented in the form of a serpent. *Paphal* is a particular pattern of a coiled serpent, and since the *paphals* are taken to be extensions (*phal*) of Pakhangba (*pa*) the *paphal* illustrations are regarded as symbolic representations of Pakhangba.[222] This serpent is believed to lay hidden in the Meitei palace of Kangla. There is a myth associated with the origin of *paphal*. It says that Sanamahi attempted to destroy the earth as a revenge against his younger brother Pakhangba at the time of formal assumption of the throne of Kangla after merely going around the throne of his father. Out of panic Pakhangba could not come out and he hid in the form of a *paphal*.[223] Any construction at Kangla requires consultation of traditional scholars because it is said that during the reign of Naophangba (428-518 A.D.) a pillar, erected for the purpose of some extension of the palace, struck the body of the *paphal* and blood oozed out of the hole.[224] The *paphals* are considered to possess supernatural powers, and this motif is drawn at the entrance of homes to protect the inmates from evil spirits.[225]

Ch. Ibohal Mangang has translated the *paphal* manuscripts from Meitei *mayek* to Bengali script. The four hundred and thirty four *paphal* illustrations portray various shapes, each with a particular scheme of colours. Some of the *paphals* also contain representations of dragon-shaped heads attached to the bodies of animals such as pigs, rats etc., embellished with horns, wings and tails. The illustrations indicate that a *paphal* need not necessarily be a serpent alone. Taoroinai Sanahal Pakhangba[226] is a *paphal* with the face of a human being and the body of a snake, the upper portion of which is comparatively large and it gradually tapers off towards the tail. A headgear is placed on the head and the upper portion of the body has some projections on two sides. Tupichiren Sana Taoroinai Pakhangba [227] is an illustration of two intertwined serpents, each biting the tail of the other. The serpents are given a pair of horns and thorn-like projections on one side of the body. Tupi Pungtro Sana Pakhangba[228] is a single serpent with tongue protruding out of an open mouth, prominent ears, horns and thorn-like projections on the anterior side of the body. The illustration of Tupi Tusang Ngamba Pakhangba[229] features a serpent head combined with the body of an animal with four legs and a tail. In Tupi Lairen Kokkrai Meisangpa[230] the *paphal* takes the form of a chameleon, the head biting it's tail, Tupi Nongkhrang Pakhangba[231] is a popular *paphal* where the coiling takes the shape of a square, with each middle point of the sides encircled by a part of the body. The head of the serpent biting its tail is placed at the centre of the square. Each *paphal* illustration gives the name of Pakhangba, the *salai* associated with it, its distinctive colour, and mentions the area under its jurisdiction. Various geometric letters and words are placed inside or outside the coiling form. In the majority of the *paphals*, the tail of the serpent is put into its mouth.

The serpent is a common object of worship among several ancient religious systems of the world. Serpent symbols are found in Persia, China and Egypt. From the earliest times the serpent has been associated with the god of wisdom. The Syro-Egyptian deity Thoth or Taaut which symbolized intelligence and life was represented by a serpent. The serpent which was the symbol of the Egyptian Kneph, the divine deity of wisdom was the presiding deity of happiness and good fortune.[232] Those *paphals* of Pakhangba, which portray the head of the serpent biting its tail, symbolize tranquility and continuity of life. Those which portray the intertwined bodies of two serpents symbolize the union of male and female as begetters of offspring.[233] The ancestor serpent-dragon residing below the surface of the earth, represents the power of fertility, veneration of which lies at the core of the Meitei religious system.[234]

Each *paphal* is related to either one *salai* or more. A *salai* may seek the blessings or protection of only that Pakhangba which concerns them. Some of the *paphals* are named according to the *salais* associated with them, such as, *Luwang Maklang Pakhangba*[235] *Khuman Sana Lairel*

Pakhangba Taoronai,[236] *Moirang Salai Pakhangba Taoronai*[237] *Angom Salai Pakhangba Naoyom*[238] *Khaba Salai Apokpa Pakhangba Langyen,*[239] *Nganba Salai Taoding Pakhangba,*[240] *Ningthouja Salai Chopista Pakhangba.*[241]

It is believed that Pakhangba, in his many forms, govern every locality of the valley. In fact, most of the *paphals* are associated with a specific area. In case a person encounters one of the form of Pakhangba, he is either blessed by the *lai* or he is inflicted with an incurable disease. The majority of the forms of Pakhangba (those which are realistic representatives of snakes) when encountered, are dangerous to men. Some of those which are supposed to cause disease include *Hangkok Kingnaiba,*[242] *Sana Chinglen Pakhangba Yurel Sanahal,*[243] *Tubisana Henba Hellu Pakhangba,*[244] *Loktak Karang Kaphut Eelel Pakhangba,*[245] *Lairel Kukra Pakhangba,*[246] and *Kaphut Pakhangba,*[247] *Chirel Nonglei Pakhangba*[248] makes a person mad, while *Hangkok Pakhangba,*[249] causes physical abnormality. Death results if a person encounters the forms such as *Lairel Pakhangba Mongyang Halpa Sana,*[250] *Chenglei Pakhangba,*[251] *Taoting Hiyang-hirel Pakhangba,*[252] *Chirel Pakhangba Apakma*[253] etc. The *Paphal* manuscripts record that *Lokya Hithangpham*[254] is a significant *lai* and if encountered, the serpent should not be killed but saved. Interestingly, this *lai* exists in both male and female forms. As a male *lai* he is known by the name of Nongpok Chingningthou, the female forms are known by the names of Laishram Lairemma and Yumjao Lairemma. Illness resulting from an encounter with a particular Pakhangba may not always be incurable. On certain occasions performance of some rituals meant to appease a particular form of Pakhangba may cure a person. The procedure to be followed is given in the *Paphal* manuscript, along with the illustrations.

There are also *paphals* which, when encountered, bring good luck to an individual, a family or a *salai*. *Sana Korou*

Yangpa Sana Pakhangba,[255] is one such form. It is associated with the Angom *salai*. This Pakhangba guards the areas around Komkeithel, Tusang Lairelpat, Uchekol, Takhok Urup Loukok, Loumanba and Kachipat. The manuscript mentions that if the *lai* is worshipped at Kongba Laikan cave, the Angom *salai* will be blessed. Speaking of the moods of this *lai*, W. McCulloch commented that "the Raja's peculiar god is a species of snake called Pakung-ba, from which the royal family claims descent. When it appears it is coaxed on to cushion by the priestess in attendance, who then performs certain ceremonies to please it. This snake appear, they say, sometimes of great size, and when he does so it is indicative of his being displeased with something. But as long as he remains of diminutive form it is a sign that he is in good humour" [256] It may be mentioned here that when Pakhangba assumes a monstrous form, signifying evil and misfortunes, the ancestral *lai* has to be appeased with blood offerings. Frequent appearance of the *lai* requires offering of the blood of a pig. At Kangla, however, it should be that of a yak.[257]

Pakhangba occupies a very significant position in the large pantheon of the Meitei *lais*. He is addressed to as *ipudhou* or grandfather.[258] The *Sakok Lamlen Ahanba Puya* reveals that he assumed the highest position in the *Konna Chak*, the last of the four human sub-periods,[259] and many of the *Puyas* place Pakhangba on top of the list of ancestral *lais*, at times describing him as the progenitor of all the *salais*.[260] According to the *Sakok Lamlen Ahanba Puya* King Khagemba inquires from three learned men about the greatest *lai* whom he should worship. The three learned men replied that in the *Konna Chak* there was none greater than Pakhangba. They also revealed that there were one hundred and eight manifestations of Pakhangba.[261] Further, they told Khagemba that Pakhangba the Immortal (Sidaba) would not be visible to the devotees unless they followed the 'way to Pakhangba', known as *Pakhangba Laining*, which was acceptable to the *lai*. *Pakhangba Laining* is a code of conduct which emphasizes the need to understand life, to acquire the ability of seeing one's true self, to do good to others even when such acts are not recognized, to be disciplined in eating and sleeping habits as well as in maintaining one's home, to be prepared to sacrifice one's body and soul, and to respect parents and elders. The *Ningthou Naophangba Puya* adds that in order to achieve self-realization, which please Pakhangba, one should be polite, sober and modest.[262]

Pakhangba is venerated with the performance of a number of rituals. The festivals organized in honour of this *lai* include *Heikru Hitongba, Ukrong Hongba* and *Ukai Kappa*. In *Lai Haraoba* Pakhangba is worshipped along with a number of other ancestral *lais*.

The serpent is not the only form of Pakhangba. That he had a dual personality is recorded in many *Puyas*. The royal chronicle says that Pakhangba assumes attributes of a god during the day and that of a man during the night.[263] In addition, the *Thiren Layat Puya* reveals that the *lai* also assumes the form of a serpent in the evening.[264] The same *Puya* further states that these three forms vary on different days of the week. On Sunday, Pakhangba takes the form of a *lai*, on Monday, Tuesday and Friday that of a serpent, and on Thursday and Saturday, he reveals himself as a human being.[265] The different forms also vary according to months. He is a *lai* during the months of *Sajiphu, Kalen, Enga* and *Engen* (from March to July), a serpent during the months of *Thawan, Langban, Mera* and *Hiyangei* (August to November) and a human being during the months of *Poinu, Wakching, Phairen* and *Lamta* (November to February). In view of Pakhangba's association with serpents in general and *paphals* in particular, some scholars have argued that snake worship was practiced by the Meiteis.[266] However, on the basis of available evidence it is difficult to establish that snake worship transformed into the veneration of Pakhangba.

A study of the Meitei pantheon reveals that Taibangpanba Mapu is the Ancestor of Ancestors and Sanamahi and Pakhangba stand out as universal *lais*. Respect for parents and elders is a code of conduct prescribed in *Pakhangba Laining*. This is best exemplified by the popular Meitei proverb *'Ima Ipadi Mitna Uba Lainido'* (mother and father are the visible gods). The Meiteis believe in the idea of re-birth.[267] Once a person is born, he is to worship his forefathers and surrender himself to *Mapa Guru*, because He symbolises life.[268] Every Meitei belongs to one of the *salais* (clans) and the progenitors of the *salais* all converge to the Ancestor of Ancestors. In the Meitei pantheon, there is no sharp distinction between gods and men, both of which are encompassed in the ancestor cult.

Notes and References

1. Ronald M. Berndt, "Traditional Morality as Expressed through the Medium of an Australian Aboriginal Religion" in R.M. Berndt (ed.), *Australian Aboriginal Anthropology*, 1970, pp. 216-217, cited in William H. Newell (ed.), *Ancestors*, 1976, p.3.
2. M. Fortes, "Some Reflections on Ancestor Worship in Africa", in M. Fortes and G. Dieterlen (ed.), *African Systems of Thought*, 1965, p.124, cited in William H. Newell (ed.). *op. cit.*, p.22.
3. Robert J. Smith, "Who are the Ancestors in Japan? A 1963 Census of Memorial Tablets", cited in William H. Newell (ed.), *op. cit.*, p.60.
4. M. Fortes, "An Introductory Commentary", in William H. Newell (ed.), *op. cit.*, p.10.
5. Chongtham Meramacha (ed.), *Leishemlon Ariba*, 1947, Introduction.
6. *Pakhangba Laihui*, (Handwritten copy), custodian L. Suresh, pp.1-2.
7. Bhagya Singh Yengkhoiba (ed.). *Leithak Leikharon*. 1988, p.3.

8. Kh. Chandrashekhar Singh (ed.). *Sakok Lamlen Ahanba Amasung Meihouron Sakok,* 1992, pp. 4-5.
9. *Ibid.*, p.7.
10. N. Ibochouba (ed.), *Thiren Layat,* 1981, pp. 23-24.
11. Chongtham Meramcha (ed.), *Leishemlon Ariba,* 1947, p.13.
12. Robert P. Gwinn, et.al (ed.*), TheNew Encyclopaedia Britannica: Micropaedia, Knowledge in Depth,* Vol.17.,1988, p.368.
13. Bhagya Singh Yengkhoiba (ed.), *Leithak Leikharon,*1988.
14. *Pudin* (Handwritten copy), custodian Y. Mohendra Singh.
15. M Laimit and L. Iboyaima (ed.), *Wakok Hilel Thilel Amailon Pukok Puya,*1972.
16. Athokpam Yaima Langdum (ed.), *Khamlangba Erengba Puwari: Neinarol,* 1993.
17. Bhagya Singh Yengkhoiba (ed.), *Leithak Leikharon,* Introduction.
18. *Ibid.*, pp. 3-4.
19. *Ibid.*, p.5.
20. *Ibid.*, pp. 5-6.
21. *Ibid.*, p.9.
22. Y. Bhagya Meitei (ed.), *Sakck Lamlen Ahanba Amasung Meihouron,* 1988, p.28.
23. Bhagya Singh Yengkhoiba (ed.), *Leithak Leikharon,* pp. 12-14. The major gods emerged from him and depending on the context either merge with or are taken as identical with him. However, functionally these gods maintain their separate identities.
24. *Ibid.*, pp.19-20.
25. *Ibid.*, pp. 21-23.
26. *Ibid.*, p.19.
27. *Ibid.*, pp. 25-32.
28. *Ibid.*, pp. 55-56.
29. *Ibid.*, pp. 44-47.
30. Robert P. Gwinn, et.al (ed.), *op. cit.*, pp. 368-370.
31. *Ibid.*, pp. 368-369.

32. B. Kullachandra (ed.), *Sanamahi Puya*, 1989, pp. 24-32; *Sanamahi Laigi Thouni Lairik; Lainingthou Sanamahi Mingkheiron; Sanamahi Ming; Sanamahi Laihui; Sanamahi Phangkhong* and *Sanamahi Thelon*. Henceforth each *Puya* will be referred to separately and *Sanamahi Puya* will be written as SP.
33. Kala Moirangcha (ed.), *Amai Laining Khuda Punshirol*, 1988, p.38.
34. Y. Bhagya Meitei (ed.), *Sakok Lamlen Ahanba Amasung Meihouron*, 1988, p.1.
35. M. Laimit and L. Iboyaima (ed.), *Wakoklon Hilel Thilel Amailon Pukok Puya*, Introduction, p.1.
36. Bhagya Singh Yengkhoiba (ed.), *Leithak Leikharon.*, p.1.
37. Malem Yaiphasang (ed.), *Khamoi Yangoi Sekning*,1974, p.1.
38. L. Iboongohal Singh and N. Khelchandra Singh (ed.), *Cheitharol Kumbaba*, 1989, p.1.
39. Y. Bhagya Meitei (ed.), *Sakok Lamlen Ahanba Amasung Meihouron*, p.28.
40. Bhagya Singh Yengkhoiba (ed.), *Leithak Leikharon*, p.4.
41. *Sakok Wakok* (Unpublished *Puya*), p.13, custodian Y. Mohendra Singh.
42. *Ibid.*, p.13.
43. Kh. Chandrashekhar Singh (ed.), *Lai Haraoba Laisol*, 1982, p.13.
44. Kh. Chandrashekhar Singh (ed.), *Loiyamba Shinyen*, 1975, p.1.
45. Thokchom Rajo Maibi, *Langol*, 1975, p.1.
46. J. Shakespear, "The Religion of Manipur", *Transactions of the Folklore Society*, 1913, p.423.
47. Kh. Chandrashekhar Singh (ed.), *Lai Haraoba Laisol* p.34.
48. R. K. Sanahal Singh, *Satjal*, 1937, p.31. There are several names for the cardinal points and directions. Obviously these were considered important and therefore, have been included in many *Puyas*, but as they were written by different people in different times these names have not been standardized.
49. Sairem Nilabir, "The Revivalist Movement of Sanamahism", in Naorem Sanajaoba (ed.), *Manipur: Past and Present*, Vol. II, p.110.

50. J. Shakespear, *op. cit.*, p.421.
51. S.N.Parratt, *The Religion of Manipur: Beliefs, Rituals and Historical Developments*, 1980, p.9.
52. Kh. Chandrashekhar Singh, "Umanglai", in Kh. Chandrashekhar Singh (ed.), *Umanglai Khunda,* 1980, p.31.
53. Y. Bhagya Meitei (ed.), *Sakok Lamlen Ahanba Amasung Meihouron*, p.5.
54. L. Kunjeswori Devi, *A Study of Archaeology in Manipur since Pre-historic Times.*,1988, pp. 177-178.
55. L. Iboongohal Singh and N. Khelchandra Singh (ed.), *Cheitharol Kumbaba,* p.36.
56. Frank Byron Jevons, *The History of Religion*, 1985 (Reprint), p.188.
57. L. Iboongohal Singh and N. Khelchandra Singh (ed.), *Cheitharol Kumbaba,* pp. 28-45.
58. Communicated by K Mangi Maiba, Selung Puren, Pandit Loisang, Sri Sri Govindajee Temple Board, Imphal, on 2nd November, 1992.
59. W. K. Bunce, *Religions in Japan*, 1955, pp. 99-100.
60. Sokyo Ono, *Shinto: The Kami Way*, 1964, p.7.
61. H. Byron Earhart, *Japanese Religion: Unity and Diversity*, 1982, p.8.
62. W. Lukhoi Singh, *Lai Haraoba*, 1989, pp. 177-184.
63. *Lai Khunta Lon,* p.1, custodian Y. Mohendra Singh.
64. Irom Amubi Singh (ed.), *Nunglon*, n.d., p.61.
65. N. Birachandra Singh, *Socio-religious Life of the Meiteis in the 18th Century A.D.*, 1987, p.210.
66. W. Lukhoi Singh, *Lai Haraoba*, pp. 177-184, see supra Appendix II.
67. Ng. Kullachandra Singh, *Meitei Lai Haraoba*, 1953, Appendix, pp. 1-10, see supra Appendix III.
68. Suvira Jaiswal, *The Origin and Development of Vaisnavism*, 1981, pp. 187-188.
69. Surajit Sinha, "Vaisnava Influence on a Tribal Culture' in Milton Singer (ed.), *Krishna: Myths, Rites and Attitudes*, 1966, pp. 72-73.

70. Bhagya Singh Yengkhoiba (ed.), *Leithak Leikharon*, p.41.
71. *Ibid.*, pp. 79-82.
72. *Leimaren Naoyom* (Unpublished *Puya*), p.1, custodian Y.Mohendra Singh.
73. S. N. Parratt, *op. cit.*, p.22.
74. Yumnamcha Budhichandra (ed.), *Imoinu Ahongbi Tungnapham*, 1963, p.25.
75. Bhagya Singh Yengkhoiba (ed.), *Leithak Leikharon.*, pp.57-58.
76. Kh. Chandrashekhar Singh (ed.), *Sakok Lamlen Ahanba Amasung Meihouron Sakok*, pp. 10-11.
77. Y. Bhagya Meitei (ed.), *Sakok Lamlen Ahanba Amasung Meihouron*, p.27.
78. N. Khelchandra Singh, *Ariba Manipuri Sahityagi Itihas*, 1969, p.100.
79. *Ibid.*, pp.103-104.
80. L. Basanti Devi, *A Study of Political History of Manipur from Pakhangba to Khagemba (33-1652 A.D.)*, 1988, p.226.
81. L. Iboongohal Singh and N. Khelchandra Singh (ed.), *Cheitharol Kumbaba*, p.46.
82. *Ibid.*, p.63.
83. *Khunung Lon* (Unpublished *Puya*), pp.14-17, custodian N. Khelchandra Singh.
84. L. Iboongohal Singh, *Introduction to Manipur*, 1960, p.28.
85. *Leimarel Sekning*, p.5, custodian N. Khelchandra Singh.
86. Yumnamcha Buddhichandra (ed.), *Imoinu Ahongbi Likhul Pomit*, 1992, p.2.
87. *Ibid.*, pp. 10-11.
88. Bhagya Singh Yengkhoiba (ed.), *Leithak Leikharon*, p. 41; *Pudin* (Handwritten copy), p.40, custodian Y. Mohendra Singh.
89. *Sakok Wakok* (Unpublished *Puya*), p.13, custodian Y. Mohendra Singh.
90. B. Kullachandra (ed.), *Sanamahi Laihui*, in *S.P.*, *op. cit.*, p.34.
91. L. Bhagyachandra Singh, *A Critical Study of the Religious*

Philosophy of the Meeteis Before the Advent of Vaisnavism in Manipur, 1991, p.36.

92. *Sakok Wakok* (Unpublished *Puya*), p.13,. custodian Y. Mohendra Singh.
93. Bhagya Singh Yengkhoiba (ed.), *Leithak Leikharon*, p.55.
94. *Ibid.*, p.38.
95. L. Iboongohal Singh and N. Khelchandra Singh (ed.), *Cheitharol Kumbaba*, p.36.
96. *Ibid.*, p.94.
97. Communicated to me by Y. Mohendra Singh on 27th May, 1993.
98. O. Bhogeswar Singh (ed.), *Ningthourol Lambuba*, 1967, p.242.
99. M. Laimit and L. Iboyaima (ed.), *Wakoklon Hilel Thilel Amailon Pukok Puya,*, p.4.
100. N. Manijao, *Pombi Lang*, 1986 (3rd Edition), p.36, fn.
101. *Ibid.*
102. O. Bhogeswar Singh (ed.), *Ningthourol Lambuba*, p.242.
103. Communicated to me by Y. Mohendra Singh on 9th June, 1993.
104. N. Khelchandra Singh (ed.), *Chingoiron*, 1982, pp. 23-25.
105. M. Chandra Singh (ed.), *Panthoibi Khongul*, 1987, (3rd Edition), p.98.
106. *Ibid.*, p.117.
107. O. Bhogeswar Singh (ed.), *Ningthourol Lambuba*, p.70.
108. Naorem Amuyaima Singh (ed.), *Panthoibi Naherol Amasung Aman Sikum Lon*, 1986, p.22.
109. R.K. Jhalajit, *A History of Manipuri Literature*, 1987 (2nd Reprint), pp. 151-152.
110. M.Chandra Singh (ed.), *Panthoibi Khongul*, Introduction, p.1,
111. *Ibid.*, pp. 2-3, 7, 9.
112. *Sakok Wakok*, (Unpublished *Puya*), p.13, custodian Y. Mohendra Singh.
113. *Ibid.*, p.53.
114. *Ibid.*, p.80.

115. N. Khelchandra Singh (ed.), *Ariba Manipuri Sahityagi Itihas,* p.75.
116. M. Chandra Singh (ed.), *Panthoibi Khongul,* Introduction, p.2.
117. L. Iboongohal Singh and N. Khelchandra Singh(ed.), *Cheitharol Kumbaba,* p.352.
118. N. Ibochouba (ed.), *Thiren Layat,* p.19.
119. M. Chandra Singh (ed.), *Panthoibi Khongul,* pp. 15, 129.
120. O. Bhogeswar Singh (ed.), *Numit Kappa,* 1986, (2nd Edition). Although the *Puyas* could not be dated with certainty comparing *Numit Kappa* with *Panthoibi Khongul,* we find that *Panthoibi Khongul* compares *Panthoibi* with Durga, an evidence showing the influence of Brahmanical religion at the time of writing the text which is not found in *Numit Kappa.*
121. R.K. Jhalajit, *op. cit.,* p.151.
122. L. Iboongohal Singh and N. Khelchandra Singh (ed.), *Cheitharol Kumbaba,* pp. 62-63.
123. *Ibid.,* p.84.
124. L. Bhagyachandra Singh, *op. cit.,* p.41.
125. *Sakok Wakok* (Unpublished *Puya*), p.13, custodian Y. Mohendra Singh.
126. N. Khelchandra Singh (ed.), *Chingoiron,* p.20.
127. *Ibid.,* p.19.
128. L. Iboongohal Singh and N. Khelchandra Singh (ed.), *Cheitharol Kumbaba,* p.38.
129. Kh. Chandrashekhar Singh (ed.), *Sakok Lamlen Ahanba Amasung Meihouron Sakok,* p.4.
130. Bhagya Singh Yengkhoiba (ed.), *Leithak Leikharon,* p.5.
131. O. Bhogeswar (ed.), *Moirang Ningthoural Lambuba,* Pt. I, 1982, p.6.
132. N. Khelchandra Singh (ed.), *Chingoiron,* p.55.
133. Bhagya Singh Yengkhoiba (ed.), *Leithak Leikharon,* p.55.
134. M. Laimit and L. Iboyaima (ed.), *Wakoklon Hilel Thilel Amailon Pukok Puya,* p.4.
135. L. Bhagyachandra Singh. *op. cit.,* p.41.
136. *Ibid.,* p.1.

137. L. Iboongohal Singh and N. Khelchandra Singh (ed.), *Cheitharol Kumbaba,* p.36.
138. N. Birachandra Singh, "Kings and Emperors who Reigned Before the Christian Era", in *Seminar on Cultural History of Manipur Before 33 A.D.*, 1990, p.7.
139. Bhagya Singh Yengkhoiba (ed.), *Leithak Leikharon,* p.80.
140. *Ibid.*, p.83.
141. *Ibid.*, p.80.
142. N. Khelchandra Singh (ed.), *Khuman Kangleiron,* 1980, p.59.
143. Kh. Yaima Singh (ed.), *Poireiton Khunthokpa,* 1971, pp.12, 13, 28, 40.
144. Ch. Manihar Singh (ed. and tr.), *Naothingkhong Phambal Kaba,* 1983, p.17.
145. *Ibid.*, p.27.
146. *Ibid.*, p.34.
147. *Ibid.*, p.38.
148. *Ibid.*, pp.55-57.
149. R.K. Jhalajit Singh, *op. cit.* p.116.
150. Thockchom Rajo Maibi, *Langol,* p.212.
151. Y. Bhagya Meitei (ed.), *Sakok Lamlen Ahanba Amasung Meihouron.*, p.76.
152. Ng. Kullachandra, *Meitei Lai Haraoba,* Appendix, pp. 1-10.
153. *Ibid.,* p.30. Y. Bhagya Meitei (ed.), *Sakok Lamlen Ahanba Amasung Meihouron.*, pp. 28-30.
154. Ch. Manihar Singh (ed. and tr.), *Naothingkhong Phambal Kaba, op. cit.*, pp. 55-56.
155. *Ibid.*, p.16.
156. L. Iboongohal Singh and N. Khelchandra Singh (ed.), *Cheitharol Kumbaba,* p.16.
157. Y. Bhagya Meitei (ed.), *Sakok Lamlen Ahanba Amasung Meihouron,* pp.36-39.
158. R.K. Jhaljit Singh, *op.cit.*, p.159.
159. Y. Bhagya Meitei (ed.), *Sakok Lamlen Ahanba Amasung Meihouron,* p.108.
160. L. Iboongohal Singh and N. Khelchandra Singh (ed.), *Cheitharol Kumbaba,* p.84, fn.1.

161. Ng. Kullachandra, *Meitei Lai Haraoba*, Appendix, pp. 1-10.
162. L. Iboongohal Singh and N. Khelchandra Singh (ed.), *Cheitharol Kumbaba*, pp.33-34.
163. *Ibid.*, p.39.
164. Bhagya Singh Yenkhoiba (ed.), *Leithak Leikharon*, p. 43.
165. *Ibid.*, p. 55.
166. J. Shakespear, *op. cit.*, p. 444.
167. B. Kullachandra (ed.), *Sanamahi Phankhong*, p.50.
168. B. Kullachandra (ed.), *Lainingthou Sanamahi Mingkheiron*, in *SP*, p.51.
169. Bhagya Singh Yengkhoiba (ed.), *Leithak Leikharon*, p.10.
170. B. Kullachandra (ed.), *Sanamahi Naoyom* in *SP*, p.10.
171. B. Kullachandra (ed.), *Sanamahi Laihui* in *SP*, p.6.
172. B. K. Kullachandra (ed.), *Sanamahi Laihui* in *SP*, p.34.
173. B. Kullachandra (ed.), *Lainingthou Sanamahi Mingkheiron* in *SP*, pp. 24-29; *Sanamahi Ming* in *SP*, pp. 36-37.
174. B. Kullachandra (ed.), *Lainingthou Sanamahi Mingkheiron* in *SP*, pp. 24, 26, 27.
175. B. Kullachandra (ed.), *Sanamahi Ming in SP*, pp. 30-32.
176. B. Kullachandra (ed.); *Lainingthou Sanamahi Mingkheiron* in *SP*, p.26.
177. B. Kullachandra (ed.), *Sanamahi Naoyom* in *SP*, p.7.
178. B. Kullachandra (ed.), *Sanamahi Naoyom* in *SP*, p.1.
179. B. Kullachandra (ed.), *Mahilen Khulumpa* in *SP*, p.55.
180. B. Kullachandra (ed.), *Sanathong Laigi Thouni Lairik* in *SP*, pp. 9, 12, 15, 22.
181. B. Kullachandra (ed.), *Sanathong Laigi Thouni Lairik* in *SP*, pp. 16.
182. Y. Bhagya Meitei (ed.), *Sakok Lamlen Ahanba Amasung Meihouron*, pp. 3-4.
183. L. Iboongohal Singh and N. Khelchandra Singh (ed.), *Cheitharol Kumbaba*, p.52.
184. *Ibid.*, pp. 67, 68, 72.
185. *Ibid.*, p. 63.
186. *Ibid.*, p. 73.

187. *Ibid.*, p. 76.

188. *Ibid.*, pp. 81, 82, 90, 92.

189. The Sanamahi temple housed at the premises of the present 1st Battalion Manipur Rifles at Imphal is said to have been built in 1891 A.D. as written on the Board kept at the *mandap* in front of the temple.

190. Sougaijam Iboyaima, *Lainingthou Sanamahina Haying Khongbal Tolong Yumphum Sana Sanggaida Lengshillakpa,*, 1987, p.1.

191. L. Iboongohal Singh and N. Khelchandra Singh (ed.), *Cheitharol Kumbaba,* p.52.

192. *Ibid.*, p.87.

193. Sougaijam Iboyaima, *op. cit.*, pp. 2-3.

194. L. Iboongohal Singh and N. Khelchandra Singh (ed.), *Cheitharol Kumbaba,* pp. 90, 93.

195. Sougaijam Iboyaima, *op. cit.*, p.3.

196. L. Iboongohal Singh and N. Khelchandra Singh (ed.), *Cheitharol Kumbaba,* pp.131-32.

197. Sougaijam Iboyaima, *op. cit.*, p.3.

198. L. Iboonghal Singh and N. Khelchandra Singh (ed.), *Cheitharol Kumbaba,* p.221.

199. *Ibid.*, p.494; Sougaijam Iboyaima, *op. cit.*, p.5.

200. L. Iboongohal Singh and N. Khelchandra Singh (ed.), *Cheitharol Kumbaba,* p.131.

201. Communicated to me by Oinam Manikchand, Manipuri Thougal Langba, Lainingthou Sanamahi Temple Board, Imphal on 19th June 1993.

202. Y. Bhagya Meitei (ed.), *Sakok Lamlen Ahanba Amasung Meihouron,* p.4.

203. Bhagya Singh Yengkhoiba (ed.), *Leithak Leikharon,* pp. 43, 55.

204. O. Bhogeswar (ed.), *Sanamahi Laihui,* (Handwritten copy), pp. 7, 9-11, custodian Y. Mohendra Singh.

205. *Census of India, 1981, (Series I), Paper (1984) - 4, India, Household Population by Religion, Head of Household,* Appendix A.

206. Y. Bhagya Meitei (ed.), *Sakok Lamlen Ahanba Amasung Meihouron*, pp. 4-6.
207. Chongtham Meramacha (ed.) *Leishemlon Ariba*, Introduction.
208. Communicated to me by N. Khelchandra Singh, on 15th June 1993.
209. Bhagya Singh Yengkhoiba, *Leithak Leikharon*, pp.58-59.
210. M. Laimit and L. Iboyaima (ed.), *Wakok Hilel Thilel Amailon Pukok Puya*, p.47.
211. L. Iboongohal Singh and N. Khelchandra Singh (ed.), *Cheitharol Kumbaba*, p.1.
212. *Pakhangba Phambal*, pp. 21-27, in Y. Mohendra Singh and N. Birachandra Singh, *Nongda Lairen Pakhangba Hourakpam Thiba*, Imphal, 1981, p.1.
213. *Amailon*, p.2; *Leithak Leikharon*, p.89; *Thiren Layat*, p.7; *Pakhangba Phambal*, p.21; *Mayang Ngamba*, p.1; *Krathong Lamlen*,p.18; *Leithak Leikharon*, p.105; *Thiren Meiram Liba*, p.15; *Ningthourol Lambuba*, Vol. I, p.1; *Ningthourol Lambuba*, Vol. II, p.1.
214. L. Iboongohal Singh and N. Khelchandra Singh (ed.), *Cheitharol Kumbaba*, p. 691.
215. Y.Bhagya Meitei (ed.), *Sakok Lamlen Ahanba Amasung Meihouron*, p.66.; Kh. Chandrashekhar Singh (ed.), *Sakok Lamlen Ahanba Amasung Meihouron Sakok*, p.5.
216. Bhagya Singh Yengkhoiba (ed.), *Leithak Leikharon*, p.79.
217. Y. Mahindra Singh and N. Birachandra Singh, *op. cit.*, p.4.
218. *Pakhangba Phambal*, pp. 17-18, *Ningthourel Seireng*, pp. 135-138, *Sendembi Cheisra*, pp. 13-15, *Sangai Phammang Latam*, p.7, *Langthaban Latam*, pp. 13-14, *Meihourol Makok Latam*, pp. 2-3 and Chekhong, p.4, in Y. Mohendra Singh and N. Birachandra Singh, *op. cit.*, pp. 4-6.
219. *Thiren Meiram Liba*, p.15, in Y. Mahindra Singh and N, Birachandra Singh, *op. cit.*, pp. 8, 10, 11.
220. *Ibid.*, p.12.
221. L. Iboongohal Singh and N. Khelchandra Singh (ed.), *Cheitharol Kumbaba*, p.1.
222. P. Gunindra Singh (ed.), *Catalogue of Manuscripts and Manuscript Paintings in Manipur*, *op. cit.*, "Introduction", n. p.

223. Dr. M. Kirti Singh, *Folk Culture of Manipur*, 1993, p.151.
224. Y. Bhagya Meitei (ed.), *Sakok Lamlen Ahanba Amasung Meihouron*, pp. 12-17.
225. P. Gunindra Singh (ed.), *Catalogue of Manuscripts and Manuscript Paintings in Manipur*, "Introduction", n. p.
226. Ch. Ibohal Mangang Pandit (tr.), *Paphal*, n.d., custodian, Manipur State Archives, Illustration No. 420.
227. *Ibid.*, Illustration No. 399.
228. *Ibid.*, Illustration No. 395.
229. *Ibid.*, Illustration No. 383.
230. *Ibid.*, Illustration No. 321.
231. *Ibid.*, Illustration No. 313.
232. Hodder M. Westropp and C. Staniland Wake, *Ancient Symbol Worship, Influence of the Phallic Idea in the Religions of Antiquity*,1972 (2nd Edition), p.46.
233. P. Gunindra Singh (ed.), *Catalogue of Manuscripts and Manuscript Paintings of Manipur*, "Introduction", n.p..
234. Lokendra Arambam, "Manipur- A Ritual Theatre State", in Naorem Sanajaoba (ed.), *Manipur: Past and Present*, Vol. II, p.62.
235. Ch. Ibohal Mangang Pandit (tr.), *Paphal*, Illustration No. 63.
236. *Ibid.*, Illustration No. 108.
237. *Ibid.*, Illustration No. 109.
238. *Ibid.*, Illustration No. 110.
239. *Ibid.*, Illustration No. 111.
240. *Ibid.*, Illustration No. 399.
241. *Ibid.*, Illustration No. 179.
242. *Ibid.*, Illustration No. 16.
243. *Ibid.*, Illustration No. 20.
244. *Ibid.*, Illustration No. 29.
245. *Ibid.*, Illustration No. 31.
246. *Ibid.*, Illustration No. 82.
247. *Ibid.*, Illustration No. 91.
248. *Ibid.*, Illustration No. 62.
249. *Ibid.*, Illustration No. 69.
250. *Ibid.*, Illustration No. 14.

251. *Ibid.*, Illustration No. 21.
252. *Ibid.*, Illustration No. 77.
253. *Ibid.*, Illustration No. 246.
254. *Ibid.*, Illustration No. 41.
255. *Ibid.*, Illustration No. 21.
256. W. McCulloch, *Account of the Valley of Manipur*, 1980 (Reprint), p.17.
257. Naorem Amuyaima Singh (ed.), *Yabirok*, 1981, pp. 7, 15.
258. Y. Bhagya Meitei (ed.), *Sakok Lamlen Ahanba Amasung Meihouron*, p.39. *Ibudhou* or *Ipu* is translated as grandfather in Ningthoukhongjam. Khelchandra Singh, *Ariba Manipuri Longei*,1978, p.12 and O. Clark, *A Vocubulary Manipuri to English Dictionary*, 1924, p.34.
259. *Ibid.*, p.39.
260. M. Laimit and Y. Iboyaima (ed.), *Wakok Hilel Thilel Amailon Pukok Puya*, pp. 49-50.
261. Y. Bhagya Meitei (ed.), *Sakok Lamlen Ahanba Amasung Meihouron*, p.39.
262. *Ningthou Naophangba Puya* (Unpublished manuscript), p. 13, custodian Y. Mohendra Singh.
263. L. Iboongohal Singh and N. Khelchandra Singh (ed.), *Cheitharol Kumbaba*, p.1.
264. N, Ibochouba (ed.), *Thiren Layat*, p.19.
265. *Ibid.*, p.28, fn.1.
266. E.A. Gait, *Census of India*, 1891, Assam, Vol. I, Report, 1892, pp. 182, 252, in G.A. Grierson, *Linguistic Survey of India*, 1904, Vol. III, Pt III, 1967 (Reprint), p.20.
267. Y. Bhagya Meitei (ed.), *Sakok Lamlen Ahanba Amasung Meihouron*, p.52.
268. *Ibid.*

4

Rituals and Ritual Specialists

Rituals cluster especially around those primary realities (such as sexuality, death, strife, and failure) that force us to face our personal limits and our merely relative existence. Rituals as such are constituted by the longing to place the self in enduring contact with absolute or source realities. W. Brede Kristensen referred to this connection of self and other (eternity, cosmic reality) as the fundamental 'compact', 'agreement', or 'covenant', 'man's law of life' that underlies all rituals, for in them humanity of the divine bind themselves together to sustain a unified and stable order of the universe.[1] Rituals deal with those sectors of experience which do not seem amenable to rational control and hence where beings can least tolerate insecurity.[2] The religious symbols must express the nature of the social structure of the group which they are a part and which they represent.

Ancestor worship among the Meiteis find formal expression in the performance of various rites and rituals which are observed for the numerous *lais* throughout the year. A Meitei life may be said to be full of prayers and other religious activities which revolve round a series of rituals. Prescribed ways of carrying on religious acts and procedures, ways of worshipping, praying, chanting, sacrificing, making offerings etc., are practiced in rituals.[3] Rituals may be said to implement beliefs. Ancestors are linked to their descendants by a chain of rituals, thus affirming the continuity of social relations through time.

In ancestor worshipping societies like the Meiteis, the troubles and misfortunes that inevitably occur in the course of human life - be they economic loss, career failure or the ultimate and inescapable afflictions of sickness and death - are often attributed to the ancestors. Conscientious ritual activities are therefore performed on appropriate occasions to make the ancestors happy and thus preventing or mitigating their anger. Rituals are also performed when the worshippers seek blessing from their ancestors.

The rituals for the ancestors may be broadly divided into two categories, viz; private and public. Private worship includes those rituals which are performed within the premises of a family. They are performed at three levels viz; *phungga* (hearth), *sagei* (sub-clan) and *salai* (clan). The public rituals, on the other hand, are observed in public places such as the premises of a local shrine, a selected site etc., to propitiate *Lamlais* (*lam:* locality or area; *lai*: god). In this chapter an attempt is made to understand the various aspects of *salai*, *sagei* and *phungga apokpa* rituals. The rites-de-passage are also taken into account since, we shall see in the discussion that the *Yumlais* (household deities) are also venerated along with the family progenitors of the *salai* concerned.

I

The traditional priests and priestesses, who preside over these rituals are called the *Maibas* and the *Maibis*, respectively. Shamanism is not an unusual feature of primitive societies. Maria Leach defines a shaman as thus: 'The term shaman is usually used by American ethnographers in reference to men or women, who through the acquisition of supernatural powers are believed to be able to cure diseases'.[4] For Herskovits 'the shaman is an individual endowed with supernatural power to hear or one who can call his spirit to find out what is beyond time and space'.[5] The definition given by Leach is useful for understanding the characteristics of the *Maibas* and that of Herskovits for the *Maibis*. Meiteis distinguish between two categories of priestly classes viz; those specially qualified for performing social and religious rituals and those who act as physicians and midwives.[6]

The *Maibis* stand apart as a distinct group in the traditional Meitei society. 'The gods and goddesses prefer to be served by women and therefore should a man become possessed while dancing at the *Lai Haraoba* festival, he is styled a *Maibi* i.e., a priestess, in contrast to a *Maiba* i.e., a priest. And while dancing before the gods he will wear woman's clothes'.[7] It is likely that the female *Maibi* came earlier than her male counterpart.[8] This is in view of the possibility that the Meiteis had a matrilineal setup at least till the time of Nongda Lairen Pakhangba.[9] The meaning and origin of *Maibi* is obscure. However, it is generally believed that they were in existence at least by the time of Nongda Lairen Pakhangba, the first 'historical' king.[10] An interesting aspect of *Maibis* role in Meitei society is that she holds a special ritual status outside of the norms of the social framework for women.[11] Yet, they are an integral part of the social organization of the Meiteis and are within the *salai* system. Therefore, they should not be misunderstood as standing apart from the Meitei traditional society.[12]

The *Maibis* used to be and still are formally initiated and registered with the *Pandit Loisang* (College of Priests), attached to the royal palace. The *Loisang* has been a strong institution and had three divisions viz; *Maiba Loisang, Maibi Loisang* and *Pena Loisang (pena*: one-stringed fiddle).[13] The *Pandit Loisang* was responsible for supervision of worship of *lais* in general and the annual *Lai Haraoba* in particular, that takes place all over Manipur. It was this institution which assigned to the *Maibis* their duty of officiating in *Lai Haraoba* festival in different localities. The *Maibis* are grouped under three categories, each having their responsibility towards particular *yeks*. The three groups are *Sanglen, Nongmai* and *Phura*. The first one officiates for the Ningthouja *yek*, the second for all the rest except Khuman and Kha-Nganba *yeks* which are looked after by the third group.[14] Further goddess Yumjao Lairembi can be served only by the Nongmai group of *Maibis*, whereas god Nongshaba is permitted to be served only by the *Phura* group of *Maibis*.[15] As far as the *Maibas* or officiating priests are concerned, the *Loiyamba Shinyen* records in detail the duties assigned to them. Each of the thirty-four *yumnaks* of *Maibas* with corresponding *lai* to be taken care of is listed in the *Puya*.[16] The same source also records the *yumnaks*, numbering thirty-seven of the *Maibas* who are assigned the duties for the invocation of and rendering service to various gods and goddesses.[17]

Ever since the institution of these ritual specialists came into being the *Maibis* and the *Maibas* hold an exalted position and are an indispensable part of the society. No worshipper could perform any rite without the intervention of a priest or a priestess who stood between him and the *lai* as a mediator. As early as the reign of Naothingkhong (653-763 A.D.), these ritual specialists occupied an important position in the society. The coronation ceremony of this king was conducted with elaborate rituals and under the strict guidance of these specialists.[18] It is rather surprising that the royal chronicle *Cheitharol Kumbaba* is almost silent about the *Maibas* and *Maibis* in the early period. The earliest references we have is of *Ametpa Loisang*(College of Traditional Physicians) acting as a physician in curing the illness of Meiteileima Serambi, the wife of King Mungyamba. This incident took place in the year 1570 A.D.[19] The traditional priests and priestesses were entrusted with the responsibility of general superintendence of all religious activities. They are supposed to be thoroughly acquainted with all the traditions regarding the appropriate worship of each divinity, understand the mysteries of numbers and be well versed in astronomy. They are expected to settle the festival calendar and determine the days suitable for transaction of business by an individual or the community. The Meitei *Maibas and Maibis* are soothsayers who warned people against forthcoming dangers. They are able to suggest modes of averting divine anger and thus saved men from evils which would otherwise have come upon them unawares. In such cases, sacrifice on a large scale or of an unusual character was commonly recommended. They also made good luck charms and acted as guides, counsellors and advisors for the well-being of the king in particular and his subjects in general.

A woman may become a *Maibi* either by being chosen at the *Lai Haraoba* or by being directly possessed by the *lai*. The signs of possession are frantic dancing, wild babblings in an unknown tongue and final collapse in a state of unconsciousness. In the instances when possession leads to one becoming a *Maibi*, the first symptom is the formation of the *iota* (hair coiling into a tangle).[20] Possession leads to abnormal behaviour. A female destined to be a *Maibi* is distinguished from other females right from a very young age.[21] She is always attracted towards other *Maibis*, desiring to be in their company and having a natural interest to be like them. Once possessed she may sing, pull her hair, refuse food and run restlessly in a wild manner. She sets out to find her own *Ima Guru* (*ima*: mother). As if revealed by the *lai* which possesses her, she sometimes accurately tells the name of the *Ima Guru* and the location of her residence. Once she meets her *Ima Guru*, the latter washes the face, feet and hands of the girl in the manner in which a child is treated. She is asked to eat *tairen* leaves (*cedrela toona*) which signifies acceptance of the young girl as a novice. The *Ima*

Guru now teaches the novice the sacred words of the *lai* and all the other rules and regulations to be followed, having become the one chosen by the *lai*. She is trained in dance, music, chanting and complex ritual procedures.[22] She has to learn the use of the most important tool of her profession, namely, a brass metal bell called *sarik*.[23] *Sarik* is used whenever a *Maibi* chants in a *senmit* or *laitongba* (act of divination). Oracles of this kind are performed with the aid of two sets of *senkhai* (ancient coins). The *Maibi* casts these coins and the oracle is read from the inscriptions on the side of the coin which is uppermost. Not all *Maibis* make use of *sarik* as a tool for delivering oracles.[24] Those *Maibis* who use *sarik* are considered to deliver accurate prophecies. She is believed to be capable of naming persons, places etc., in delivering oracles. She sometimes even predicts the day, date and time of death of an individual. The oracles are taken to be the words of the *lai* and therefore the *Maibis* act as mediators between gods and men. *Maibis* are respected by the people. Those *Maibis* who do not use *sarik* are considered to have limited powers of prophecy. The limitations include her inability to deliver oracles at any shrine or in any locality. Her ability to foretell is limited to individuals i.e., she is not capable of prophesising for a whole clan or a village. Further, she can deliver oracles pertaining to general issues only. Nevertheless, these *Maibis* are no less significant than those who use the *sarik*. On certain occasions these *Maibis* are particularly called to perform some rituals.

When the novice completes her training under the *Ima Guru* she is asked to appear before the *Pandit Loisang* where her superior powers and skill are tested. If found suitable, the novice undergoes the *Kandha Epal Thaba* rite symbolizing the purification of the novice. From then on she becomes a full fledged *Maibi* and can practice her profession on her own.[25]

As a general rule *Maibis* are not expected to marry. She is subject to certain taboos. She is not expected to eat a particular variety of fish which has spines on its head e.g., *ngakra* (*clarius batrachus*), commonly known as catfish. She cooks her own meals and uses clean fire i.e., fire made by flint and steel or friction of a band of cane drawn across a piece of dry wood. If a woman becomes possessed after marriage, she cannot lead a normal married life. *Maibis* are believed to be the wives of the *lais* who possess them and are therefore treated as special persons even by their husbands. The *Maibi* occupies that side of the bed which is usually occupied by the husband. The *lai* is believed to visit the *Maibi* at night and on particular nights of the month she has to sleep alone. On such occasions, the *lai* may approach her in the form of a human or an animal. *Koubru* takes the form of an elephant, Marjing a horse, and Sanamahi a bull.[26] If the *Maibi* bears a child by her husband, the *lai* may become angry. The *Maibi* will then lose natural affection for the child and sometimes ill-treat and neglect the child.

The *Maibis* deliver oracles whereas the *Maibas* are priests who officiate in religious ceremonies. They conduct the minute details of the ceremony, and act as partners of the *Maibis* on many occasions of ancestor worship. When the *Lai Haraoba* ritual is performed, only the *Maibas* are permitted to adorn the Lainingthou with a new dress. The *Maibi* does the same for Lairembi. Throughout the various stages of the function the place of the *Maiba* is at the side of the *Maibi*.

The other category of priests are the traditional physicians and midwives who are also known by the terms *Maiba* and the *Maibi*, respectively. These physicians and midwives have no role in the religious life of the Meitei community, although a group of *Maibas* indulge in acts of witchcraft and sorcery and are greatly feared by the people.[27]

The significant role of the *Maibis* and *Maibas* in the everyday lives of the Meiteis can hardly be overemphasized.

Like the *Brahmana* priest, the traditional priests and priestesses of the Meitei society enjoyed a special ritual status. They are kept busy throughout the year conducting various rites and ceremonies at home, in the locality or the village. The function of the *Maibis* as diviners in a society which greatly depends on their powers of prediction, further enhances their position in the traditional religious set up.

II

Ancestor worship is essentially a family affair. But wherever such cults are found, - they also include the worship of the community's gods. The family is a comparatively late institution in the history of society, and therefore, it is probable that the family imitated the community's rituals than the other way round.[28] Among the Meiteis, the *lais* worshipped in the house as also in the community are all ancestral *lais*. The difference between the private and the public rituals lies in the fact that the former can be performed only by those groups of families, sub-clans or clans for whose ancestors the ritual is initiated. There is no such restriction for the public rituals. In all ancestor worshipping societies, the worshippers are drawn from the family and are united by the natural bonds of blood. It therefore seems appropriate that an understanding of the veneration of ancestral *lais* requires an initial study of its private rituals.

It has already been mentioned that the Meiteis evoke their ancestors for almost every event that take place in their everyday lives. The formation of a bee-hive, an usually large collection of termites or a plantain trunk branching into two are considered *khudam peeba* i.e., indication that the *apokpas* (ancestors) should be appeased by performing the appropriate rites.[29] Ancestors may also be evoked when the worshippers ask for the grant of specific wishes. In case the ritual is to be performed in connection with granting of offsprings, it is performed in the month of *Langban* (August-September), for long life in the month of *Poinu* (November-December) and for wealth in the month of *Enga* (May-June).[30]

Veneration of ancestors with appropriate rituals is expressed by the term *'Apokpa Khurumba'* (*apokpa*: ancestor; *khurumba*: to bow before, to pay respect to and to pray to) i.e. to bow before and pray to ancestors with reverence. The private cult and its associated rituals may be grouped under three categories. They are the following:

(1) *Salai Apokpa Khurumba* for clan progenitors.

(2) *Sagei Apokpa Khurumba* for sub-clan progenitors.

(3) *Phungga Apokpa Khurumba* for family progenitors.

Salai Apokpa Khurumba as the name implies relates to the worship of the *apokpas* of each of the seven *salais* of the Meitei social organization. The descendants of each *salai* worship them on the Meitei calendrically fixed days and months of a year with appropriate rites. The worshippers seek blessings for general prosperity, well-being and protection of the whole *salai*. Each *salai* venerates its *apokpa*(ancestor) by the offering of particular fruits, flowers, fish, animal etc. *Thiren Meiram Liba Puya* gives an exhaustive list of the various items to be offered to each *Salai Apokpa* along with the particular direction and *lai* associated with each *salai*.[31]

The prescribed rules for ritual observance are followed strictly. The *Maibas* and *Maibis* as the ritual specialists are the main functionaries in these ceremonies. *Salai Apokpa Khurumba* for each *salai* is performed at different months of the year viz; Moirang *Salai Apokpa – Lamta* (February-March), Khuman *Salai Apokpa - Sajiphu* (March-April), Khanganba *Salai Apokpa - Kalen* (April-May), Mangang *Salai Apokpa - Enga* (May-June), Angom *Salai Apokpa - Engen* (June-July) and Luwang *Salai Apokpa - Wakching* (December- January).[32] Sarang-Leishangthem *Salai Apokpa* is worshipped in the month of Phairen (January-February).[33] Therefore, we find that each *salai* propitiates its progenitor in its own distinct way. It may be mentioned here that there are also particular colours associated with a particular *salai* viz; Khuman - black, Khanganba - mixed shades of green, Mangang - red, Angom - white, Luwang - blue, Sarang-Leishangthem- a light shade of green and Moirang - mixed shades of yellow.[34]

The worship of a clan progenitor is generally attended by all the members of the clan. However, when a clan consists of hundreds of families it becomes impossible for a full participation of all the members. It is at this juncture that *Sagei Apokpa Khurumba* acquires great significance. Here, the *Sagei Apokpa* is evoked along with the *Salai Apokpa.*[35] Therefore, for all practical purposes *Sagei Apokpa Khurumba* emerges as the most widely observed ritual and thus representing the Meitei ancestral rites and rituals.

The main ritual of *Sagei Apokpa Khurumba* is performed at the *phura* (shrine) which is housed at the courtyard of the house of the *Sagei Piba*. Inside the *phura* is kept a *thinbi* and a *khallong* which are both made of iron.[36] The *thinbi* represents the mother and the *khallong* the father of each *sagei*. The *thinbi* is kept buried in the ground while the *khallong* is kept over it above the ground. Each *Sagei Piba* will ensure the safe-keeping of these two items. If on account of any reason such as flood, migration etc., where the *thinbi* and *khallong* of the *sagei* cannot be traced, the two items will be replaced and kept in the *phura* accompanied by rituals conducted by the *Maiba* and *Maibi* officiating the ceremony. It may be mentioned here that only the Thangjam *sagei* has the sole right to cast these iron items of *thinbi* and *khallong* for the whole community. There is an interesting aspect of this installation of *thinbi* and *khallong*. The two items are brought from the place of casting to the *phura* assigned to it by a bearer who has to maintain strict silence throughout the journey. Any conversation required is done for the bearer by an attendant who accompanies him. In such cases where the original place of *thinbi* and *khallong* are known but the items untraceable, a small portion of mud from the original place may represent *thinbi* and *khallong* in the shrine newly assigned to them.

The main ritual of *Sagei Apokpa Khurumba* is the *Lai-Chaklon Katpa* i.e., offering of food to the *lais*. A *Sagei Apokpa Khurumba* ritual may be said to follow the procedure of a *Lai Haraoba* ritual, although on a less detailed scale. The *Maiba* and the *Maibi* are the two leading experts officiating the ritual. The *pena* (one stringed fiddle) singer accompanies the rite performances with the song of *Ahonglon*. The central theme of the song is *'hongnemse'*, an archaic Meitei word translated as 'let us offer food'.[37] The *pena* singer first sings in respect of the *Salai Apokpa* and then the *Sagei Apokpa* of the sub-clan in question. If the ritual is performed for the *Laisram sagei*, the *Ahonglon* song runs as thus: "*Hei Khuman Apokpa Ibudhou , hei, hou, hei hongnemlo ....*".[38]

At the start of the ritual, the ancestors are evoked from the water. The *Maiba* and the *Maibi* accompanied by the *pena* singer perform the *'Lai Ikouba'* or *'Lai Loukhatpa'* ritual from the river.[39] This 'calling up of the *lai*', performed by the river-side is an essential aspect of the *Lai Chaklon Katpa* ritual. The significance attached to this *Lai Ikouba* ritual is that the *lai* is now given life and the other rituals can now follow. As the *Maibi* approaches the water, two preliminary rites are carried out by her. The first of this is called *Leirai Yu-khangba* and it consist of the offering of *yu* (rice beer) and powdered rice with water to the *lai*. The *Maiba* then offers the *konyai* i.e., gold and silver pieces by throwing them into the water. He then invokes the *lai* by name. The *Maibi* then dances holding the *ishaifus* (cultic pot) of the Lainingthou and Lairemma facing the four cardinal points guarded by Thangjing, Marjing, Wangbren and Koubru. The *ishaifus* which are handed to the *lai*-bearers are carried to the shrine after the completion of the *Lai Ikouba* ritual. The *lai*-bearers should have an unblemished marriage line. The *Piba* or head of the *sagei* carries the *ishaifu* of Lainingthou whereas the next eldest male carries the *ishaifu* of Lairemma.[40] After the *lai* has been given life, they are brought to the *phura*(shrine) and offered the appropriate number of *langthrei* buds . The main feature of offering meal to the ancestors takes place. The food to be offered to the *lai* must be cooked only by the *Piba* i.e., head of the *sagei*.[41] The *lais* include besides the *Sagei Apokpa*, that of *Salai Apokpa* concerned and the Ultimate Father along with the Ultimate Mother (Leimaren Sidabi). A yet significant part of this *Apokpa Khurumba* is *Laibao-chenba* i.e., divination which is delivered by the *Maibi*. The members participating the *Lai Chaklon Katpa* ritual pay great attention to this because the *Maibi* foretells the forthcoming events concerning the *sagei*. Any sacrificial rites required for thwarting evil if any or impending dangers etc., are all predicted by the *Maibi*. The ritual of *Apokpa Khurumba* complete, the members of the *sagei* join a feast. It is a tradition that *Sagei Apokpa Khurumba* should be held at least once a year.[42] This must have been done to enable the *sagei* members to meet at least once a year renewing the bonds of kinship.

Perhaps the close link between the dead ancestors and the living descendants are best kept alive in the observance of the *Phungga Apokpa Khurumba*. Here, a family worships its immediate ancestors without the participation of anyone else outside the *phungga* group.[43] The fire of the *phungga*(hearth) symbolizes the root of social relations, a family dining together from the food cooked out of one *phungga*. A *phungga* may consist of a couple, their children and grandparents. In case families share the same *phungga*, such as extended family they also fall under the purview of *Phungga Apokpa Khurumba*.

The *Phungga Apokpa Khurumba*, unlike the *Salai Apokpa Khurumba* and *Sagei Apokpa Khurumba* can be performed on any auspicious day. The day and month is, however, fixed according to the Meitei calendar if the family desires to pray for specific grants such as offsprings, wealth etc.[44] Some considerations have to be taken into account for the *Phungga Apokpa* ritual. The date selected should not fall on *i-khudeng* and *lai-khudeng* which are considered ominous. Following the *saka* era, the dates on which the ritual may be performed are 1, 2, 3, 5, 11, 12, 21, 22, 23, 25 and 26.[45] A day before the appointed day, the ancestors are invited to a small rite. If the occasion falls in the month of *Langban* (August-September), the place for the ritual is the South-East portion of the courtyard of a home. A plantain leaf is cut in a circular shape and three white flowers are placed on it. The three flowers are meant for the great grandfather, grandfather and father, inviting them to attend the ceremony to be performed the following day.[46] In case the ritual is performed on other months of the year, the procedures may vary. However, it is the great grandfather, grandfather and father who are the main invitees through the last male deceased member of the family.

On the appointed day, the preliminary important rite of *Anam-Athou* is performed. This is done to drive out any evil spirit that may disturb the ritual. Some food items are placed on the left side of the verandah of a typical Meitei home. The items include a bunch of bananas of even number and some grains of rice. They are placed on a plantain leaf. Alongside, seven *lukmais* (round baskets with short legs) filled with *kabok* (parched rice) are also kept. Thus, this makes sure that no evil spirit disturbs the ritual.[47]

The main ritual is conducted in the *laplel-ka* or the second room of a typical Meitei house. In the southern side of the room, near the foundation pillar of the house is erected an altar called *khuda*. This symbolizes the seat of Lainingthou and Lairembi, the Ultimate Father and Mother who are also venerated during the ritual. This *khuda* faces North. A white cloth called *phiroi-ashuba* covers the *khuda* of the divine couple.[48] Three *langthrei* buds are placed before the *khuda*. This is known as *Leihun Tamba*. Then the seven flowers associated with each of the seven *salais* are offered to the *lais*. Along with it a variety of raw food items are also offered to the *lais*. These include banana, sweet smelling fruits, betel nut and leaves, *sareng* fish, rice grains, vegetables, salt, oil, spices etc. A lamp and incense are also kept along with the items. Where the *Apokpa Khurumba* is for long life, gold and silver pieces are also included. The *Naheiba* (purification rite) and *Anam-Athou* (driving off evil spirits) are performed. The first stage of offering is now over.

The raw items are then cooked in a fire place kept ready for the occasion. Fuel and water to be used for cooking are to be collected from specific areas traditionally accepted for each *salai*. The goddess Imoinu Ahongbi whose abode is at the hearth is then evoked by offering fruits, betel nut and money asking her to cook the rice and curry. There are certain rules to be followed in the process of cooking. Exact amount of water should be put since the excess water, if any, cannot be drained out. There should be a minimum of three items for offering to the ancestors. The cooked food is now served to the ancestors and their attendants (*khaobunai*) on a double layered plantain leaf which is being used as a plate. The part of food set aside for the *khaobunai* is kept beside the foundation pillar of the house. Further away three places are set aside for the great grandfather, grandfather and father in order of seniority. Before the *apokpas* come to eat it is essential that all the lights be extinguished. After bowing to the ancestors, they are left to themselves for a while to relish the meal. The *Maiba* and the head of the family subsequently re-enter the house and chants *mantras*. When the lights are re-lit, the three meals offered to the *apokpas* are taken by the head of the house, his wife and eldest son. The portions allotted to the *khaobunai*, together with what remains of the *apokpa* offering are placed in a piece of cloth and buried in a hole near the foundation pillar of the house.[49]

Just about the time when the *apokpas* are expected to finish eating the meals, that is the time when the worshipper asks them for the boon. The sequence of asking begins with the request by the worshipper to the father who in turn is requested to ask the grandfather and in turn the great grandfather. Likewise the boon will also be granted first by the great grandfather to the grandfather, grandfather to the father and finally the father will grant it to the son or the worshipper.[50] After the ancestors have been fed with the food cooked for the purpose, they are offered betel nut and leaf in the *phamel* i.e., the South-West side of the front verandah of the house.[51] This is the last act of meal offering to the ancestors.

The sending off ceremony is done by the officiating person. If the *Maiba* is the officiator, he will instruct the head of the *phungga* to lead the three *apokpas* and their attendants out of the house up to the edge of the verandah. In case it is the worshipper himself who has officiated the ritual, he will go up to the gate to see them off. The ancestors are requested to take with them *lai-amangba* (*lai*: god; *amangba*: impure) or evil spirit, if any, obstructing their way out. Once all these are complete the final ritual is that of making sure that the dead forefathers have left the house and its compound. A ritual is conducted by the *Maiba* for this purpose where he closes the door of the house.

The food which was offered to the *apokpas* can be consumed only by the members of the *phungga*. Any food remaining which has to be thrown will be put in a hole dug in the last room of the house. It is to be remembered that the *Maiba* who conducted the ritual is also prohibited from eating the food offered to the *apokpas*. The ritual of *Phungga Apokpa* being conducted for the exclusive unit, the *Maiba* stands outside this family group. There are certain rules to be followed. The *Maiba* will have to spend the night in the house where the *Phungga Apokpa Khurumba* took place. He can accept gift given for his service for the ritual only the next day.

The indications given by the lamp lit and the rice cooked for the occasion reveals the omens of the family. If the flame of the lamp displays three colours it is sign that ancestors are pleased with the worshippers. The opposite is indicated if the flame are flickering and does not burn uniformly. As for the rice, while cooking if it is raised it is a sign of prosperity. The directions reveal prosperity for the daughters if raised on the left side of the cooking pot, if on the right side it is for the sons, back side for the children in general and the front side for the elderly members of the family. Further, if the rice rises at three different spots on the surface, the family's wishes will be fulfilled. There are also bad omens such as diminishing wealth of the family in case the center of the surface of the rice sinks, rice grains falling out of the pot indicate that the children will be injured or die. If water overflows from the pot it is a bad omen. In case the surface of the rice cooked cracks into four parts it is a sign that the house will be ruined. The crack in two parts only will result in quarrels in the family. Finally, the family will earn a bad name or receive bad news if insects are found in the rice cooked for the *apokpas*.[52]

III

Ancestor worship among the Meiteis finds its place in every aspect of life. The rites of passage - birth, marriage and death all take place in accordance with the wishes and blessings of the ancestral *lais*. All activities associated with these ceremonies distinguish three major phases: separation, transition and incorporation.[53]

Right from the conception of a child the ancestors are venerated so that smooth delivery is ensured. Meiteis believe that a man possesses five *thawais* (souls) and a *mi* (shadow).[54] Each *thawai* is none else than five gods viz; Koubru, Thangjing, Marjing, Wangbren and Apanba.[55] The ritual of *Kokthok-chamthokpa* is performed once during pregnancy so that the five souls and the shadow do not leave the body. It may be performed on the fifth or seventh month of pregnancy. On the appointed day, a *Maiba* is called to conduct the ritual. In this, the mother is seated and her husband stands behind her moving a burning piece of pine wood behind her head. He manipulates this torch until the shadow of his wife's head falls on her lap. The *Maiba* brings a pot of water, places it in the center of the house and then prayer is offered along with some betel nut and fruits. The sacred water is used to wash the woman's hands and face to enable the woman to retain her strength during pregnancy and childbirth. When the child is to be delivered, a special house is constructed for the purpose known as *chaboksang*. In case of the royal family it was called *wangongsang*. At the time of delivery, the *Maibi* (midwife) cuts the umbilical cord with a bamboo knife. Before doing this, she invokes the five souls and the shadow to take up their place in the child: 'O five souls - The shadow also a sixth - O come'.[56] It must be remembered here that a traditional Meitei house is the abode of three *apokpas* viz; Sanamahi, Leimaren and Imoinu Ahongbi. Therefore acts such as delivery of a child which are considered impure are prohibited within the premise of the sacred household. Another significant ritual is the *Ipanthaba* or *Yupanthaba* ritual which is carried out on the morning of the sixth day of the birth of a child. The first *Ipanthaba* ritual was performed at the divine birth of Konchin Tukthaba, son of Lainingthou and Leimaren.[57] The new born and the mother are purified by a *Maibi*.[58] Along with this ritual, the whole house is also sanctified which is known as *Yumsengba* (*yum*:

house; *sengba*: clean, purify). The first *Yumsengba* was performed on the sixth day after the birth of. Konchin Tukthaba.[59] The *Thaloi Nongkhailon Puya* mentions that *Yumsengba* takes place on the tenth day following the birth of a child.[60] The requirements are a pot of water filled to the brim, two round discs of salt, a basketful of paddy, a garland of flowers having the colour of the particular *salais*, a garland of dried fish, coins, a piece of gold, fruit and betel nut.[61] The *Ipanthaba* ritual is done by a *Maibi* who sprinkles holy water i.e. water in which *tairen* leaves are dipped, to the mother and the child. On a *yangkok* (winnowing fan) is placed uncooked grains of rice, vegetables, *heibi* (medlar, a fruit), roast *ngamu* (common mud fish), chilly and salt on six pieces of plantain leaf. After the child is bathed and covered with a fresh cloth, the *Maibi* who officiates the ritual pretends to feed the child with the materials placed on the *yangkok* as many as six times accompanied with traditional hymns. This is repeated five times with the words: 'Father's food, grandfather's food, human food: eat this'. On the sixth occasion the wording is changed: 'O five souls and the shadow, this is the food of life: eat this'.[62]

The materials on the *yangkok* are offered to the *sarois* (evil spirits) so that the child is protected from these evil spirits.[63] For the Chakpas, believed to be the preservers of the traditional customs, the *Yupanthaba* ritual takes place on the fifth day for a female child and the sixth day for a male child. Purification of Sanamahi Kachin, the mother and child and subsequently the whole house is done by sprinkling of the sacred water by *tairen* leaves. *Yu* (rice beer) forms a very important item in Chakpa rituals and is offered to the *lais*.[64]

During the *Ipanthaba* ritual, the primal elements of fire, water, air, earth and heaven are worshipped with the singing of traditional hymns by the *Maibi*. These primal elements are the various manifestations of Taibangpanba Mapu himself. The *Maigei-Ngakpas* or the guardians of the four directions are also evoked. Later in the day the maternal uncle of the child shoots arrow on the four directions (North-East, South-East, North-West and South-East) for the purpose of driving away evil spirits from the child.[65]

Once the child is three months old, the *Chakumba* ceremony may take place.[66] The *Chakumba* or first feeding of the child can also be performed on the first month for a female child and sixth month for a male child.[67] Before the main ritual of feeding the child, a ceremony invokes Sanamahi and Imoinu Ahong Achaobi and they pray for the welfare of the child and for long life. A feast is prepared where there should be seven items of fish, meat or vegetables. Fruits and flowers are offered to the *lais*. Then, the mother is made to sit on the verandah of the house with the child on her lap. The child is fed the cooked food five times by the father. This represents the five souls of man.[68] Usually three dishes are prepared for *Ibudhou* Pakhangba (*ibudhou*: grandfather), the *salai* ancestor and the grandfather of the child descended from the *salai* ancestor. The food from the three dishes will be offered to the *lais* and fed to the child.[69] The final stage of the ritual is prediction of the child's future. Five items viz; earth, gold, silver, paddy and a book are kept in front of the child. The first item the child touches determines the course of life of the child.[70]

Marriage rituals of the Meitei society are conducted with the veneration of the *Salai* and *Sagei Apokpas* of the two parties concerned. The party of the groom-to-be brings *Apok-Asa* for the *Sagei Apokpa* of the bride-to-be. They may bring five, seven or more baskets of fruits for the purpose. Each basket must include two fruits viz; *heikru* and *heining*. A *phanek* and *laiphi* (garments for *lai*) are offered to the household *lai* along with fruits, *kabok* (parched rice), betel nut and leaf. The gods venerated are the *lamlai* (the *lai* of the area where the girl resides) and the *sagei lai*.[71]

L. Bhagyachandra mentions another ritual to be performed at the *Heijingpot* (ritual when marriage is made known formally by inviting guests known as *Heiching Kharai Puba*). Seven kinds of fruits of which *heikru* is compulsory are placed on a *kharai* (a carrier made of thin bamboo pieces) and offered to the *apokpas* of the girl's *sagei*. This food item can be consumed only by the people of the same ancestry.[72]

On the day of the marriage, the groom is sanctified by a priest. Prior to leaving for the residence of the bride, the groom will pray to the Ultimate Ancestor and the immediate seven ancestors under ritualistic formalities. Then he prays to his parents. The groom party then starts for the bride's place carrying fruits, sweets and other items to be offered to the ancestral *lai* of the bride, the *lamlais* i.e., *lais* of the locality and Sanamahi. The *chengluk nungshang* (a basketful of rice) and the items meant for the ancestral *lai* are kept at the place of Sanamahi and Imoinu Ahongbi in the bride's house. At the main ritual officiated by the *Maiba*, a seat is specially prepared with ritualistic formalities for the Ultimate Ancestor. The primal deities of fire, water, air, sky, earth, the *Lainingthous, Lainuras,* Sanamahi and Pakhangba are also worshipped for the welfare and long life of the new couple. When the marriage function at the residence of the bride is complete with the final veneration of Sanamahi, Leimaren and the *Salai Apokpas* of the bride, the couple pays their respect to the parents of the bride and then leaves for the residence of the groom. It is significant to note that the bride on entering the new house first pays obeisance to the Sanamahi and Leimaren of the husband's house.[73] At every stage, therefore, ancestral *lais* play a very important role in the maintenance of the social bond whether it is between the bride and the groom, the parents of the two parties, the *sageis* or the *salais*.

Death is an event which marks the passage of an individual from the world of man to the world of spirit.[74] The

Meiteis believe that there is a cycle of birth and death. *Khamoi Yangoi Sekning Puya* refers to *pokpa* (to be born) as *lang-ol-lakpa* (to be reborn).[75] In *Sakok Lamlen Ahanba Puya*, it states: *'Meeoiba ! poklabadi poklaga si-o, siraga amuk pok-o'* (O man! if you are born, you are born to die, and you die to be reborn again).[76] Death ritual acquires great significance in that death is the preliminary stage for an individual to be raised to the level of an ancestral spirit. There is no definite evidence recorded in the *Puyas* about the form of disposal of the dead practiced in pre-Hindu Meitei society. *Poireiton Khunthok* claims that cremation by fire was practiced in Manipur as early as the time of Poireiton who was a contemporary of Nongda Lairen Pakhangba (33-154 A.D.). Poireiton and his band of men reached a *Chakpa* village where he noticed some smoke at a distance. He inquired a villager as to the reason for emission of the smoke, on which the villager replied that it was the smoke emanating from a cremation of the dead body of Sangphu Raba.[77] The same event is also mentioned in *Ningthourol Lambuba*.[78]

According to *Sakok Lamlen Ahanba Puya*, the early Meiteis practiced four forms of the dead viz; air, water, earth and fire. During *Haya Chak* or the first human age, the dead body was disposed off by throwing away in the open only to be taken by *Khingpaingamba Thinungkhak*, the King of Birds. This divine bird was believed to carry the body to Heipokching where the dead body joins the rest of the corpse in the river. Once the dead body is thrown in this river, the departed joins the divine world.[79] The disposal of dead by burial was introduced by King Moriya Phambalcha in *Haya Chak* or second human age.[80] The same *Puya* mentions the disposal of dead by fire which was started during the last human age.[81] The *Cheitharol Kumbaba* records that from the time of King Garibniwaz the Meiteis started the practice of cremation of dead by fire: 'On the 20th day, Sunday of the month of *Lamta* (February-March) in the year 1724 A.D., the king went to Ningthee river to exhume the bones of his ancestors.[82]

According to tradition, no individual should be allowed to die inside a house since death is taken as an impure event. It is important to mention that a Meitei house is the abode of Sanamahi, Leimaren and Imoinu Ahongbi and hence no impure event should take place. At the Sanamahi Kachin, fruits and betel nuts are offered to the household *lai* Sanamahi. A lamp is also lit and kept beside the offerings. The *lai* is prayed to so as to save the dying person from leaving the human world. The dying person is kept on the right side of the *phungga* (hearth) for sometime. When the *Maiba* anticipate death, the body is taken out and kept at the *khangpoksang* (hut for the dying person).[83] Once declared dead by the *Maiba*, a *kai* (coffin) is prepared. A *tairen* leaf is placed in the *kai* near the head of the dead body, symbolizing sanctification of the body. After the bath and other rituals for the dead body, the *Maiba* offers flowers to Taibangpanba Mapu asking him to accept the departed soul in his abode. Finally, the *Maiba* offers the departed soul to the Ultimate Father.[84] All these rites completed, the dead body kept in the *kai* is tied with *paya* (a strip of bamboo) at three places. The one around the chest symbolizes fire, one at the navel symbolizes air and the one around the knee, water. The Meiteis believe that a body consists of five constituent elements viz; fire, air, water, earth and sky.[85] It is to these elements that the body returns after the soul departs from the body.

Cremation begins with the selection of a site. A *sel* (bell metal coin) is dropped at the site as a symbolic gesture of seeking permission from the *lamlai* (*lai* of the locality). A pyre is prepared at the site by laying firewood longitudinally (East-West) with seven cross layers. According to Y. Gourmani, the seven layers represent the seven *Lainuras* (divine girls). These *Lairunas* will protect the departed soul in the heavenly abode.[86] For L. Bhagyachandra, they represent the seven *salais* which constitute the Meitei society.[87] Yet another view is that of Sairem Nilbir who suggests that the seven layers represent the seven days of the week.[88] Above the pyre is placed a white canopy which is hoisted by fixing it to four green bamboo holes placed at the four corners of the assembled firewood. The four holes represent the *Maigei-Ngakpa lais*. It is believed that these guardians of directions will guard and direct the soul on its journey to the abode of the dead. The *kai* is always kept on the funeral pyre with the head in the North-West direction and the feet towards the South. The fire used to kindle the pyre is produced by striking two bamboos. A fire hymn accompanies the worship of the god of fire, praying that the departed soul is taken into its fold.[89] The fire is lit by the nearest male kin of the deceased amidst chanting of '*ha, hung, hei, he hing*' and sprinkling of holy water. On completion of the cremation, the holy name of the Ultimate Father is uttered at the grave for the peaceful union of the departed soul with Him.[90] The ashes are then collected and buried in a hole at the same spot of the cremation. A small mound is made and fruits and flowers offered to Leimaren,[91] the goddess of earth (*malem*).[92]

Purification of those persons who attended the funeral takes place by the sprinkling of holy water i.e., water in which *tairen* and *pungphai* leaves are dipped. This is to ward off any evil spirit that may have followed the person from the *mongfam* (cremation site). On the tenth day after the death of the person, *Yumsengba* ritual (*yum*: house; *sengba:* to sanctify) is performed. The *Maiba* who conducts the ritual makes an altar for Taibangpanba Mapu in the middle of the front courtyard of the house. Some items such as flowers and fruits are offered to the Supreme Father, Supreme Mother, Sanamahi, Pakhangba, the guardian of directions and also the primal elements of fire, water, air, earth and sky.[93] This purification rite is an important aspect of death rites and the same was practiced since very early times by the Meiteis as revealed by *Sakok Lamlen Ahanba Puya.*[94]

The *Lanna-thouram* ritual is performed on the eleventh day, which ensures safe journey of the departed soul to the abode of the dead. L. Bhagyachandra mentions that *Chupsa Moithem* is observed on the seventh day after the death of the person, to offer to the Ultimate Father to give a new birth to the departed soul.[95]

Food offering, which forms an important aspect of ancestral worship is done once every month for a whole year. The last rite for the deceased is the *Phiroi* ,earlier known as *Kumon Yangelba.* A grand feast is prepared which is attended by members of the *sagei*. The *Kumon Yangelba* rite signified the *Mung-thong-thingba* or the closing of the door of the dead.[96] The importance attached to the number of months i.e., twelve for the observance of the last rite of the dead is explained by *Khamoi Yangoi Sekning Puya.* According to the traditional belief, the conception of a child starts with the father who nurtures it for two months, after which the mother takes over the care of the unborn child. This takes a total of twelve months. The same time span is required for the dead to be reborn again.[97] Death which is caused by unnatural circumstances viz; suicide, burning etc., are considered bad omen. *Chupsaba* rite is observed for this category of the dead. The *Piba* of the *sagei* prays to Taibangpanba Mapu, Leimaren and the nine *Laibungthous* (divine youths) so as to prevent the occurrence of such undesirable deaths in the clan in the future.[98]

IV

It has been seen that the Meiteis attach great importance to the worship of their *apokpas*. The close ties of families are chiefly maintained by conducting the *Apokpa Khurumba* rituals on auspicious days throughout the year. The *Phungga Apokpa Khurumba*, apart from anything else, gives the family a sense of oneness, security and discipline in that the *phungga* is united as a unit without the interference of any outside group. The central point is the solidarity of the group who share the food cooked of a *phungga*. At the *sagei* level, the enactment of the *Sagei Apokpa* ritual maintains the kinship bond of the various sub-clan. The idea of the *Maibi* predicting good or bad omens concerning the members of the *sagei* again reinforces the idea of the same concern of families for the good or bad of the particular *sagei* they belong to. At the highest and broad level of ancestor ritual is the *Salai Apokpa Khurumba*. This is the highest expression of common ancestry among the numerous Meitei families. It must be remembered here that each level of ancestor worship is exclusive to the particular family or families in concern, thereby maintaining solidarity from the *phungga* to the final integration of the Meitei family of the *salai* level. Food offering forms an important aspect in the ritual of ancestor worship, the significance attached to food being that food dependence is from the moment of birth the vital bond that unites child to parent. Food is the basis of all life, biological, psychological and social and therefore of all action.[99] To share a meal is an expression of unity and trust and what is more important about it is that it presupposes the co-presence of all who share it. The purpose is to reunite all the sibling members of the group, sometime also the deceased, in the same way that a clan which has been broken by the disappearance of one of its links must be rejoined.[100] It is at the moment of sacrificial offering that the presence of ancestors is most immediately felt. Originally, the dead were supposed to suffer from hunger and thirst as the living do and to require food - for which they were dependent on the living. The *apokpas* are held with great awe and fear and they have to be constantly appeased by the living. This may be taken as expressing a sense of gratitude which entails the obligation to make a return for the protection the living gets from their ancestors.

A typical Meitei home is the abode of the *yumlais* (*yum:* house; *lai*: gods) . The Sanamahi Kachin functions as the private shrine and therefore at birth, marriage and death this *lai* is always venerated. Imoinu Ahongbi with her abode at *Phungga Lairu* plays an important role at *Apokpa Khurumba*. The food items which are cooked for the family ancestors are believed to be the handiwork of Imoinu. Since the divination of the cooked food forms an important aspect of the *Apokpa Khurumba*, the role of Imoinu can hardly be overemphasized. It is to be noted that Supreme Father and the Mother are always invoked at all the rituals whether they be held in honour of the *Phungga*, *Sagei* or *Salai Apokpas* or even in the rites of passage. The *Maigei-Ngakpa lais* drive off evil spirits which may harm any performing ritual. However, it is interesting to note that the Meiteis also propitiate Pakhangba at birth and death rituals although it is generally believed that Pakhangba is a state deity. We may assume that before the Ningthouja *salai* raised Pakhangba to the position of a state deity, the *lai* must have been venerated as any other ancestral *lai* in the Meitei pantheon.

All rituals, even that of *rites-de-passage* involve four elements: purification, an offering, prayer and a symbolic feast. Purification may be done by the worshipper, *Piba*, *Maiba* or *Maibi* depending on the occasion. This act of *Naheiba* is done by sprinkling of holy water by *tairen* or *langthrei* leaves. Pandit N. Khelchandra informs us that each *salai* is associated with a plant or a tree, leaves of which are used for the purification rite for the function of each *salai*. However, due to extinction of some of the species, *tairen* or *langthrei* leaves being still available came to be used for all the purification rites.[101] The offerings to the ancestral *lais* in general include offerings of *hei-lei* i.e., fruits and flowers. There are of course certain items of flowers, fruits etc., which have to be offered at specific rituals of the *salais*.[102] The ceremonial prayers, hymns and songs are usually recited, read or sung by the officiator of the ritual whether it is the *Piba, Maiba* or *Maibi*. The accompaniment of the *pena* (one stringed fiddle) by a *pena* player is also meant to sing the praises of the ancestral *lais*. At the end of most rituals, there is the dining of the participants and the guests. More often than not, the feast forms an essential part of every ritual. Offering of food to the ancestors and the subsequent idea of sharing a meal with the dead forebear dramatize the dependence of the ancestors on the continual care of the descendants and on the other hand, it symbolizes the coercive power and authority attributed to the ancestors by the descendants.

Notes and References

1. W. Brede Kristensen, The Meaning of Religion, 1960, in Mircea Eliade (ed.), *The_Encyclopaedia of Religion*, 1987, pp. 408-409.
2. Clyde Kluckhohn, "Myths and Rituals: A General Theory", in William A. Lessa and Evon Z. Vogt (ed.), *Reader in Comparative Religion: An Anthropological Approach*, 1958, p.146.
3. William, A. Lessa and Evon, Z. Vogt, "Myth and Ritual: Introduction", in William, A. Lessa and Evon, Z.Vogt (ed.), *Reader in Comparative Religion: An Anthropological Approach,* 1958, p.134.
4. Maria Leach (ed.), *Standard Dictionary of Folklore, Mythology and Legend,* 1950, p.1002.
5. Melville, J. Herskovits, *Cultural Anthropology*, 1974 (Reprint), p.228.
6. It may be noted here that the distinction is still valid and the *Maibas* and *Maibis* continue to function as priests and the priestesses, respectively in the present Meitei society. Therefore, although the data is mostly based on the *Puyas*, we discuss them in the present tense.
7. J. Shakespear, "The Religion of Manipur", *Transactions of the Folklore Society*, 1913, p.429.

8. S. N. Parratt, *The Religion of Manipur: Beliefs, Rituals and Historical Developments*, 1980, p.96.
9. Bhagya Singh Yengkhoiba (ed.), *Leithak Leikharon*, 1988, pp. 79-82.
10. Communicated to me by Pandit N. Ibochouba, Pandit Yaima, Pandit Loisang, Sri Sri Govindajee Temple Board, Imphal, on 28th October 1992.
11. Manjusri Chaki-Sircar, *Feminism in a Traditional Society: Women of the Manipur Valley*, 1984, p.168.
12. S. N. Parratt, *op. cit.*, p.96.
13. Communicated to me by Pandit N. Ibochouba, Pandit Yaima, Pandit Loisang, Sri Sri Govindajee Temple Board, Imphal, on 28th October 1992
14. S. N. Parratt., *op. cit.*, p.97.
15. Ng. Ekasini Devi, *Meitei Amaibisingi Lai Tingi Oiba Mahei*, 1988, p.25.
16. Kh. Chandrashekhar Singh (ed.), *Loiyamba Shinyen*, 1975, pp. 23-24.
17. Kh.Chandrashekhar Singh and Naorem Sanajaoba 'Ancient Meitei Written Constitution: Loiyamba Shinyen',(tr.) in Naorem Sanajaoba (ed.), *Manipur: Past and Present*, Vol. 1, p.300.
18. Ch. Manihar Singh (ed. and tr.), *Naothingkhong Phambal Kaba*, 1983, p.49.
19. L. Iboongohal Singh and N. Khelchandra Singh (ed.), *Cheitharol Kumbaba*, 1989, p.28.
20. Pandit O. Bhogeswar, cited in Manjusri Chaki-Sircar, *op. cit.*, p.176.
21. Communicated to me by Pandit N. Ibochouba, Pandit Yaima, *Pandit Loisang*, Sri Sri Govindajee Temple Board, Imphal, on 28th October 1992.
22. Manjusri Chaki-Sircar, *op. cit.*, p.175.
23. Ng. Ekasini Devi, *op. cit.*, p.32.
24. *Ibid.*, p.32.
25. Communicated to me by Pandit N. Ibochouba, Pandit Yaima, Sri Sri Govindajee Temple Board, Imphal, on 28th October 1992.

26. S. N. Parratt, *op. cit.*, p.97.
27. Communicated to me by K. Mangi Maiba, Selung Puren, Pandit Loisang, Sri Sri Govindajee Tample Board, Imphal, on 2nd November 1992.
28. Frank Byron Jevons, *The History of Religion*, 1985 (Reprint), p. 188.
29. Ngariyambam Kullachandra Singh, *Apokpa Thourinol*, 1992, Introduction.
30. Konjengbam Dhan Singh, *Meitei Puya Wari Machang*, 1978, p. 153.
31. Pebam Ibomcha Singh (ed.), *Singkaklen Mikouron Khanggoi Yangoi Sekining and Thiren Meiram Liba*, 1992, pp. 40-41.
32. Yumnamcha Buddhichandra (ed.), *Thaloi Nongkhailon Enat Kanba Amasung Semgat Sagatpalup*, 1985, pp. 5, 10, 12, 15, 19, 41.
33. Yumnamcha Buddhichandra(ed,), *Emoinu Ahongbigi Tungnapham*, 1963, p.34.
34. *Ibid.*
35. Communicated to me by Pandit N. Khelchandra Singh on 14th June 1993.
36. *Thinbi* is made in the shape of an hour glass, although not too constricted in the middle. *Khallong* is made in the shape of a spoon. The information on *thinbi* and *khallong* is given to me personally by Pandit N. Khelchandra Singh on 14th June 1993.
37. Communicated to me by Ibomcha Singh, *pena* singer, and former fellow . J.N. Dance Academy, Imphal, on 16th June 1993.
38. The full text of *Ahonglon* is published in N. Khelchandra Singh, *Thainagi Seireng*, 1966, pp. 42-46.
39. Mayanglambam Gourachandra (ed.), *Erat Thounirol*, 1988, pp. 32-33.
40. S. N. Parratt, *op. cit.*, p.69.
41. Communicated to me by Pandit N. Khelchandra Singh on 14th June 1993.
42. Communicated to me by Laisram Gopal Singh, *Piba* of the Laisram *sagei* on 29th May 2003.

43. Ngariyambam Kullachandra Singh, *op. cit.*, Introduction.
44. Konjengbam Dham Singh, *op. cit.*, p.153.
45. N. Birachandra Singh, "Ancestor Worship Among the Meiteis with Special Reference to Family Ancestor", *Proceedings of the North-East India History Association*, 1982, p.78.
46. *Meihourol Lathup* (unpublished *Puya*), p.1, cited in N. Birachandra Singh, *op. cit.*, p.79.
47. *Ibid.*, p.79.
48. *Ibid.*, p.82.
49. S. N. Parratt, *op. cit.*, p.72.
50. *Apokpa Thounirol*, p. 11, custodian N. Ibochouba, cited in N. Birachandra Singh, *op. cit.*, p.81.
51. *Ibid.*
52. N. Birachandra Singh, *op. cit.*, p.82.
53. Arnold Van Gennep,(tr. Monika B.Vizedom and Gabrielle L. Caffee), *The Rites of Passage*, 1966 (Fourth Impression), p.vii.
54. Malem Yaiphasang (ed.), *Wachet Lon Pathup*,1974, p.7.
55. Bhagya Singh Yengkhoiba (ed.), *Leithak Leikharon*, 1988, p. 55 fn.
56. S.N. Parratt, *op. cit.*, p.78.
57. M. Laimit and Y.Iboyaima(ed.),*Wakoklol Hilel Thilel Amailon Pukok Puya*,1972, p.36.
58. Y. Gourmani, *Ancient Cult and Culture of Manipur*, n. d., p.42.
59. M. Laimit and Y. Iboyaima (ed.), *op. cit.*, p.36.
60. Yumnamcha Buddhichandra (ed.), *Thaloi Nongkhailon*, *op. cit.*, p.53.
61. L.Bhagyachandra,"The Meitei Rites and Rituals", in Naorem Sanajaoba (ed.), *Manipur: Past and Present*, Vol. II, 1991, p.128.
62. S.N. Parratt, *op. cit.*, pp. 78-79.
63. L. Bhagyachandra, *op. cit.*, p.128.
64. A. Mangi Singh, *Chakparol*, 1972, p.22.
65. Nongmaitham Naran, *Angang Epan Thaba Thouram Pareng Asuba*, 1976 (Reprint), pp. 5-7.

66. *Ibid.*, p.53.
67. L. Bhagyachandra Singh, *A Critical Study of the Religious Philosophy of the Meeteis before the Advent of Vaisnavism in Manipur*, 1991, p.115.
68. Yumnamcha Buddhichandra (ed.), *Thaloi Nongkhailon, op. cit.*, p.54.
69. L. Bhagyachandra. "The Meetei Rites and Rituals", *op. cit.*, p.129.
70. Yumnamcha Buddhichandra (ed.), *Thaloi Nongkhailon, op. cit.*, p.54.
71. S.N. Parratt, *op. cit.*, p.81.
72. L. Bhagyachandra, "The Meetei Rites and Rituals", *op. cit.*, p.129.
73. *Ibid.*, pp. 130-131.
74. Francis L. K. Hsu, *Under the Ancestor's Shadow*, 1971, p.154.
75. Malem Yaiphasang (ed.), *Khamoi Yangoi Sekning*, 1974, p.3.
76. Y. Bhagya Meitei (ed.), *Sakok Lamlen Ahanba Amasung Meihouron*, 1988, p.52.
77. Pandit M. Chandra Singh (ed.), *Poireiton Khunthok*, 1979, p.29.
78. Oinam Bhogeswar Singh (ed.), *Ningthourol Lambuba*, 1967, p.234.
79. Y. Bhagya Meitei (ed.), *Sakok Lamlen Ahanba Amasung Meihouron*, pp. 4-5.
80. *Ibid.*, p.5.
81. *Ibid.*, p.10.
82. L. Iboongohal Singh and N. Khelchandra Singh (ed.), *op. cit.*, p.85.
83. Sairem Nilbir, "Meitei (Sanamahi Laining) Ahibagi Mari Leinaba Leihousing", *Seminar on Death Rites of Manipur*, 1990, pp. 3-4.
84. *Ibid.*, p.5.
85. Nongthombam Naran, *Ahalna Nahada Laining Lambigi Paotak*, 1984, p.27.
86. Y. Gourmani, *op. cit.*, p.48.

87. L. Bhagyachandra, "The Meetei Rites and Rituals", *op. cit.*, p.133.
88. Sairem Nilbir, *op. cit.*, p.6.
89. N. Khelchandra Singh, *op. cit.*, pp. 14-15.
90. L. Bhagyachandra, "The Meetei Rites and Rituals", *op. cit.*, p.133.
91. Sairem Nilbir, *op. cit.*, p.8.
92. *Leimaren Naoyom* (unpublished *Puya*), p.1.
93. Sairem Nilbir, *op. cit.*, p.9.
94. Kh. Chandrashekhar Singh (ed.), *Sakok Lamlen Ahanba Amasung Meihourol Sakok*, 1992, pp. 8,9.
95. L. Bhagyachandra, "The Meetei Rites and Rituals", *op. cit.*, p.133.
96. Yumnamcha Buddhichandra (ed.), *Tahloi Nongkhailon*, p.63.
97. Malem Yaifasang (ed.), *Khamoi Yangoi Sekning*, p.7.
98. L. Bhagyachandra, "The Meetei Rites and Rituals", *op. cit.*, p.134.
99. H.L. Seneviratne "Food Essence and the Essence of Experience in R.S.(ed.),*The Eternal Food: Gastronomic Ideas and Experiences of Hindus and Buddhists*, 1992, p.188.
100. Arnold Van. Gennep, *op. cit.*, pp. 164-165.
101. Communicated to me by Pandit N. Khelchandra Singh on 29th May 1993.
102. Pebam Ibomcha Singh (ed.), *Thiren Meiram Liba, Singkaklen, Mikouren, Khanggoi Yangoi Sekning, op. cit.*, pp. 40-41.

5

Lai Haraoba and Other Festivals

Community rituals and the observance of festivals in the Meitei society are also aimed at ancestor veneration. A community is a collectivity of actors sharing a limited territorial area as the base for carrying out the greatest share of their daily activities.[1] Assuming that a community has a specified territorial base, the concept is applied to such varying units as a village, a pioneer settlement, a tribe or a nation.[2] In the context of ancestor worship among the Meiteis, the term community will be used in reference to the kingdom, a group of villages, a village or a locality. The public worship of the gods of the community acquires significance in that the public worship of the gods must have been the origin of ancestor worship in the early tribal community. With comparative safety of village life and the beginning of family as an institution, the community gods must have assimilated the family gods. Apart from the immediate ancestors of the *phungga* i.e. the father, the grandfather and the great grandfather who are venerated in the private household, the *Umanglais* are worshipped in the various festivals which are participated by the whole community. While *phungga* ritual focuses on the expression of individual sentiments and continued relations between descendants and particular deceased individuals, public rituals of ancestor worship express the sentiments of obedience to the authority of ancestors and elders as a group. The festivals of the Meiteis which were celebrated in honour of the ancestral *lais* are: *Cheiraoba, Chinggoi Iruppa, Heikru Hidongba, Kwak Tanba, Lai Keithel Kaba, Mera Mentongba* and *Lai Haraoba*. Out of these festivals, those which are celebrated even today are *Cheiraoba, Heikru Hidongba* and *Lai Haraoba*. The festivals of *Chinggoi Iruppa, Kwak Tanba, Lai Keithel Kaba* and *Mera Mentongba* became relatively obsolete. Although the state plays a central role in all the festivals, the participation extends to families and communities in the case of *Cheiraoba, Heikru Hidongba* and *Lai Haraoba*. This may explain the continuity of these festivals even today.

I

Cheiraoba

The *Cheiraoba* festival is celebrated in Manipur on the first day of the month of *Sajibu* (March-April) in order to herald a new year. Popularly known as *Sajibu Cheiraoba*, this traditional festival was originally celebrated under the name *Poireigi Lakyen Taiba*.[3] It was also known as *Khungi Lakyen Taiba* or *Sajibu Lakyen Taiba*.

The word *Cheiraoba* is derived from two words viz., *chei*: stick and *laoba*: to announce; to cry out. *Cheiraoba* therefore literally means 'to announce by a stick' or 'to cry out by means of a stick'. From the time of King Naophangba (428-518 A.D.), this festival was held publicly on the first day of the first month of the Meitei year through announcement of the beginning of the new year by the *Lakpas* (Divisional Officers).[4] Later, the close of the previous year and the beginning of a new year was proclaimed by the respective heads of the four *panas* (territorial divisions) of Khurai, Wangkhei, Khwai-Wangthoubi and Yaiskul.[5] Dressed in their respective costumes, the head of each *pana* carried a bamboo stick with a small flag and a bell at the top, proclaiming *Cheiraoba* with the stick. This practice carried on till the time of King Kyamba (1467-1508 A.D.) who introduced the system of *Cheithaba* in the year 1485 A.D.[6] *Cheithaba* (*chei*: stick; *thaba*: counting) literally means 'the counting of sticks.[7] According to Meitei custom, a day was counted as one *shing* i.e. firewood: stick. Thirty sticks represented one complete month and twelve months made one *chei*. A year was therefore counted by using the symbols of *chei*.[8] The heads of the four *panas* was replaced by a *Cheithaba*. He was selected by a process of comparing his individual horoscope with that of the king. The *Cheithaba* was meant to bear all the misfortunes that would befall the king and his subjects for the particular year he is proclaimed the *Cheithaba*. The symbolism of the stick is best explained by J.C. Higgens in his account of the *Cheithaba* of the year 1926 A.D. The account is as follows: 'Let all the evils such as war and battle, enmity and struggles, fall down at the advent of the new year in which the seasons of the ancient god Pakhangba who is the head of gods, fallen from the sky at a happy place, and the god Chingshomba the white, who reigns in the North-East, are invested with the ceremony of *Cheithaba*, in which the *Cheithaba* man performs it with a stick on his shoulder - the stick which exempts the *Cheithaba* man from the burden of public work when he is seen to carry it on his shoulder on the public road - the stick which can make one conquer great and small kingdoms in battle, the stick which is attached to the bamboo tube in the time of coronation at Kangla, the stick which is used by warlike young men in fight, the stick which was the hilt of the god Thangjing, the stick of which the head is known at the first touch, the stick that opens the door of the earth and fills up the underground pit in the month of *Sajibu*, in the reigns of all kings according to ancient custom'.[9] The royal chronicle mentions that the first *Cheithaba* was *Hiyangloi*.[10] It was from the year 1485 A.D., starting with the year of *Hiyangloi*, that every year came to be associated with the *Cheithaba* of the year. The rituals performed at *Cheiraoba* may be studied under three broad heads viz; the state, the village or locality and the family.

The first category includes the significant act of installing the *Cheithaba* of the year. This takes place on the eve of the new year i.e. on the last day of the month *Lamta* (February-March). The ceremony was performed in the presence of the king since the time of King Kyamba. As a tradition, the outgoing *Cheithaba* usually sat on the right side of the king and the incoming *Cheithaba* on the king's left side. The two *Cheithabas* then exchange places. They address the king and the public in archaic Manipuri language.

The Meiteis believe that the gods assemble on every Saturday of the month of *Lamta* (February-March), the last month of the Meitei calendar, to estimate the number of persons who are going to die in the coming year. Each such individual was represented by a *shing*, hence the ritual was called *Shingsatpa, Shingthaba* or *Shingthekpa* which means generally 'to count with sticks'. The ritual specialist is the *Maiba* who prays to the *lais* to spare the lives of those designed by the sticks. The ritual of *Thouniba* (appeasement) takes place at Heibok Ching. Certain offerings have to be made to the *lais* which consist of a complete set of garments intended for Lainingthou and Lairembi, seven bamboo barrels of *kabok* (parched rice), milk, an earthen pot of molasses, a piece of cloth joined in the middle, iron and gold pieces and seven candles made of beewax. In addition to this are also included flour, fruits, flowers, vegetables and rice.[11] The ritual of *Shingsatpa* was performed initially only for the royal family.[12] On the day of *Cheiraoba*, every member of the royal family was given *shingnang* (a piece of reed). The person concerned ought to keep it intact for the whole year as if it were his or her soul. The *Maiba* who conducts the ceremony hands over the sticks to the individuals whose lives they represent. The stick is tied with a coin and wrapped in a new cloth. The Meiteis also believed that taking bath in sacred streams a day before *Cheiraoba* will ensure a happy and peaceful life for the coming year. The streams are Khakhong, Laithong, Malangthong, Thaknakha, Lamgkhol and Punshikhong.[13]

A very important aspect of *Cheiraoba* is divination. For this purpose two rituals are performed for the state viz; *Kongba Leithong Phatpa* (digging the hole at Kongba) and *Sajibu Leikhun Phunba* (closing of the hole at *Sajibu*). At Kongba, Pakhangba and Pureiromba are worshipped by offering certain food items and new cloth for the two deities.[14] Two *laiphams* (sacred spots) are dug up with the help of iron implements and the contents of the earth are wrapped in a cloth. The *Maiba* carries this around his neck to the shrine of the *Yumjao Lai* (household deity) in the palace. Here it is kept in an earthen pot where offerings are made consecutively for five days to the *Yumjao Lai*. The offerings include *sareng* fish (*wallago atu*), gold and silver discs and customary flowers and fruits. Divination is done when the earthen pot is opened five days later and the signs are read and predictions made for the king and the state for the coming year.[15] The materials are then brought to the original place wherefrom it was collected and the hole from which the earth was taken is filled again. *Usin* (a form of divination) is conducted for the king by the *Maibas*. A *ngamu* fish (common lata fish), representing the king, is let loose in the pond. The movements of the fish determine good or bad fortune for him. The ceremony is followed by the offerings of a pot filled to the brim with water, flowers, fruits, betel nut and money.[16] The purpose of this offering to the *lai* is to secure the prosperity of all the people in the kingdom. At Langol hill there is a shrine of *Thongngak Lairembi* (a goddess associated with death).[17] The Lairembi is offered clothes along with gourd from which the dead are believed to drink. After the offering is done, a fire is lit. The *Maiba* then makes predictions for the king and the state from the insects drawn towards the flame. The *Amaiba Loisang* at the royal palace also pray to the three deities Mangang, Luwang and Khuman Chinggu Sidaba.

On the morning of *Cheiraoba* day, flowers and fruits are offered to Nongshaba, Pakhangba and Yumjao Lairembi at their respective shrines. The deities are also adorned with a new attire. The *Pibas* of Laithangba *sagei*, Laisram *sagei* and Thaoboijam *sagei* render their services to the three *lais* respectively. The *Yoirengshang* (a department in charge of *pena*, one stringed fiddle) performs a ritual before Poireiton by way of playing the *pena*.[18]

At the village level, the ritual of *Saroi-ngaroi* (evil spirits) takes place.[19] The Meiteis believe that these evil spirits follow the *lais* in their assembly at mount Heibok Ching. They are perpetually hungry and demand food from human beings. In order to appease them and prevent them from entering the village or locality the propitiation of the *sarois* take place. Elderly women of the locality collect food items such as rice, vegetables etc. from every household to be offered to the deities of the four directions viz; Thangjing, Marjing, Wangbren and Koubru. The ritual is performed in late evening of the first Saturday of the month of *Lamta* (February-March) and may be performed by the *Maibas* or the *Maibis* at the junction where three roads meet. When the ritual is performed by the *Maiba* of the *Pandit Loisang* for the protection of the kingdom as a whole, the *sarois* are propitiated by offering food items at the junction of the four *panas* i.e. Khurai, Wangkhei, Yaiskul and Kwai-Wangthoubi. This is performed to protect the kingdom as a whole. The appropriate time for this ritual is in the late evening of the first Saturday of the month of *Lamta* (February-March). The items include cooking pots, spoons, rice, vegetables, salt, chilly, oil, *sareng* fish , new clothes for Lairemma and a canopy.[20]

Cheiraoba festival is also associated with the worship of the household deities Sanamahi and Leimaren. On this occasion, every house is cleaned and all utensils are to be washed and replaced by new ones.

At the Sanamahi Kachin, the *Piba* leads the household members in worshipping the deities.[21] The Leimaren *ishaifu* (*ishaifu:* earthen pot) is filled with fresh water on this New Years day. Flowers, fruits, rice and vegetables are offered to them. A meal is prepared and offered to the deities which is done at the gate of each house to seek their blessings, protection from any harmful events of the year and pray for the prosperity of the family. All professional activities are suspended for five days from the date of *Cheiraoba*. This is known as *Shilhenba*. The five days are spent in playing *kang* (an indigenous game).

The deities venerated at the *Sajibu Cheiraoba* festival include, besides the domestic *lais* Sanamahi and Leimaren, a host of other deities such as Pakhangba, Pureiromba and Nongshaba, Poireiton, Thangjing, Marjing, Wangbren and Koubru.

Chinggoi Iruppa

This festival of *Chinggoi Iruppa* usually takes place on the 28th day of *Lamta* (February-March) every year. The Chinggoi stream is believed to have originated from the western hillock of the Nongmaijing hill. This Nongmaijing hill is traditionally the abode of the divine couple Nongpok and Panthoibi. The *Naothingkhong Phambal Kaba Puya* accounts for the origin of the *Chinggoi Iruppa* (a dip in the Chinggoi stream).[22] A holy dip in this sacred rivulet was made into a religious duty by King Naothingkhong (663-763 A.D.) to atone for the suicide of a Selloi girl named Pitanga Liklu Louthibi. The story has it that Naothingkhong was saved by Pitanga from grave danger at the hands of Selloi-Langmai tribe when they wanted to kill him, on realizing that

Naothingkhong belonged to the Ningthouja *salai*, the traditional rivals of the Selloi-Langmais. At that time the king fell in love with Pitanga and had promised to marry her. Years later when Pitanga went to the palace in the hope that she would be united with her lover, she was shocked to learn that the king had forgotten her and that he was already married. Filled with remorse, Pitanga killed herself in front of the king and those present at the royal court. The mortal soul as the bard describes was transformed into that of a deity.[23] Pitanga made her eternal abode in a forest at the foot of the Langmai Hills, near the Chinggoi stream. From this time onwards, every year at the approach of spring when the hill-sides are aflame with *chingthrao* flowers, the Meitei king with his subjects used to march to that spot for a holy dip.

The ceremonial rite of taking a dip at the Chinggoi stream is a preliminary necessity for proceeding to climbing the Nongmaiching Hill. The Meiteis believe that a holy dip here purifies the person by washing away all his sins.

Heikru Hidongba

The *Heikru Hidongba* festival derives its name from *heikru: emblica officialis*, a small edible fruit, and *hidongba:* crew leaders. The main feature of the festival is the popular boat race *Hiyang Tannaba* which is practiced till today. It is generally believed that this festival was observed from the reign of King Irengba (984-1074 A.D.).[24] The myth has it that two evil deities Huni and Narot tried to destroy the country of the Meiteis when one Maichou Langol Lukhoi controlled these evil designs. When they failed in their attempt they informed the king of the many ways by which the king and his subjects could become secure and prosperous; the *Heikru Hidongba* ritual was one of them.[25]

A more popular explanation of the origin of this festival takes the ritual to the time of King Thawanthaba (1195-

1231A.D.). The *Cheitharol Kumbaba* records the use of *Hiyang Hiren* boat by the king for the purpose of warfare.[26] The boat itself seems to have been in use since the time of Luwang Ningthou Punshiba.[27] The *Hijing Hirao Puya*, written during the reign of King Naothingkhong (7th century A.D.) records the construction of *Hiyang Hiren* by Luwang Ningthou Punshiba and the beginning of the boat race since the time of King Naothingkhong. The first *Hiyang Tannaba* recorded in *Cheitharol Kumbaba* took place in the year 1641 A.D. during the reign of King Khagemba. It was King Khagemba who introduced a new feature to this boat race, that of the king and god being made to sit on the same boat.[28] The *Thaloi Nongkhailon Puya* records that in the *Hiyangei* month (October-November) the festival of *Hiyang* is celebrated. The king sat on board the *Hiyang Hiren* boat and journeyed to the Chakhaba Langmeitemba site. The *Amaiba* and *Amaibis* also travel to secret spots and venerate various *lais*. They are then received warmly by the king on their return. The king and the nobles of the kingdom, dressed in their courtly attire, celebrated the festival.[29]

The *Hiyang Hiren* boat which is used in this festival has to be of a particular type. Initially, the boat was exclusively meant for the kings of Manipur who used it in boat races and other state functions. Apart from decorations and colourful and attractive painting of the boat, significant is the figure of the artistic head of Khuman Kwakpa at the end of the boat.[30] Spreading its loose hair and having a long moustache, the neck of Kwakpa was flanked by two wooden leaves, painted with yellow colour. At the helm of the boat is the two horned dragon known as Chinglai.[31] Scale like engravings cover the neck. The decoration of long chain like structure represents the body of Taoroinai, the vehicle of Pakhangba.

Hiyang Tannaba is essentially a water festival. It bears mythological significance of the creation of the earth and its beings.[32] One day ahead of the festival, pieces of gold and silver are placed over a funnel-shaped article made of clay called *nganthak* and offered to the *lai*. The *Lamyenba* rite is a necessary ritual. Here the two boats which are tied together go to every *Hiden Tapham*. The *changsaba* (personal bodyguard who accompanies the crew leader), two *naourungbas* (front rowers), *naomangthaba* (real rowers) and *hinaosaba* (coxswain) represent a soul signifying fire, water, wind, heaven and earth. The formation of the universe is manifested by the *Tangmailappa* (leader of the boat race) sitting in the boat. He was so called because he executed the tasks entrusted by the Almighty Lord, as he decided the direction of the boat.[33]

Over the years, this festival became more elaborate. Great preparations are made for it and games such as *lamchel* (foot race) and *mukna* (Manipuri style of wrestling) are played during the four day festival. Pakhangba is the presiding deity of this festival. The *Maiba* chants *mantras* while the boat is kept inside its shed called *Hijagang*. He prays for the steerer of the boat so that the evil power of *Hiren* is appeased and that he gains the power of Pakhangba.[34] One string of 108 *heikru* fruits, a leaf separating each fruit, and one string of 108 whole grains of rice are offered to *Pakhangba* in order to ensure good harvest and protection from evil. The two strings are placed round the necks of the two men who lead the boat race i.e. *Tangmailappa*. In this way *heikru* is placed over the boat. This was followed by a boat race.[35] The six *panas* of the kingdom send in a boat each and the *panas* compete in a fixed order viz; Ahallup *vs*. Naharup, Khabam *vs*. Laipham, Hidakphanba *vs*. Potsangba.

All means are permitted to the competitors including attempts to overthrow the boat. The *Hiyang Tannaba* takes place at Thanggapat, the moat around the palace.[36] The winning boat indicated the state affairs, good or evil consequence of the year for the entire kingdom.

The significance of the festival lies in the fact that Pakhangba is venerated for the prosperity and welfare of the king and the subjects of the Meitei kingdom. The casting of *konyai* (gold and silver pieces) in the ritual is to pray to the *lai* that the king may be able to subjugate the neighbouring kingdoms and extend his suzerainty over them.[37] The festival is also held in honour of the Almighty as thanksgiving to him for the creation of the universe and mankind.[38] *Heikru Hidongba* is described in the royal chronicle as a very big festival. R. Brown observed that this festival was the most important held in Manipur.[39] Every year on the eleventh day of *Langban* (August-September) this boat race festival continues to take place at the Sri Sri Bijoy Govinda moat at Sagolband.[40]

Kwak Tanba

Kwak Tanba (kwak: crow; *tanba:* to drive off) literally means 'driving off the crows'. The main purpose of this ritual is the divination of good or bad omen of the year for the king and the subjects which is determined by observing the direction of the flight of birds. Every year on the tenth day of the month of *Mera* (September-October), this ritual is performed with great pomp and grandeur. It is also an opportunity for the high officials and nobles to display their awards and decorations received from the king.[41]

A suitable site where the ritual is to be performed is determined within the area of particular places viz; Chingga, Nongmeibung and Lalambung.[42] A few days before the *Kwak Jatra,*[43] food items such as parched rice (*kabok aphaba*) and prawns *(khajing)* are scattered at the selected site to entice the crows. On the *Kwak Jatra* day, a loud sound of a gun shot disperses the crows. This day is known as *Kwak Tanba* day.[44] Good result is anticipated if the birds fly towards the direction of North (*Awang*), North-East (*Chingkhei*), East (*Nongpok*) and North-West (*Koubru*).[45] Flight in other directions anticipates bad omen for the year.

When exactly this *Kwak Tanba* ritual began to be performed is not known. N. Khelchandra Singh suggests that it was King Garibniwaz who introduced this festival.[46] Some scholars believe that the original ritual was called *Ukai Kappa.*[47] This used to take place on the tenth day of *Mera* (September-October). A *Kwakshang* (*kwak*: crow; *shang*: hut) is built. This however should not be built in the *Thasi Maigei* (direction of the *Thasi* i.e. the new moon) as well as *Thaban* (opposite side of *Thasi*). The king and the nobles led by a *Bor Senapati* (Commander-in-Chief) comes to this hut dressed up as warriors.[48] Ritually, an idol was erected in the form of a human being and the king shoots an arrow aimed at the idol. The spot where the arrow hits indicate possible bad or good omen of the year.

The *Kwak Tanba*[49] ritual is accompanied by amusements like sword dancing, spear dancing, *mukna* (Manipuri style of wrestling) etc. Then, for the prosperity and the welfare of the state a ritual song called *Ougri* is chanted. The king used to cast *konyai* (gold and silver pieces) in the *Mityengphu* (a pot filled with water towards which one's vision is focussed). The king then returns to his palace whence the *Bor-Senapati* (Commander-in-Chief) gave to him an account of an imaginary war. He then used to communicate the tidings of the war to god Nongshaba, Pakhangba and goddess Yumjao Lairembi. At last, the *Maichous* performed skull burying ritual at Nungoibi. Outwardly, the *Kwak Tanba* ritual is believed as the auguring of omens, the black colour being compared to evil idea or spirit. The king went out on an imaginary war path on that day and performed an imaginary skull burying ritual of captives called *Sharon Chanba* at Nungoibi. However, this ritual was a secret for the subjugation of enemies, neighbouring rulers and native courtiers and nobles. The heads represented by betel nuts were buried at Nungoibi with due ritual. Although the Meitei ritual of *Kwak Tanba* has multiple significance, the essential motive is political.

Lai Keithel Kaba

This festival is believed to have originated during the divine age when there was no clear demarcation between the *lais* and human beings. Tradition has it that in early Meitei history, there prevailed chaos and anarchy on account of enmity between mankind and the *lais* over the possession of this country. The myth goes on to say that eight goddesses[50] viz; Pukshikhombi, Thungpaileihomba, Angaibi, Thonghaibi, Kotinleima, Thareima, Yuchengleima and Chingleima made an effort to bring peace and harmony. By the effort of these goddesses, men and gods together attended the divine market and the food stuffs sold by the eight goddesses were bought and cooked.[51] This was then arranged into eight *chakluks* (food-shares) for the eight *Pibas* (male head of a *salai*) of eight clans i.e. Mangang, Luwang, Khuman, Angom, Moirang, Khaba, Nganba and Sharang Leishangthem. The addition and grouping of these *chakluks* in a sequence is known as *Salai Luptinba.*[52] A slightly different version is related by N. Birachandra who understands that the king on this day invites all clan chiefs, nobles and *Pibas* to his court and interdined with them. Then they take a vow among themselves to live in peace and harmony. The *Lai Keithel Kaba* ceremony was observed on the tenth day of *Lamta* (February-March) in the present Kangla, the seat of Meitei kingdom.[53] Another probable date is the twentieth day of *Lamta.*[54]

Although the beginning of this ritual is pushed back to pre-historic times,[55] this festival seems to have been performed by the time of Pakhangba the first 'historical king'. This festival has now become almost extinct. The myth of *Lai Keithel Kaba* makes us believe that there is a significance attached to the interdining or rather the integration of the previously anarchic and separate ethnic communties in Meitei history. Perhaps, it symbolizes the integration of the clans and the acceptance of the Ningthouja clan as the suzerain.

This is expressed by the term *Salai Luptinba* i.e, integration of the clans. While observing this rite, people sing the hymn of *Mihourol* (creation). The *Lai Keithel Kaba* ritual aimed at bringing a peaceful co-existence between the *Lairup* (community of gods) and *Mirup* (community of human beings). Feasts and merry making at this integration ceremony forms an important aspect of the ritual.

This ritual acquired new importance in the later years when the king performed the ritual when there was anarchy in the kingdom and there required a need to remind the people of peaceful co-existence between the kings and the subjects. Whatever be the origin, it is clear that the ancestral heads of the clans are remembered on this occasion and a feast in their honour forms an important feature of this *Lai Keithel Kaba*.

II

Lai Haraoba

The *Lai Haraoba* festival may be said to mirror the rich indigenous belief of the Meiteis. The religious significance of this festival lies in the worship of Lainingthou and Lairembi, the male and female manifestations of the supreme deity Taibangpanba Mapu. *Lai Haraoba* is 'the festival of gods'.[56] Col. J. Shakespear described it as 'the pleasing of god'.[57] The word *Lai Haraoba* literally translates as thus: *lai*: god; *haraoba*: to rejoice.[58] N. Khelchandra[59] refers to it as a festival to 'satisfy' Lainingthou and Lairembi by worshipping them. It is also an occasion to pray for the prosperity and well being of the worshippers.

It is to be mentioned at the very outset that unlike the festivals discussed so far the *Lai Haraoba* festival does not take place at the initiative of the king. The festival is a living tradition of the Meiteis. This may explain why there are no *Puyas* dealing with this subject, although a few of them make passing reference to certain aspects of the festival viz; myth of the creation of the Universe, worship of certain deities etc. *Panthoibi Khongkun Puya* mentions that this festival was associated with the Khaba clan who started worshipping the dual deities Nongpok Ningthou and Panthoibi.[60] A myth connected with the beginning of *Lai Haraoba* runs as thus:[61] It was decided by all the gods that they would participate in a festival to recollect their past activities. In order that their future generation may keep it in their memory, the gods replayed each event reminiscent of their past contribution to the creation of earth. This happy union of gods took place at Koubru hill in the month of *Mera* (September-October). There is yet another myth of the origin of *Lai Haraoba* as believed by the Chakpa Leimaram people. It is said that during the *Hayi Chak* i.e. the first of the four human ages, Lord Sorarel appeared before the village folk of Leimaren in the form of a *yarou saji* (a species of deer). On seeing it people chased the animal until it went out of sight. After chasing it for a long distance, they heard the sound of drums, singing and merry-making nearby. Going in the direction of the sound, the people reached a site where they saw a number of *lais* rejoicing. They forgot about the deer and soon returned home for the day. However, one fine day, the Lord revealed to the Chakpas that the deer they were chasing was none other than Himself and that it was His plan to show the people the happy union of gods. He asked them to worship him. Since that event, the people of Leimaram have never neglected the *Lai Haraoba* festival to honour Lainingthou and Lairembi, through whom Sorarel is worshipped.[62]

The *Lai Haraoba* rituals depict creation of the universe and life and the gradual development of society as conceived by the Meiteis. The gods became happy at the creation of the earth by the will of the Supreme Lord.[63] This expression also appears in the *Leithak Leikharon Puya*. The primal elements came out of the womb of Atingkok with the *cry "Ahei Hei*

Hoiru Hoiru Nakese" and Atingkok sang in happiness "*Ha Hei Hei Ha ha Hei Hai Ha Ha Ha Herinl Herinla Hayute Khulate Heiyase Ashibu Thoina Haraopa Leipane. Tahou Hou He Heiya Naketas*".[64] This unintelligible cry marks the beginning of *Laipou* dance of the *Lai Haraoba* festival till today.

The *Lai Haraoba* may broadly be classified into four main forms viz; *Kanglei, Chakpa, Kakching* and *Moirang*, derived from the place names with which they are associated.[65] This classification may be explained as related to the attempt at integration of comparative distinct separate social groups.[66] The *Kanglei Haraoba* is patronized by the royal clan and takes the name of *Kanglei* from Kangla, the seat of the Ningthoujas. The Chakpas have always maintained their distinct culture. According to their own tradition and also of the Meiteis, Chakpas are said to have been descendants of the autochthons of the country. But later on "when the Meitei (Ningthouja clan) became the most powerful they defeated the Chakpas and drove them off the fertile lands".[67] The history of the Moirangs reveal that they remained a homogeneous group for a very long time. As Hodson observes, the Moirang tribe preserved a fair amount of independence upto the advent of the British authority. He further says that the Moirangs have not shared in the progress in the development of the civilization of the country to quite the same extent as the other tribes.[68] There is no specific inference which can be drawn for *Kakching Haraoba*. However, we may assume in general that the four forms of *Lai Haraoba* must have been the result of distinct traditions preserved by each of the tribal groups. Out of these four, the Chakpas are considered to preserve the oldest form of the *Lai Haraoba* in dance, rites and language. They are again subdivided into the *Andro, Leimaram, Phayeng* and *Sekmai* festivals, which are the names of the villages of the Chakpas.[69]

A study of the various forms of *Lai Haraoba* reveal that the basic pattern underlining the festival is the same everywhere, although slight variations may be observed. Some deities are worshipped annually while others are worshipped at the interval of some specific years. The majority of the festivals take place in the month of *Kalen* (April-May) before the season's work of planting starts. The festival is also held during the months of January and March.[70] It commences on one of the days of the month which contains the numbers 1,2,3, 5, and 8.[71]

The *Lai Haraoba* festival is held in honour of the *Umanglais*. These ancestral *lais* now numbering three hundred and seventy-eight[72] are worshipped by the respective *salais*, locality or villages in different parts of the land. These *Umanglais* originally numbering nine are none other than the manifestations of the Supreme Deity. Therefore, in worshipping the *Umanglais* the Meiteis are worshipping Lainingthou and Lairembi, their divine ancestral parents.

The *lai* itself is represented in many ways but never by any image. The Meitei deities have no specific forms because they are believed to belong to the original being who is formless and boundless.[73] At the *Lai Haraoba*, the *lais* are represented by wooden or brass masks which are made to look like human forms with pieces of cloth above and below it.

Kanglei Haraoba

Kanglei Haraoba, performed in the valley of Manipur is largely drawn from the *Lai Haraoba* as performed in the royal palace. The festival commences on an auspicious day which is decided by the *Pandit Loisang* (College of Priests) according to the lunar calendar or the *Thaban* system. The preparation for this festival begins well before the appointed day when the shrine is cleaned and the courtyard prepared for the occasion. Candles are lit in the locality at night as a measure to ward off evils that may cause hindrance to the festival. Before the appointed day, the *Lai Phi Setpa* or dressing of the *lai* is done by the priest and the priestess. Here, the mask of the god and goddess are adorned with cloth and flowers. The priest and the priestess attending the Lainingthou and Lairembi place the deities on a throne made of wood or cane. This representation of the *lais* is the preliminary and an important aspect of the *Lai Haraoba* without which no festival of this kind can commence.[74] It should be noted here that all the participants of *Lai Haraoba* i.e. the *Maibas, Maibis* and those taking part in the festival have to come suitably dressed for the occasion. The 'calling up of the *lai*' from water is called *Lai Ikouba*. This is an elaborate ritual performed by the *Maiba*, the *Maibi* and the *pena* singer by the side of a river or a pond. It symbolizes giving life to the *lai*. At the very outset is performed the ritual of *Leirai Yu Khangba* where *yu* (rice beer) is offered to the nine *Laibungthous* and the seven *Lainuras*, and the *lais* who assisted Taibangpanba Mapu in the creation of the universe. Prayer is offered to them to ensure smooth running of the festival. Since the *lai* is to be given life by calling it up from the water, a procession from the courtyard of the shrine to the river-side forms an important aspect of the ritual. Performed with great paraphernalia, the procession is led by two men carrying swords. They are followed by four women in rows of two. The first two women carry brass vessels while the latter carry a fan and a traditional vessel called *kausel*. The *lai*-bearers follow suit. The *lai*-bearer has to be a person whose parents are not divorced or married outside the permissible norms of the society. In case where the *Lai Haraoba* is performed for the *Sagei Lai*, the *Sagei Piba* is the *lai*-bearer for Lainingthou and the *Piba's* younger brother is the *lai*-bearer for Lairembi. The respective wives of the *lai*-bearers carry ritual pots.[75] The *lai*-bearers carry two *ihaifus* (an earthen pot with a plantain leaf placed inside it;

the leaf is thrust out at the neck of the pot and then bent down and tied with a thread), decorated with *leiyoms* (a package of *langthrei* i.e *eupatorium burmaniacum*, flower buds covered by three layers of plantain leaves which are attached to the *ihaifu*). The *ihaifu* for Lainingthou is tied around the neck with nine strands of hand woven thread of a fathom's length. At the end of the thread is tied a *leiyom* which has fourteen buds facing downwards. The *ihaifu* for the Lairembi uses seven strands of thread with a *leiyom* of seven buds facing upwards and tied at the end of the thread. Behind the *lai*-bearers, two women carry *phida* (a piece of cloth used for sitting on it) on their left shoulders and with their right hand a wooden *lepsoom* (mortar; a cultic object). The fruits and flowers which are to be used at the *Ikouba*, called *Turel Heiruk* are carried by two women. Just before the procession to the river-side, the *lai*-bearers stand on plantain leaves and face the shrine. The pots containing the sacred thread are given to them by the *Maibi*, who then gives a dance performance. After this, the *lai* - bearers join the other participants in the line of procession already formed. The *Maiba*, the *Maibi* and the *pena* singer also join the procession to the river side.[76]

On reaching the river-side, the participants form two lines facing the river. Here, the *Maibi* performs the *Kontharol* ritual.[77] The *Kontharol* hymn is sung by the *Maibi* and this is followed by casting of the *konyai* in the water. The *konyai* which consist of gold and silver pieces are thrown in such a manner that they do not by any chance float in the water. At the same time of throwing the *konyai*, *khayoms* (a package of rice, egg and three buds of *langthrei* wrapped in plantain leaves) for the Lainingthou and Lairembi are also thrown into the water. The *khayom* of Lainingthou has nine strips of bamboo while that of the Lairembi has seven strips. For the Lainingthou the *khayom* is placed facing downwards while that of the later faces upwards. A dance ritual follows in which the *Maibi* emphasizes leg movements. She holds the *ihaifu* of Lainingthou on her right and that of Lairembi on her left and dances facing the four cardinal points of the earth, thereby venerating the four *lais* associated with the directions.[78] In continuation of the *Lai Ikouba* ritual, the *Maibi* takes out the *hiri* (thread) from the *ihaifu* held by the *lai*-bearers and tie the *leiyoms* and a *hirichei* (a short stick) together. Taking precaution that the thread does not fall on the ground, she passes the thread over her shoulder. She is positioned slightly on the left of the *lai*-bearers. Covering her head with a white cloth and holding a bell (*sarik*) with her left hand, she takes the *leiyoms* on her right hand. Then she dips the *leiyoms* in the water singing the traditional hymn of creation. At this stage, the *Maibi* is possessed by the *lai* and she starts delivering divine oracles. This completed, she places the *sarik* on a plantain leaf, in a manner so that it does not touch the ground. The two *leiyoms* are then put back in the respective *ihaifus*. The *leiyom* of Lainingthou is placed in the cultic pot by the *Maiba* while that of Lairembi is done by the *Maibi*. As soon as the *Maibi* utters the words of the *lai*, it indicates that the *lai* has woken up. The *pena*, drum and bell accompaniment then comes to a stop.[79] With this *Lai Themgatpa*, the *Lai Ikouba* ritual is completed. The symbolic coming out of the *lai* from the water to participate in the *Lai Haraoba* festival is called *Higaba*. A special dance called *Khunjao Laijao* is performed and the procession returns to the shrine, following the same sequence as earlier.

In the procession back to the shrine, the two *lai*-bearers face each other - the one carrying Lairembi stands on the left and the Lainingthou bearer on the right. Once the courtyard of the shrine is reached, the thread around the *ihaifu* is unwound. It is then placed in the *ishaifu* by the two women carrying it. The *ishaifu* contains water collected from the river. Great care is taken not to break the thread or accidentally touch the ground lest the *Ikouba* ritual has to be repeated.

The participant of the procession on reaching the courtyard is made to step over certain items placed for the purpose of purification and to dispel all evil. The items include fish, salt, coin, iron pieces, duck and pigeon. The Lainingthou group steps over the item with their left leg while the Lairembi group steps over with their right leg. The *pena* singer plays the *Higaron* and the *Maibi* ringing the bell accompanies the *pena*. The next ritual is called *Hiri Phanba*. The thread around the *leiyom* is now unwound. The Lainingthou *leiyom* is taken out by the *Maiba* and that of Lairembi by the *Maibi* from the respective *ishaifu*. The *Maiba* and the *Maibi* hold the respective *leiyoms* and accompanied by three men and three women approach the throne of the *lai*. At this stage, the *Hiri Laoba* (*hiri*: thread; *laoba*: to shout) takes place. The *Maiba* shouts "*O:O:O:Leo*". The *Maibi* and others respond "*He He*". The *Maiba* shouts again "*A:A:A:Ole O*". The others respond "*He He He*". The *ishaifu* is now placed on a plantain leaf. With the *leiyom* the *Maiba* and the *Maibi* touch the portion of the pot which is supposed to be the navel of the *lai*. Thus the *lai* is given life.[80] The two *ishaifus* are kept on the side each appropriate to the two deities. The thread of the *leiyom* is wrapped around the *ishaifu* and kept there. Once the *leiyom* is unwrapped, the *Maiba* places five *langthrei* buds for the *guru* between the two deities. These flowers are called *Namnga lei*. Nine *langthrei* buds for the Lainingthou and seven for the Lairembi are placed before them in such a way that they touch the pot. After this, the five buds for the *guru* are distributed between the two deities - three for the Lainingthou and two for the Lairembi. This is followed by the *Lei Hunba* (*lei* : flower; *hunba*: to throw) ritual.[81] In front of the *lais*, three plantain leaves join together make up the *luklen*. On the right side of this *luklen* is placed nine plantain leaves facing downwards for the *Laibungthous*. On the left side is placed seven leaves facing upwards for the seven *Lainuras*. These leaves of nine and seven should be placed facing each other. On these leaves are placed some fruits, sugarcane, banana and parched rice.

The *Luklen Thaba* is followed by a ritual to ward off evil spirits. This is called *Anam Athou.* A cloth stitched in the middle (about 5 feet by 14 inches) is folded three time and placed on a plantain leaf. On it is kept some fruits, rice, a bunch of banana (two or multiples of it), flowers and parched rice. Four coins are then placed on these items. This is followed by throwing of *konyai* to the *lai.*[82] The *pena* singers praise the *lais* worshipped and the *Maibi*, possessed by the *lai*, performs the *Saroi Khangba* ritual. This is done to propitiate the evil spirits who are always watching to disturb the religious rites. Some items of food and flowers are offered to them. The *Maibi* carrying a sword in her hand acts out as if she is chasing the *sarois* towards the direction of the South where Lord Wangbren, the guardian of evil spirits, reside. If the *Kanglei Haraoba* carries on for many days the *Saroi Khangba* takes place on the 3rd, 15th, 17th and 19th day of the ritual.

An interesting feature of this form of *Lai Haraoba* is the *Lai Kanglei Thokpa*,[83] which is choosing a wife for the *lai* (*Lai Nupi Thiba*). *Kanglei Thokpa* is performed by the *Maibi* to propitiate Lai Khoriphaba. She enacts the story of how Khoriphaba chose his wife. This ritual takes place on the 5th , 7th , 9th and 11th day of the festival. She dances to the tune of the *pena* and the drum until she is possessed by the *lai*. After delivering oracles, she enacts *mukna* (Manipuri style of wrestling) in which Khoriphaba is believed to participate. The *mukna* comes to a close and the *Maibi* now declares her intention to play *Sagol Kangjei* (Manipuri polo). She takes the *kangchei* (a stick resembling the present day hockey stick) and the *kangdroom* (ball made out of bamboo root) and strikes the ball in the directions of the four cardinal points of the earth. She starts with the South-West (Thangjing), and then moves to the direction of the North-East (Marjing), South-East(Wangbren) and North-

West(Koubru). At last she sends the ball rolling into the shrine after which she sings some ancient hymns after putting the stick on her left shoulder. A search for the *lai's* wife begins. She throws seven sticks in the front direction. The direction pointed by the stick which falls farthest determines the area from where the girl is to be chosen. The *Maibi* runs into the audience and selects a girl with the help of a *kangchei*. Leading the chosen girl by hand, the *Maibi* guides her to the *Leishi* dance, a dance form which can be performed only by the *Maibis*. One being the chosen one, she is presented with a *phanek* and an *enaphi*. These clothes are kept near the deities before presenting it to her, suggesting that it is a gift from the *lai*. The girl is sanctified by performing the *Anam Athou* ritual. The next morning the parents of the girl offer flowers and fruits to the deities for the welfare of their daughter. At the end of the festival, the *Maibi* holds the sword, dances and sings while the *pena* is played. The song sung by the *pena* singer describes how out of a tree a boat is made for the *lai* to ascend to heaven. Through rhythmic clapping by those attending the *Lai Haraoba*, the *lai* is guided to his abode.[84]

Chakpa Haraoba

The Chakpas preserve the oldest form of the *Lai Haraoba*. The four forms of *Chakpa Lai Haraoba* are *Andro, Leimaram, Phayeng* and *Sekmai Haraoba*. The people of Andro village worship Panam Ningthou, who is a manifestation of Atiya Guru Sidaba. It is believed that Atiya Guru Sidaba revealed himself in four incarnations, Panam Ningthou being the last. The other three are Nongpok Ningthou, Tarang Lainingthou Sidaba Kabaw Yangdow Leihallaba Khuya Echotlaba and Nongmai Kaina Chingsomba.[85] There are again four forms of *Andro Lai Haraoba* viz; *Panam Haraoba, Chaoren Haraoba, Chingpak Hongba* and *Pureiromba Haraoba*. They are celebrated for five days, nine days, one day and nine days respectively.[86] However, *Pureiromba Haraoba* can be performed for thirteen days. The *Andro Lai Haraoba* is celebrated in the months of February and April.

In the *Leimaram Haraoba* the deities worshipped are Loiyarakpa and Nungthil Leima. This festival is performed every alternate year. However, certain rituals are to be performed every year viz; *Lai Chaklon Katpa* (offering food to the *lai*), *Lamta Thangja Saroi Khangba* (warding off evil spirits on a Saturday of the month of *Lamta* i.e. February-March) etc.[87] Cooked pig and chicken used to be offered to the deities. The *lais* are housed in a hut constructed for the purpose. Two gongs (9 feet by 7 feet each) are kept here to summon the village folk. Seating arrangements are made for the *Ahallup* (elder group of the village folk) and *Naharup* (younger group of village folk). The five oldest men are offered separate seats. Firewood representing the living people of the village are kept pilled up near the shrine. A death in the locality reduces one stick while the birth of a child increases the number of sticks by one. There are seven thrones for seven deities, four for the gods of the four directions and the other three for Lainingthou, Lairembi and Emoinu Ahongbi.[88] A fire is kept burning in a corner of the hut. This fire is not extinguished till the completion of the festival, for Emoinu Ahongbi, the goddess of fire, is venerated on this occasion. The same is also used for cooking food to be offered to the deities. During the *Leimaram Haraoba*, no marriage alliance can take place and any death in the locality calls for closing of the shrine.

The people of Phayeng village worship Koubru and Loiyarakpa as also Soraren whom the Chakpas consider to be their creator. This festival takes place three times in a year. It is essential to have a *Phamnaiba* (a person honoured with a title by the kings of Manipur) participate in the festival. The clothes to be used for dressing the *lai* are washed only by married elder women of the locality. Thirteen unmarried females and six unmarried males become the servants of the *lais*. Dressed in white attire, they become the attendants of the deities during the *Lai Haraoba*. Unlike other *Lai Haraoba* festivals where the *lai*-bearer is a *Piba*, here the *lai*-bearer for *Ikouba* ritual is a *Khullakpa* (leader of *Naharup* or younger village folk). The items of *Lai Ikouba* ritual such as sword, fruits and flowers are carried only by men. The two *lai*-bearers, on return to the shrine, perform the *Lai Khong Hamba* ritual (*lai*: god, *khong*: feet, *hamba*: to wash). *Soraren*, considered to be the Ultimate Ancestor, is offered a pig, which can be killed only by a multiple pronged weapon. The meat may be offered raw or cooked. This offering takes place just before dawn. No vegetable dishes are offered to this deity. *Phayeng Lai Haraoba* has the special feature of the performance of *Lai Keithel Kaba* ritual (attending the divine market).[89] Another feature of this festival is that men dance naked before the deities worshipped. Females are not allowed to be present on this occasion. This is performed from the second night of the festival up to the last day. From the fourth day, the deities are not taken out of the shrine for any ritual. The festival comes to a close with discarding of the dress of the *lai* and keeping it folded on the throne. Unmarried women sing songs of farewell to the deities. The shrine is closed till the next *Haraoba*.

Popularly known as *Awang Sekmai Haraoba*, twelve deities are worshipped here. A myth about the Lord of Sekmai migrating towards *Awang* (North) is associated with the name of this festival. The names of the deities venerated are Koubru, Leimaren, Chingjanungnang, Loiyarakpa, Nungthil Leima, Nongpok Ningthou, Panthoibi, Soraren, Erem Tubi, Eime, Tampha Lairembi, Ekop Ningthou and Laisna.[90] The celebration starts towards beginning of the month of Phairen (January-February) on an auspicious day which has to fall either on a Monday or a Friday.

Kakching Haraoba

In this *Haraoba* seven *Umanglais* are worshipped. Khullen Khamlangba and Wairi Khamlangba are the two gods worshipped by the whole village. The other five are *sagei* gods and worshipped only by particular family groups belonging to the *sageis*. They are Eroom Ningthou, Sekmai Ningthou, Ethat Ningthou, Naohal and Yengkhom Pakhangba.[91] Khullen Khamlangba and Wairi Khamlangba are worshipped in the second half of the month of *Kalen* (April-May) and the other five *lais* between the months of Langban (August-September) and Phairen (January-February).[92]

The auspicious day for the commencement of the festival is decided by the *Maibas*, the *Maibis*, the village chief, the village elders and other important personalities of the village. The fetching of *nungarei* flowers to be offered to the *lai* forms a central aspect of the *Haraoba*. The person selected for this purpose and an attendant who has to accompany him prays to the deity at the shrine before setting out for the journey. He carries with him flowers, betel-nut, dried fish and a piece of fire-wood. During the journey he is not supposed to speak to anybody. Any communication required is done by his attendant. Traditionally, the flower is believed to grow at Heipung hill in Purum village. The village folk are told about the arrival of these men, who keep themselves free of any occupation on the appointed day. On reaching the village, the items brought by the men are laid out in front of the chief of the Purum village. The chief welcomes him and sends a guide along with them. The *nungarei* flowers plucked from Heibok hill are carefully wrapped in a plantain leaf. Two flowers are plucked for the two *lais* at the shrine. After this he takes a bath and all restrictions are removed. He can collect other varieties of flowers for the deities back at the shrine. On returning home, he cannot enter his house, and has to await the performance of the *Lai Ikouba* ritual when he offers the *nungarei* flowers to the *lais*. This is a distinct feature of this *Lai Haraoba*.

Moirang Haraoba

The people of Moirang venerate Lord Thangjing, the presiding deity of Moirang from whose name the festival came to be popularly known as *Moirang Thangjing Haraoba*. Legend has it that the last of the seven 'god kings' and the first of the human kings of Moirang were told in their dream to worship Thangjing and to celebrate *Lai Haraoba* festival in his name. The king then announced to the village folk about the wishes of Lord Thangjing. From then onwards this festival began to be celebrated by the people of Moirang. Along with this deity nine *Laibungthous* and seven *Lainuras* are also worshipped. Each of the *lais* is associated with a localities of Moirang. They are as follows:[93]

Laibungthous	**Localities**
1. Maharaba	*Khuman Leikai*
2. Sorarel	*Konjengbam Leikai*
3. Leikoi	*Mairembam Leikai*
4. Nongshaba	*Laishungbam Leikai*
5. Khana Chaoba	*Leikhrakpam Leikai*
6. Khoriphaba	*Philem Leikai*
7. Thongnang Ningthou	*Thongam Leikai*
8. Sanamahi	*Ahanthem Leikai*
9. Uithongrang	*Kiyam Leikai*

Lainuras	**Localities**
1. Ayangleima Kabok Chaibi	*Khoiyangbam Leikai*
2. Ayangleima Kabok Chaibi Atombi	*Moirangthem Leikom Leikai*

3&4. Pithrabi and Khongdraibi	*Khoiram Moirangthem Leikai*
5. Lalao Leima	*Phairembam Leikai*
6. Waikhu Leima	*Thingiyam Leikai*
7. Khundenbi	*Ahongbam Leikai*

These sixteen deities, each riding a palanquin, come to the courtyard of the shrine of Lord Thangjing from their respective localities. The nine gods face the Southern direction whereas the seven goddesses face the North. For this *Haraoba,* the *lai* is evoked from the Nanbi river of Moirang. The assembly of gods are welcomed by the *Maiba* and the *Maibi* and they also invite all gods of heaven and earth to join in this great union. This welcoming ritual is expressed in the *Pot Lanba* (exchange of items) viz; flowers, flour, fruits, parched rice etc. The *Pot Lanba* takes place between the many representative of *lais*. The *konyai* and *khayom* rituals follow. *Moirang Thangjing Haraoba* has three forms viz; *Khongchingba, Lam Thokpa* and *Yum Phamba.*[94] Only one of these forms is performed annually.

Khongchingba (khong :leg; *chingba*: to pull) literally means pulling the leg of the *lai*. The leg of each of the palanquins on which the deity is seated is tied with a rope kept in a straight line. Each deity is attended to by their respective *lai*-bearers. The *Maiba* sings the *Ougri* (an archaic song for the prosperity of the land) and the palanquins are moved around the shrine three or five times. In *Lam Thokpa* also the deities ride the palanquin, but no rope is attached to its legs. *Yum Phamba (yum*: house; *phamba*: to sit) the third form, literally means sitting at home.

III

Having discussed the four main forms *Lai Haraoba*, it will be worthwhile to mention certain features unique to some of the festivals.[95] The *Andro Chakpa Haraoba* is exclusive to the people of Andro. No outsiders are allowed to participate or watch the proceedings of the festival. *Lai Ikouba* in this case is performed not from a river or a pond but from a hill. Of all the *Chakpa Haraoba* festivals, that of Andro is more elaborate whether in dance or in ritual.

The *Lai Kanglei Thokpa* where the *lai* chooses a wife is a characteristic feature unique to *Kanglei Haraoba*. As for the Kakching festival, the collecting of *nungarei* flower is important and the *Haraoba* cannot commence before the flower is available and kept ready for offering to the *lai*. The *Maibi* unlike in other festivals, take a dip in the river during *Lai Ikouba* ritual. *Ngaprum Tanba* is also unique to this *Lai Haraoba*.[96] The ancestors invited to attend the festival are symbolically given lives by a special ritual in which seven sticks represent the dead. At the end of the festival, these seven sticks are offered to the deity.

In the case of *Moirang Haraoba*, the *Khong Chingba* ritual is unique to this festival only. The sequence of the *lais* is that Sanamahi leads the procession of seventeen *lais* while Thangjing completes it.[97] All the deities ride the palanquin except Sanamahi who rides a horse. This *Haraoba* is performed every year and cannot be neglected. The deities of the other three directions viz; Marjing, Wangbren and Koubru will also have to be worshipped every year.

Among tribal societies around the globe, dancing is a favourite passion.[98] To a layman the *Lai Haraoba* festival is perhaps synonymous with the dance which forms an important aspect of the festival. The Meiteis delight in the participation and is attended by all age groups. The dances are imitations of some actions of the gods. The myth connected with the origin of dance runs as thus:[99] When the nine *Laibungthous* and the seven *Lainuras* were engaged in the creation of the earth, the *Laibungthous* tried to cut jokes with the *Lainuras*. The goddesses felt shy at the gods and moved coyly away from them. This movement of the goddesses is referred to as *Chat Koi* (*chat*: to move, *koi*: in round manner). From this *Chat Koi* is derived the word *jagoi* which has become synonymous with the word dance. Manipuri dance with which Manipur is better known to the outside world, traces its origin to this dance form relating to the divine period of the history of Manipur. The dance performed by the *Maibi* just before the *Ikouba* ritual reminds the people of the one performed by Nongthangleima, the daughter of the Divine Parents. It is believed that she rescued the earth from Haraba, the evil character, who kept on destroying the newly created earth till it got its final shape. There are many forms of dances where the *Maibi* emulates the movements of the *lais* who created the earth. Led by the priests and priestesses, men, women, boys and girls participate in the *Laibou* dance enacting the process of formation of the earth and man, birth of a child, construction of a house, plantation of cotton on a hill, plucking of the cotton, weaving of cloth and finally offering of the finished article to the *lai*. The *Lairen Mathek* dance literally means the dance depicting the curves of a python. The curves are believed to represent the meandering veins of a human body. Hence care is taken not to break the curves at any stage of the dance, lest the snapping of a vein could cause harm to the body.[100]

Ch. Manihar Singh has discussed some of the significance attached to symbolism of the rituals of *Lai Haraoba*. The preliminary and important ritual of Lai Ikouba is essentially done to give life to the *lai* for whom the merrymaking is conducted. The packet of *khayom* immersed in the water are wrapped in three layers of plantain leaves. The symbolic meaning attached to the *khayom* is that the egg represents the universal father Atiya Guru Sidaba, the pieces of gold and silver representing the male and female elements of the father. The egg is surrounded by grains of rice meaning that the Lord remains constantly surrounded by heavenly bodies.

The three layers of plaintain leaves represent the primal elements of fire, water, and air which envelop the heavenly bodies. The thread which connects the *ishaifu* pot to the *leiyom* (a packet of *langthrei* buds) is symbolic of the force which attracts the various universal objects.[101] The flowers which are offered at the *Lai Haraoba* always maintains the number nine for *Laibungthous* and seven for the *Lainuras*. The creation myth of the Meitei cosmogony attributes the levelling of the earth and the resultant making of the earth fit for habitation to the *Laibungthous* and *Lainuras* who were nine and seven in number respectively.

The performing art of *Lai Haraoba* draws its significance from the fact that through it the people are continuously reminded of the creation of the universe and mankind, the need to express their gratefulness to the creators.

Mera Mentongba

As the name suggests, this festival takes place in the month of *Mera* (September-October). The two presiding *lais* of the Meitei pantheon Sanamahi and Pakhangba are worshipped for five days commencing from the full moon of the month of *Mera*. Along with these two deities are worshipped the nine *Laibungthous* and the seven *Lainuras*. The seats are prepared one each for Sanamahi and Pakhangba. One plantain tree is placed in front of these two seats. An *ishaifu* is also placed near the two seats. This pot is surrounded by seven seats for the seven *Lainuras* which is again surrounded by nine seats for the nine *Lainingthous*. A flag of the *yek/salai* representation with its seven distinct colours is used for the ritual. Candles and *khoichu-laikham* (local herbs used as incense) are used in the ceremony. Sanamahi, Pakhangba, seven *Lainuras* and the nine *Laibungthous* are worshipped in this sequence. *Mera Mentongba* is also another ritual of the Meiteis where the divine will of the Ultimate Lord and his manifestations are emphasized. Men are reminded again and again of the need to praise their Ultimate Father Taibangpanba Mapu from whom everything emerges and in whom everything dwells and ultimately retires.

IV

There are in general four main aspects of every ritual viz; purification, prayer, offering of food and flowers and that of amusement such as dance, games etc. The participation in these amusements such as climbing the Baruni hill in *Cheiraoba*, climbing the Nongmaijing hill in *Chinggoi Iruppa*, dance and games in *Lai Haraoba*, boat race and games in *Heikru Hidongba* etc., are all intrinsic parts of the festival. It is a way of amusing the *lai* and thereby paying service by the very act of participation. The action of a ritual typically consists of two parts viz; the things that have to be done and the things that have to be said. Myths recited as part of the rituals recapitulates the origin and benevolence of the deities. This must have been done to win the support of the *lais* for the present. The main purpose of the recitation and enactments of myths is to confirm and maintain the memory of and provide authority for tribal customs and institutions.

Unlike monotheistic religions such as Christianity and Buddhism, Meitei shrines are not the sites of weekly service. However, this does not diminish their importance. Periodic festivals are the expression of the whole village or section of the village whereby it serves as unifying force which links individual homes with a larger religious group. The local festivals with its carnival atmosphere is typical of Meitei religiosity.

A significant purpose of communal worship is that they uplift and give comfort to all spirits who have no living descendants and may be roaming about the village. The community rituals are performed so that the spirits leave the vicinity and thus not be potential sources of trouble for the living.[102] The Meitei identification with ancestral *lais*, the importance attached to the family,the significance of rituals, the prominence of individual cults—all bring religion into a natural and close relationship to everyday life.

In tribal societies, lineage and clan ties are strong. However, if all the clans with a strong sense of identity have to be brought together and infused with a common identity that subsumes the fragmented clan identities, then a mediating agent which has secular authority over them all is required. This task is performed by the state symbolised by the king, palace, *Pandit Loisang* etc. It is for this reason that for almost all the major festivals, the king assumes the leading role re-enacting legendary and/or actual history of Manipur, when the state or the solidarity of the community was threatened and eventually the crisis was overcome. In *Heikru Hidongba* the *panas* (territorial divisions) take part in the boat race in which the king himself participates.[103] The integration of *salais* is re-enacted by the performance of *Salai Luptinba* in the *Lai Keithel Kaba* ritual.[104] By ritually recreating these incidents the solidarity is symbolically and periodically reinforced. The community rituals of the Meiteis involve their history though myths. The *Chinggoi Iruppa* festival reminds the people of the strained relations that existed between the *Ningthouja salai* and *Selloi Langmei* tribe.[105] Unlike private rituals, the public rituals recount the myths, fixing a past to safeguard the present. The reason for this is that community festivals are more elaborate and therefore have the space to accomodate this. Further, they involve greater number of people which serves the purpose of these recreations better. The *Lai Haraoba* with its four froms of Kanglei, Chakpa, Kakching and Moirang as also the *Heikru Hidongba* with the participation of the *panas* in the boat race are examples of participation of the whole Meitei community. Public space are also free from the exclusivity of individual homes. The myths of creation which is re-enacted at the *Lai Haraoba* and the *Lai Keithel Kaba* ritual of the integration of the *salais* both justify the present by remembering the times of crisis and the resolution of the past. They also emphasize cohesion and bonding.

The purpose of the public festivals is to integrate the Meitei community and this takes place either actually or through legends. The four cardinal points presided over by the four guardians of directions are repeatedly emphasized in their veneration.[106] In the *Kanglei Lai Haraoba*, the *Maibas* holding the cultic pots of Lainingthou and Lairembi dances facing the four cardinal points to invoke the Supreme Divine Parents and the guardians of the four cardinal points, thereby symbolising the participation of the entire community, where each guardian is the tutelary deity of a sub-region and sub-community. The *Cheiraoba* festival, by propitiating of the *Saroi-ngarois* at the village level at the junction of the four *panas* once again highlights the central purpose of public rituals for the integration of the community from the village to the state level.[107]

The unification of the *Salai* is symbolised in the representation of the distinctive colours the *salai* flag in the *Mera Mengtongba* ritual.[108] The same idea is exhibited in the sharing of meal by the *salais* in the festival of *Lai Keithel Kaba*. The *chakluks* (food share) are arranged in a particular sequence indicating the very sequence of grouping of the *salais*.[109]

Community rituals held under the auspices of the state brings into play the sacred geography of the hills and rivers which are not specific to any particular clan group, but of the entire land. The climbing of Nongmaiching hill and taking a holy dip at Chinggoi stream at the *Chinggoi Iruppa* ritual, the travelling of king, *Amaibas* and *Amaibis* to various sacred spots only to return to the main ritual spot all convey the idea of integration of the kingdom. In the *Kakching Lai Haraoba*, the *nungarei* flower plucked from Heipok Ching and the association with Purum village renews the ties between Kakching and Purum and Heipok Ching at the different levels.[110]

Where the history of Manipur is the history of clan chiefdoms each having involved in inter-clan and intra-clan struggles to exert their supremacy, it is possible to assume that the public rituals seek to repeatedly instil in the minds of the people the constant need for a stable, peaceful and united kingdom. Indeed, there is a hierarchy implicit in the performance of the festivals i.e., from a family, to a locality, to a village, to a cluster of villages, to a *salai* and finally the entire region with the capital at the centre. The complex and intricate relationships between these social units are worked out in these festivals.

Notes and References

1. T. Parsons, *The Social System*, 1951, p.91 in Julius Gould and William L. Kolb (ed.), *A Dictionary of the Social Sciences*, 1964, p.114.
2. R.M. MacIver and C. Page, *Society: An Introductory Analysis*, 1949, p.8, in Julius Gould and William L. Kolb (ed.), *op. cit*, p.115.
3. Irom Amubi, *Sajiphu Cheiraoba : Shingsatpagi Maong*, 1990, Introduction.
4. L. Bhagyachandra Singh, *A Critical Study of the Religious Philosophy of the Meeteis before the Advent of Vaisnavism in Manipur*, 1991, pp. 92-93.
5. Koijam Dhiren, *op. cit.*, p.226.
6. L. Iboongohal Singh and N. Khelchandra Singh (ed.), *Cheitharol Kumbaba*, 1989, p.20.
7. T. C. Hodson, *The Meitheis*, 1989 (Reprint), pp. 104-105.
8. Koijam Dhiren, *op. cit.*, p.226.
9. J. C. Higgens, "Notes on Meithei (Manipuri) Beliefs and Customs Recorded from Various Sources", p.50, cited in S.N. Parratt, *The Religion of Manipur*, 1980, p.47.

10. L. Iboongohal Singh and N. Khelchandra Singh (ed.), *Cheitharol Kumbaba*, p.20.
11. S.N. Parratt,_*op. cit.*, p.50.
12. N. Birachandra Singh,"Traditional Rituals of the Meiteis", *Seminar on Ancient History of Manipur*, 1987, p.4.
13. Koijam Dhiren, *op. cit.*, p.228.
14. Irom Amubi, *op. cit.*, Introduction.
15. S.N. Parratt, *op. cit.*, p.51.
16. *Ibid.*, p.52.
17. Irom Amubi, *op, cit.*, p.5.
18. *Ibid.*, p.5.
19. *Ibid*, pp.1-2.
20. *Ibid*, p.1.
21. T. Bokul, *Cheiraoba Ishaiphu Latpa, Meitei Marup*, 1968, p.11.
22. Ch. Manihar Singh (ed. and tr.), *Naothingkhong Phambal Kaba*,1983, pp. 56-57.
23. *Ibid.*, p.3.
24. Y. Bhagya Meitei (ed.), *Sakok Lamlen Ahanba Amasung Meihouron*,., p.32.
25. Koijam Dhiren, *op. cit.*, p.235.
26. L. Iboongohal Singh and N. Khelchandra Singh (ed.), *Cheitharol Kumbaba*, p.12.
27. Luwang Ningthou Punshiba was one of the kings of Luwang *salai*. It is said that he ordered his chief artists Nungban, Wangmitkhu and Luwang Wamgmanao Sinheiba to bring a straight and tall *Uningthou* tree. They found from Kouba Ingen Ching and made a boat which was the first ever made for a king of Manipur. It is customary to make a Hiyang Hiren out of one *Uningthou* tree only. Keisham Sobita Devi, *Hiyang Hiren*, 1988, p.1.
28. L. Iboongohal Singh and N. Khelchandra Singh (ed.), *Cheitharol Kumbaba*, pp. 39-40.
29. Yumnamcha Buddhichandra (ed.), *Thaloi Nongkhailon*, p.34.
30. There is a historical event associated with the installation of the head of *Khuman Kwakpa* which accured during the

time of Meitei king Thawnathaba. The *Thawanthaba Hirel Puya* states thus: The Meiteis and the Khumans were enemies. However, the Khuman king on conspiracy requested the Meitei king Thawanthaba to invade Heirem Khunjan, planning to ambush the Meiteis on the return from this war. As planned before Khuman Kwakpa caught hold of the Hiru of the huge boat. It was Taoriya Elangba, the great Meitei warrior, who realised this action first and beheaded Khuman Kwakpa with the edge of a big oar. The chopped head was placed on the stern as a victory sign.

31. E. Nilakanta Singh, "Manipur - a land of dance", *Folklore*, 1960, p.226.
32. *Cultural Heritage of Manipur*, Introduction.
33. Keisham Sobita Devi, *op. cit.*, p.10.
34. N. Birachandra Singh, *op. cit.*, p.11.
35. T.C. Hodson, *op.cit*, p.51.
36. Keisham Sobita Devi, *op. cit.*, p.9.
37. N. Birachandra Singh, *op. cit.*, p.11.
38. Koijam Dhiren, *op. cit.*, p.236.
39. R.Brown, *Statistical Account of Manipur*,1975 (Reprint), p.82.
40. L.Iboongohal Singh and N. Khelchandra Singh (ed.), *Cheitharol Kumbaba*, p.173.
41. N. Birachandra Singh, *Socio-religious Life of the Meiteis in the 18th Century A.D.*, 1987, p.237.
42. N. Birachandra Singh,"Traditional Rituals of the Meiteis", *op.cit*, p.5.
43. The marching of the king, the Senapati and all the courtiers in day time, riding on horse back and elephant, accompanied with drums and music towards *Kwakshang* is traditionally known as *Kwak Jatra*.
44. L. Iboongohal Singh and N. Khelchandra Singh (ed.), *Cheitharol Kumbaba*, p.110.
45. Koijam Dhiren, *op. cit.*, p.234.
46. N. Khelchandra Singh (ed.), *Ariba Manipuri Longei*, 1978, p.22.
47. S.N. Parratt, *op. cit.*, p.44; *Pakhangba* had a son named

Khui who rebelled against him and for a time seized the throne. Eventually *Pakhangba* defeated his rebellious son in a single combat and decapitated him. His spirit thereupon entered the rare *Wakambong* (a yellow bird). In commemoration of this event the practice was instituted.

48. N. Birachandra Singh, "Traditional Rituals of the Meiteis", *op. cit.*, p.5.
49. *Ibid.*, p.6-7
50. Koijam Dhiren, *op. cit.*, p.246.
51. It was believed that the divine ladies sold heads of human beings and cats and these items were purchased by the deities and human beings for a grand feast.
52. Koijam Dhiren, *op. cit.*, p.246.
53. N. Birachandra Singh, "Traditional Rituals of the Meiteis", *op. cit.*, p.9.
54. Koijam Dhiren, *op. cit.*, p.246.
55. R.K. Hiranya, Lai Keithel Kaba, Meitei Harao Kumei, p.26, quoted in N. Birachandra Singh, "Traditional Rituals of the Meiteis", *op. cit.*, p.10.
56. E. Nilakanta Singh, *op.cit.*, p.227.
57. J. Shakespear, "The Religion of Manipur", *Transaction of the Folklore Society,* 1913, p.428.
58. O. Clarke, *A Vocabulary Manipuri to English Dictionary,* 1924, pp. 8, 17.
59. N. Khelchandra Singh, *Ariba Manipuri Longei,* 1978, p.169.
60. H.Pramodini Devi, *Numit Kappa and Panthoibi Khongkun: A Study of Socio-Economic and Politico-religious Aspects of Early Manipur*, 1988, p.33.
61. W. Lukhoi Singh, *Lai Haraoba*, 1989, p.3.
62. L. Temba Mangang,"Chakpa Leimaram Lai Harobagi Hourakpam Amasung Haraobagi Samlappa Warol", *Lai Haraoba Seminar*, 1987, p.1.
63. M. Laimit and L. Iboyaima (ed.) *Wakoklon Hilel Thilel Salai Amailon Pukok Puya,* 1972, p:43.
64. Bhagya Singh Yengkhoiba, *Leithak Leikharon,* 1982, pp. 13-14.
65. W. Lukhoi Singh, *op. cit.*, p.2.

66. A look at the location of place names of the festivals reveal that the *Chakpa Haraoba* relates to the North, Moirang South West and Kakching South East of Kangla, the centre or seat of Meitei capital.
67. R. K. Saha, "State Formation among the Meitei of Manipur," in Surajit Sinha, *Tribal Politics and State System in Pre-Colonial Eastern and North Eastern India, 1987,* p.217.
68. T. C. Hodson, *op.cit,* p.59.
69. E. Nilakanta Singh, *op.cit.,* p.228.
70. *Ibid,* p.1.
71. S. N. Parratt, *op. cit.,* p.56.
72. W. Lukhoi Singh, *op. cit.,* pp. 177-184.
73. S. N. Parratt, *op. cit.,* p.56.
74. Ng. Kullachandra Singh, *Meitei Lai Haraoba,* 1963, p.2.
75. Ng. Kullachandra Singh, *op. cit.,* pp.4-5.
76. *Ibid.* pp.2-3.
77. Khullem Chandrashekhar Singh, *Lai Haraoba Laisol,* 1982, pp.1-2.
78. Ng. Kullachandra Singh, *op. cit.,* p.7.
79. *Ibid,* pp.7-8.
80. *Ibid,* p.10.
81. *Ibid,* p.11.
82. *Ibid,* p.12.
83. W. Lukhoi Singh , *op. cit.,* pp.91-93.
84. L. Bhagyachandra Singh, *A Critical Study of the Religious Philosophy of the Meiteis before ? Advent of Vaisnavism in Manipur,* 1991, p.112.
85. Leisungbam Chaitanya Singh, "Androgi Haraoba", in N. Jugindro (ed.), *Chakpa Haraoba,* 1992, p.29.
86. Rajkumar Achouba Singh, "Andro Haraoba", *Lai Haroba Seminar,* p.5.
87. L.Temba Mangang, *op.cit.,* p.3.
88. *Ibid.,* p.6.
89. L. Bhagyachandra Singh. *op. cit.,* p.97.
90. W. Lukhoi Singh, *op. cit.,* p.230.

91. *Ibid*, p.264.
92. Naorem Amuyaima Singh, "Kakching Haraoba", *Lai Haraoba Seminar*, p.1.
93. W. Lukhoi Singh, *op. cit.*, pp. 240, 243.
94. *Ibid*, p.259.
95. Kullachandra Singh "Moirang Haraoba", *Lai Haraoba Seminar.*, pp. 1-4.
96. W. Lukhoi Singh, *op. cit.*, p.309.
97. *Ibid.*, Illustration, p.261.
98. W. Robinson, "A Descriptive Account of Assam to which is Added a Short Account of Neighbouring Tribes",1841 in Verrier Elwin (ed.), *India's North-East Frontier in the Nineteenth Century*, 1959, p.29.
99. H. Bilashini Devi, "Folk Musical Instruments of Manipur Since Pakhangba", in L. Kunjeshwari Devi (ed.), *The Manipur University Museum Bulletin*, 1988, p.3.
100. *Ibid.*, p.7.
101. Ch. Manihar Singh, "Lai Haraoba", *International Cultural Festival*, 1991, p.6.
102. Francis L.K. Hsu, *Under the Ancestors' Shadow*, 1971, p.193.
103. T.C. Hodson, *op. cit.*, p.51.
104. Koijam Dhiren, *op. cit.*, p.246.
105. Ch. Manihar Singh (ed. and tr.), *op. cit.*, p.3.
106. Ng. Kullachandra Singh, *op. cit*, p.7.
107. Irom Amubi, *op. cit*, p.2.
108. Ch. Manihar Singh, "Lai Haraoba", *op. cit.* p.7.
109. Koijam Dhiren, *op. cit*, p.246.
110. Naorem Amuyaima Singh, "Kakching Haraoba", *op.cit*, p.1.

6

Conclusion

The preceding pages are an attempt at a reconstruction of early Meitei history based primarily on the mass of old narratives called *Puyas* and extensive field survey of the living tradition as expressed in private and community rituals. The *Puyas* acquire utmost importance in view of the fact that they are the only major written source for the study. The tradition as recorded in the *Puyas* reveal that Manipur witnessed struggle for supremacy among the various independent principalities or chiefdoms before Nongda Lairen Pakhangba (33-154 A.D.) is believed to have brought elementary order and set up a kingdom in the valley. Chiefdoms are characterized by a central leadership legitimized on the basis of birth. That the clan (*salai*) status and ancestry were officially and systematically co-ordinated is clearly reflected in the genealogical records of the Meiteis. The *pana* and *lallup* systems were aimed at allotting administrative and economic functions to each sub-clan (*sagei*) indicating the genealogical basis of organizational divisions. Each member of the Meitei community was integrated into the largest social unit i.e. the state.

The core of the religion of the Meiteis is ancestor worship which is firmly linked to the social, economic and political system. *Puyas* such as the *Leithak Leikharon* record the myths of creation and the progenitors of the seven clans. Incorporation of gods and goddesses of different social groups in myths created, and the stories of deification of human personalities indicate deliberate attempts at integration. For example, the guardians of directions are gods of communities brought under the Meitei pantheon through formulation of myths in the *Puyas*. Wangbren, the guardian of the South resides in Loibi Lamngang with his four wives. The invasion of the Meitei king and the marriage of Wangbren to an Anal lady show the attempt to integrate the various communities under one canopy. Another instance at integration is that of Thangjing being made the ruler of Tripura, Cachar and Bengal. The introduction of worship of Nongshaba, associating him with the prosperity of places such as Wangu, Chothe and Moirang and then bringing the idol to the Meitei king who in turn built a temple for him also shows that such myths created help to bring the people of far off regions closer to the central authority i.e., the Meitei kingship. Another example is that associated with the beginning of worship of the goddess Imoinu during the reign of King Chalamba in the 16th century A.D. An old lady believed to have been an incarnate of the goddess was brought to the Meitei palace from the palace of the Khuman king. It may be mentioned here that Khuman and Moirang remained comparatively powerful, even maintaining its identity for a long period of time. The Moirang king was the last to be subdued by the Meitei king in as late as the 18th century A.D. In the deification of Pitanga, we have the interaction of the social groups viz; Selloi-Langmais, Ningthoujas and Khuman. Though the Selloi-Langmais and Khumans were traditional rivals of the Ningthoujas, the Ningthouja king was given protection by a girl from Selloi-Langmais. Later, the king married a princess of the Khumans, thereby establishing the close relation among them. In *Konthoujam Nongaren*, the myth raises a Konthou girl to the status of a goddess. Konthoujam clan, therefore, became famous due to this mortal who came to be worshipped later as Konthoujam Lairemma.

Ancestor worship broadly consists of two worlds; that of the human beings and the spirits, both of which are directly related to the ancestors. It is society that accords or denies ancestors their social and religious status. Although there is no absolute correspondence between social structure and patterns of worship in any society, the ways in which a particular society structures relationships within the boundaries of significant social groups, such as the family, illuminate how it conceives the social role of the deceased within those groups. Thus, if the ancestors become the primary object of veneration in a given society, the origin and significance of this practice will have to be sought within the organising principle of that society itself.

The intricate network of *salai* system among the Meiteis have sustained the cult of ancestor worship in Manipur. This clan system can best be understood as a vast network of member families, living and dead, which are all related by blood lineally and collaterally. The smallest unit of *salai* is represented by the *phungga* (hearth). The *salai* and *phungga* are linked by the *sagei* (sub-clan) which consists of groups of families bearing the same family name. Ancestral spirits both divine and human are designated as *Umanglais*. In describing the origin of the seven *salais,* the *Puyas* reveal that all the clans trace their roots to the Ultimate Parents, Taoroinai and Atingkok. Nine *Laibungthous* (divine youths) and seven *Lainuras* (divine girls) were brought forth to assist Him in the creation of the universe. The nine divine youths have often been referred to as the original nine *Umanglais.* In course of time the Meitei *lais* increased in number with the proliferation of lineages, resulting in the present list of about four hundred. The social order is legitimated through its location within a sacred and cosmic frame of reference which gives it a semblance of security and permanence. In the various myths relating to the origin of the *salais*, we find a consistent attempt to relate the *salais* to known units of time, direction, parts of the human body etc. The Ultimate Father is the highest object of worship in the Meitei religion. Beyond this, there seems to have been no fixed hierarchy among the other *lais* which assumed significance at particular sub-periods of Meitei history.

Kinship is a positive factor in state-local relations. It is kinship which maintains its web-like quality and its character as a widely cast net subsuming many different geographical areas and peoples. The social relationships, marital customs, and behaviour of one individual towards another are all governed by kinship rules. Indeed, it is this kinship network which binds the entire Meitei society which includes both the living and the dead. The parent-child relationship or the ancestor-descendant linkage is built into the terms of address to the *lais*. For example, Pakhangba is referred to as *ipudhou* (grandfather), Sanamahi as *panthou* (father) and Leimaren and other goddesses as *ima* or *palem* (mother). All animate and inanimate objects are associated with the *salais* in one form or another. The seven ancestresses of the *salais* are believed to be associated with totems such as serpent, egg, goat, elephant, buffalo, deer and tiger. Other items are tree, grass, water, fire, wind, earth, cotton, fish etc. These associations are attempts to bring about a sense of unity, belongingness, togetherness and common affinity not only among the members of the Meitei social groups, but their entire universe.

The Meiteis practice clan exogamy. The identity of each clan is maintained through the exclusive private rituals of *Apokpa Khurumba* at various levels such as the family, *sagei* and *salai*. Although this may act as a disintegrative force, it is counterbalanced by the veneration of the Ultimate Parents at all the rituals. This reminds them of their inseparable link with their dead forebears reinforcing the idea of belonging to the same roots. The initiative of integration of the disparate groups is taken by the state with the help of agencies like the *Pandit Loisang* and the *Puyas.* This is done through the creation of a pantheon, which is diverse, accommodating the deities of various groups, and also converging on at least two universal deities, cutting across clan loyalties. Thus Sanamahi, the household god, looks after the smallest unit of social organization - the family, and Pakhangba, the royal deity, looks after the largest unit of social organization - the state. It is important to note that Pakhangba is credited with the first systematic attempt at unifying the Meitei people. The purpose of public festivals such as the *Lai Haraoba* also indicates an obvious attempt to assimilate social groups under one overarching canopy of the state. These rituals, participated by members of all social groups, re-enact the creation myth as a ritualized reminder of a fundamental order that derives from a common origin or ancestry.

The position assigned to the goddesses in the Meitei pantheon may be understood in the light of the status which a Meitei woman occupies in the traditional setup. Women as an agricultural worker, weaver, dyer or trader controlled the economic life of the kingdom. Since the menfolk had to render their services to the state under the *lallup* (forced labour) system, it was left to the women to look after the production activities. Women, therefore, had the opportunity for economic autonomy and as bread earners of the family acquired an important status in the family in particular and society in general. Women have a right of residence in their natal home. The widowed, unmarried, divorced daughters and sisters, therefore, have a strong sense of security, a remarkable feature in a patrilineal set up.

The most unusual aspect is seen in the role the Meitei women play as ritual specialists (*Maibis*). Treated as 'wives of the *lais*' they are the chief functionaries in the society possessing the power of divination. Being the chief intermediary between gods and men, they are the symbolic points of contact between the historical and spiritual worlds. The *Maibis*, married or unmarried are not bound by the social rules followed by other Meitei women. The *Maibis* as indispensable priestesses in the religious life of the Meitei society reflect the role of the women vis-à-vis the men in the traditional setup. The marked feature of male-female partnership in the patriarchal Meitei society has raised the question of the possibility of a matrilineal society prior to the known patriarchal one. The *Puyas* such as *Leithak Leikharon* also strengthen this hypothesis by giving a list of genealogy of the progenitors of the clans through the matrilineal side.

While emphasizing the status assigned to women, the role of men in the society should not be underestimated. The gods as compared to the goddesses emerge as the protector and ultimate giver of security. The guardians of the directions who protect the cardinal points of the earth are all male deities. In the social structure it is the father-son relationship which forms the basis of all relationships. This is clearly demonstrated by the traditional architectural plan of a Meitei house. It reflects a patriarchal ideology with priority of place assigned to the father, the eldest son, the wife and the daughter-in-law. The *piba* i.e. head of the clan, may officiate as the priest in the veneration of ancestors in case he is conversant with the functions. At the state level, the *Pandit Loisang* to which are attached the *Maibi* and *pena* institutions are entirely a male's concern. The *Loisang* supervises the general functioning of the religious rituals in community or village levels and also allocate duties to the *Maibis* and *pena* players. The significant role of the male is observed at the time of funeral rites of the dead forebear. The sons have the right to the larger share of the inherited property. It may be worthwhile to mention that the *Cheitharol Kumbaba* i.e. the state chronicle, a very important source for the study record the genealogy of the Meitei kings from the father's side.

Ancestor worship provides men with a frame through which he is able to face a mortal existence. The ancestors worshipped are thought to confer positive benefits to the descendents. But should they be neglected, they will in resentment inflict distress and sufferings. Therefore the *apokpas* are held with great awe and fear and they have to be constantly appeased by the living. This insight then finds a more or less exhaustive representation in the rites or rituals. They vary in great complexity from the simple individual acts of worship at the Sanamahi Kachin in every home to the *Salai Apokpa Khurumba* which is performed with procession and much paraphernalia. Public rituals in contradistinction to the private ones are meant for the community as a whole. It must be emphasized that the many *Umanglais* are brought alive through the many community festivals throughout the year. The community rituals create an occasion for remembering and paying homage, offering food etc. to the deceased who have no descendants who could perform the function at the family level. Thus, the Meitei community as a whole performs the functions for which there is no scope at the more pragmatic level. The rites and rituals are intended to ward off any misfortune and secure or augment the co-operation of the *Umanglais* in promoting the happiness and peace of the individual and the community.

The declaration of Vaisnavism as the state religion during the reign of King Garibniwaz (1709-1748 A.D.) is a watershed in the history of Manipur. The *Puyas* record the earliest migration of *Brahmanas* to Manipur during the reign of King Kyamba (1497-1507 A.D.). The ancestor cult so intricately wound with the social structure would have been made to be replaced by Vaisnavism only if the whole social structure were to be replaced by a new one. This was definitely not an easy task. The result is that ancestor worship has remained dominant throughout in the history of the religion of the Meiteis.

Ancestral cults and beliefs have played significant roles throughout Meitei history. The rite of ancestor worship seems to be a legitimate and comforting belief which may serve to stimulate piety and virtue. It ensures that ties of kinship in the community are strengthened. Every individual is reminded through the periodically held rituals of ancestor veneration the status he may one day attain. The relationship of the ancestor and the descendant occupies the central place in the study of ancestor worship, for the obvious fact that household and marriage offer the inviolable prerequisites. The social organization persisted so long since it is convenient for both the individual communities and the state. In a tribal set up, group identities are strong and the ancestor cult only strengthens it. The interest of the state was to keep the groups united, without submerging their identities. In fact the status of the ruling family also depends on its belonging to a *salai*, which it succeeds in projecting as the first among equals. Moreover, the resource of the state is based on the *lallup* system which is organised around the *salai* structure. Without reducing the system therefore to necessarily cause and effect relationships, the social organization, the state and the ancestor cult reinforce one another.

In every respect, clans and lineage play a significant part in the Meitei society, thereby forming the basis of the various stages of development of Meitei philosophical thoughts, resulting in the emergence of the cult of ancestor worship. Everybody is destined to become an ancestor, a fact which provides the crucial link between the living and the dead and ensures continuity of the present structure. Indeed, the dead are thought of as having a stake in the continuity i.e. in the future persistence of the society to which they belonged in life. In ancestor worship this is accepted as just and natural; it is this that, paradoxical as it may sound, gives ancestor worship a future orientation, rather than, as might superficially be thought to be the case, a fixation of the past.

The continuity of the lineage system has been a successful mechanism for incorporating a diversity of clan groups where each maintained its identity in a relationship of juxtaposition to each other. It also helped in preserving the identity of the Meiteis as an ethnic community. Ancestor worship, therefore, derives the meaning from the society in general and human beings in particular who produce and reproduce it in their ongoing lives.

Map of Manipur Showing Clan Principalities

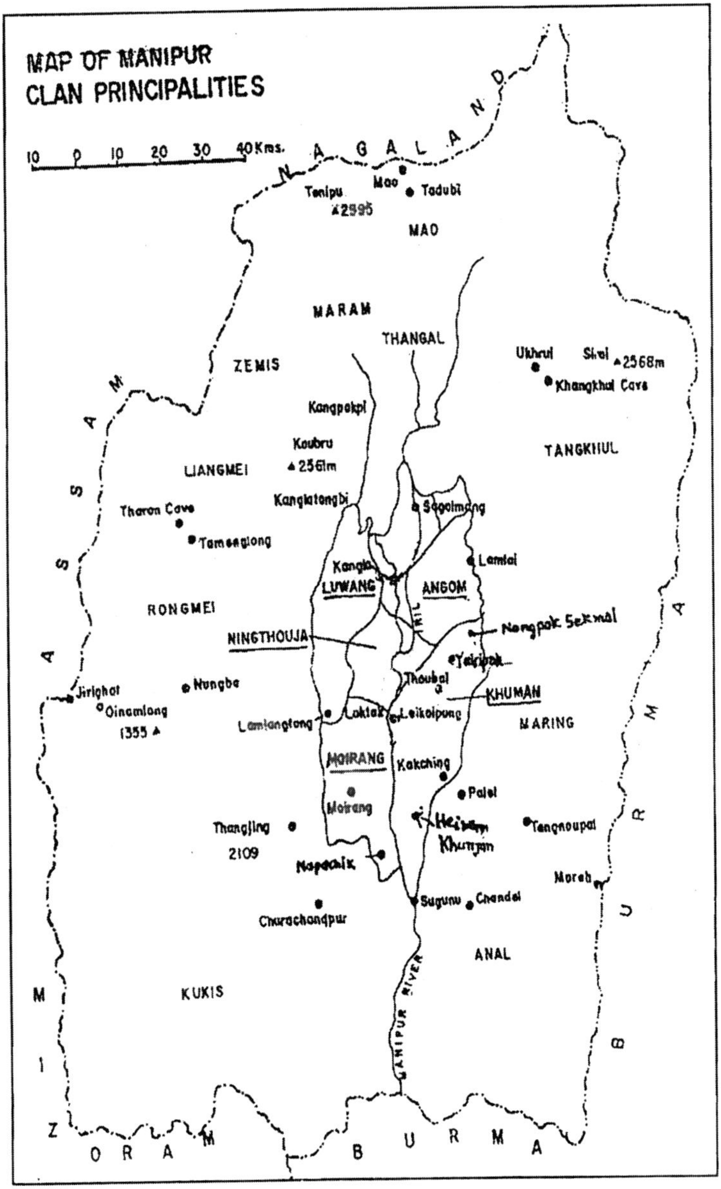

Map of Manipur Valley Showing Clan Principalities

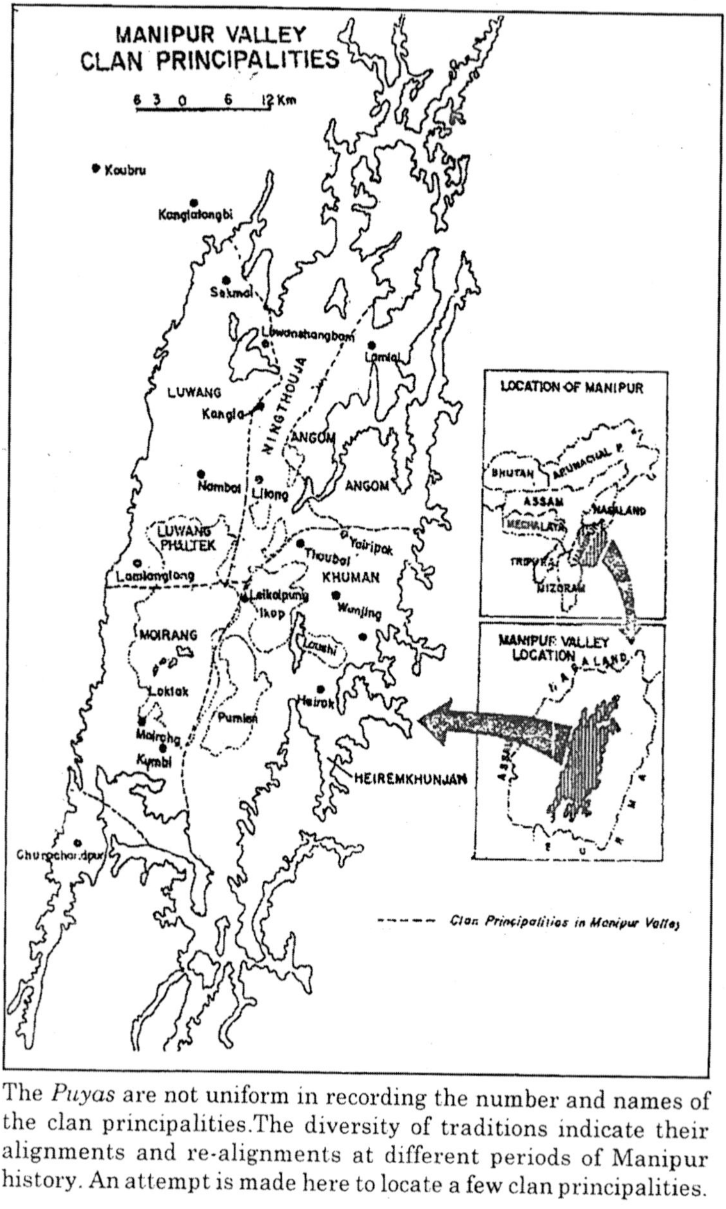

The *Puyas* are not uniform in recording the number and names of the clan principalities.The diversity of traditions indicate their alignments and re-alignments at different periods of Manipur history. An attempt is made here to locate a few clan principalities.

Social Structure and Sacred Symbols

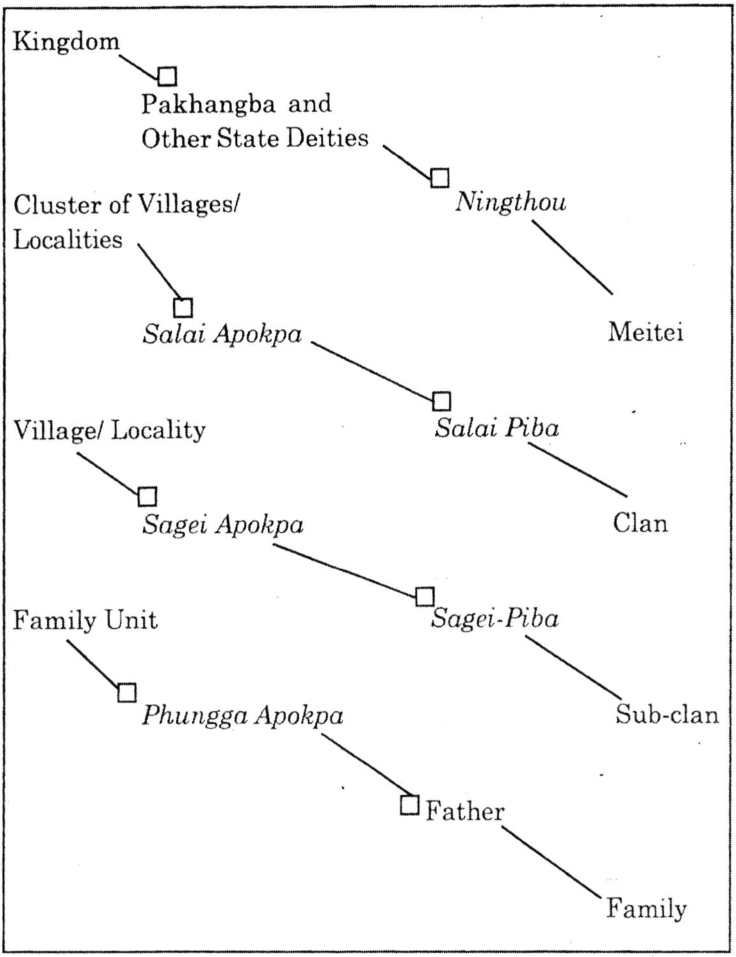

Social Hierarchy

King

|

Aristrocratic Lineages
(Belonging to the royal families)

|

Salai and *Sagei*
(Constituting the majority of the Meitei population)

|

Lowest Social Group such as Lois and Yaithibis
(Performing menial services for the royal household)

THE MEITEI PANTHEON AS EXEMPLIFIED IN THE CREATION MYTH

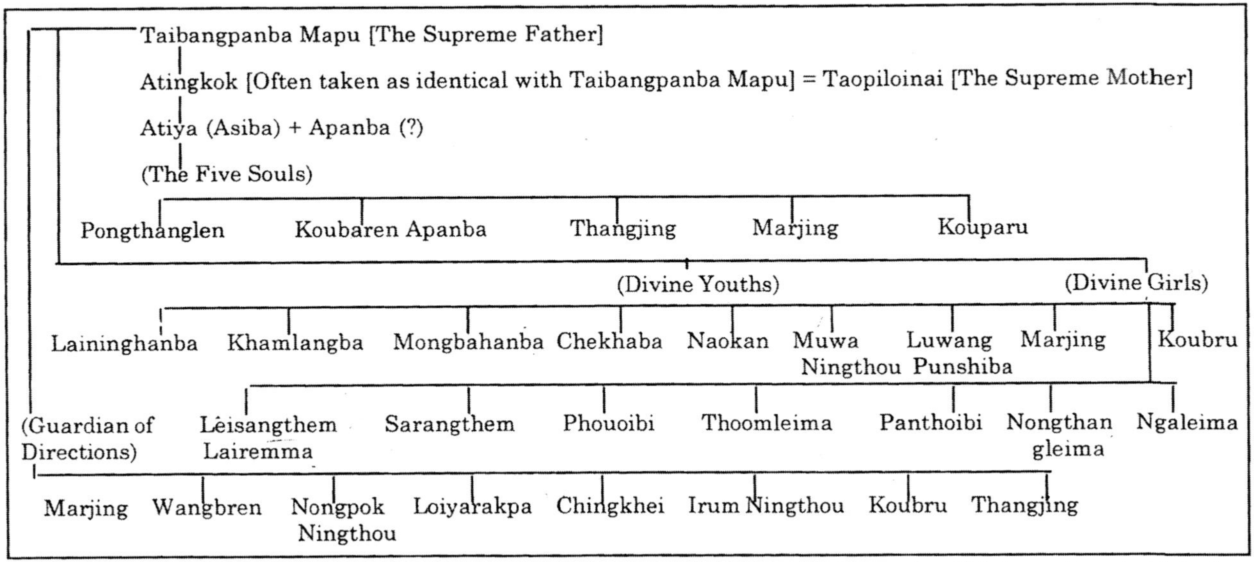

Note: It is to be noted that innumerable *Puyas* supply different and therefore confusing version. This is an attempt at bringing about an elementary order on the basis of the fuller versions contained on the *Leithak Leikharon Puya*. Even then there are certain inconsistencies in this text such as an overlap of names in lists of the divine youths and the guardian of directions.

SALAI APOKPAS (CLAN ANCESTORS)

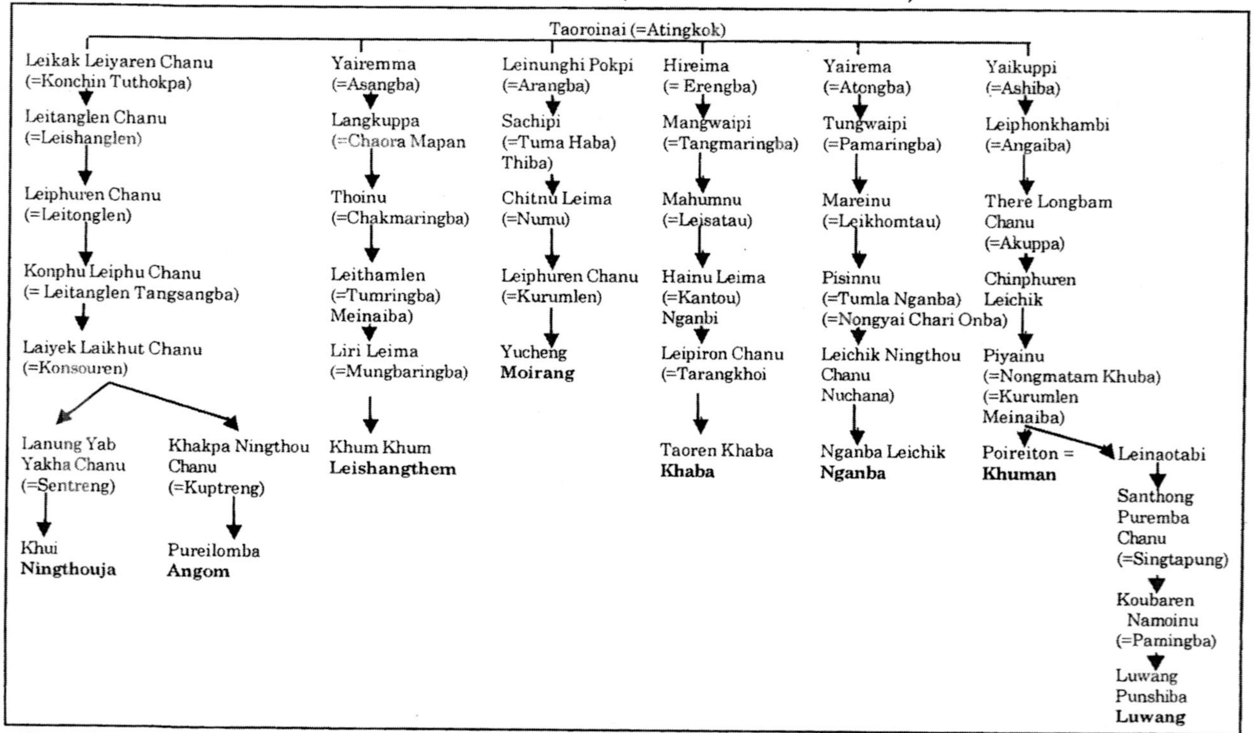

Note: The above list is the version as given in *Leithak Leikharon Puya*. Originally nine, the number of *salais*(clans) were later reduced to seven The genealogical tree indicates a matrilineal descent group up to the head of each clan after which it changes over to patrilineal descent.

Appendix-I

List of names of some *lais* and the many other names by which they are known as given in Irom Amubi Singh (ed.), *Laichan Puya*, pp. 27-31, in *Laihou Naophamlon*, 1981.

ASIBA: Samton, Khakpa, Pulang, Pureiromba, Nongpok Soraren, Puthiba, Loiyalakpa, Mayangnaha, Sarei Thekpa, Yoimongba, Sanamahi, Thongnang Ningthou, Taoroinai, Kuptreng, Khumu Tunginnaba, Rangtha Meiroinaba, Waikok Sariba, Laiyingthou Hanba Yenlangba, Hanggoi Ningthou, Sengpan, Wangbren, Wakhalakpa, Keirao Lakpa, Khongching Lakpa, Aroinung, Lokningthou, Esing Chaiba, Nongkacheng, Wangouba, Nungka Singpak.

KONCHIN TINGTHOKPA: Konglouren Apanba, Pakhangba, Naohan Ahanba, Khamlangba, Muwa Ningthou, Taothingmang, Yangkoi Ningthou, Tubu Chingningthou Achaba, Yangoi, Thangjing, Sentreng, Ekop Ningthou, Aayapa, Leikacheng, Wanmuba, Nungjongba, Nongthil Chaiba, Yaongaiba.

ATIYA SIDABA: Nongshaba, Chakhaba, Marjing, Luwang Ningthou, Langpum Ningthou, Sambum Ningthou, Thawaren, Ponbi Luwangba, Singtabung, Poireiton, Khunthiba, Pudangkoi, Nungpokpa, Nungang Maharaba, Chingkhei Ningthou, Mahou Ningthou, Untin Uphang Ningthou, Yipunlen, Yetairen, Sakuren, Thongthokaran, Andro Khullakpa, Chinga, Thawai, Koubru.

LEIMAREN: Yabirok, Hireima, Eraileima, Hikubi, Tarung Leima, Yumjao Leima, Usoi Leima, Petanga, Chinpan Leima, Erong Leima, Nongku Leima, Yumchum Leima, Chengleima, Chinga Leima, Heipok Leima, Hiyangthang Lairemma.

NONGTHANGLEIMA: Panthoibi, Tanthong Leima, Lemthong Leima, Lamteng Leima, Heinoupok Leima, Thangjing Leima, Chaning Leima, Nungkoibi, Kolloi Leima, Thoomleima, Ngareima, Thareima, Phouoibi, Yotleima, Watrei Sinheibi, Konleima, Khakpa Ningthou Chanu, Moinu Chanu, Pithet Leima, Lera (Laiwa) Leima, Laisan Thanbi, Khabi Lukok Chanu, Likla Picha, Yaibileima, Pithrai Khongdraibi, Sarik Leima, Pusari Leima, Leima Nunglaobi, Khambi Yiyengcheng.

LAIKHUREMBI: Leinaitabi, Laisana, Chitnuleima, Thamnuleima, Ahumnu, Areinu, Therelongbam Chanu, Tonthangnu, Soubon Leima.

Appendix-II

List of *Umanglais* in W. Lukhoi Singh, *Lai Haraoba*, 1989, pp.177-184.

Moirang Thangjing
Heingang Marjing

Awang Sekmai Koubru

Sugnu Sanamahi

Koirengei Pakhangba

Top Chingtha Enamung

Kodompokpi Sorarel

Yambem Yairi Ningthou

Phanknung Chingkhei Guru

Khurai Puthibi

Ningel Nongpok

Andro Panam Ningthou

Tangjeng Lokningthou

Nachou Sorarel

Ningthoukhong Okrel

Oinam Nongshaba

Laishram Ereima

Tongbram Lairemma

Wairi Khamlangba

Eranpal Erum Ningthou

Sugnu Wangbarel

Yaiskul Nongsaba

Thanga Chingningthou

Maibam Lokpaching Loiyarakpa

Yairipok Ningthou Panthoibi

Yurembam Unam Sorarel

Tairenpokpi Koubru

Awang Yumnam Khunou Puthibi

Wangu Wangparel

Chandrakhong Yenthurakpa

Andro Pureiromba

Phayeng Koubru

Kha Potsangbam Panganba

Ething Thangjing

Haobijam Chairelakpa

Moirangthem Thangjing

Kakching Khoriphaba

Aarapti Ereita

Paonam Eshijmng Chaibi

Toubul Yangoi Ningthou	Kangamung Khujai Loiyarakpa
Ngairangbam Loiyarakpa	Waiton Puthiba
Khundrakpam Marjing	Tingri Marjing
Sapam Solai Khongjom Ningthou	Thoubal Nongangthong-Thoubal Ningthou
Keikru Nongpok Panthoibi	Chabungkampani Wangbarel
Erun Siphai Ngangourakpa	Mutum Phiphou Erongleima
Kakwa Naorem Panthoibi	Eroisemba Thongakmacha
Naran konjin Koubru	Mayang Imphal Khumanpokpa
Lairenjam Lairemma	Thangbijrou Thangba
Maitram Seibu Leima	Sagol Tongba Pakhangba
Keinou Lhulleima	Thongam Mondum Khulleima
Samram Khongjom Ningthou	Lourembam Lairemma
Top Langmai Leima	Thongam Panganba
Thaoroijam Yumjaoleima	Uripok Turembam Huidompokpi
Elangbam Panganba	Mayang Langjing Mamang- Koubru
Mayang Langjing Maning Koubru	Langmeithet Panthoibi
Kumbong Panthoibi	Awangkhunou Koubru

Phoijing Chaning Leima	Tauthong Koubru
Uripok Khamlangba	Akham Khamlangba
Uripok Laikhurembi	Elangbam Khanpokpi Panganba
Luker Khoimom	Lairemma Lamboikhul Ereima
Gobindagram Puthiba	Khonghampat Luwangpokpa
Khonghampat Koubru	Parnam Khul Loiyarakpa
Ngariyanbam Koubru Loiyarakpa	Nambol Khoriphaba
Phoukakchou Phouoibi	Kha Thounaojam Panthoibi
Uchekol Moriba	Nambol Konkham Loiyarakpa
Khundrakpam Panganba	Meisnam Lairemma
Achanbikei Marjing	Kangamung Meisnam Loiyarakpa
Keirao Langdum Keirao Lakpa	Wahengbam Yumjao Leima
Tekcham Ekop Ningthou	Langmeidong Pakhangba
Engourok Nongpok Ningthou	Keinoupok Loiyarakpa
Chingga Makha Maisnam Luwangpokpa	Pukhao Ahallup Ereima
Khurai Lai Awangba	Wangbal Ekop Ningthou
Hiyangthang Lairemma	Huirem Chingbal Leima
Naharup Pureiromba	Pungdongbam Panthoibi
Nungoi Puthiba	Sagolband Pakhangba
Lamding Wangjing Ningthou	Chingtham Khongjom Ningthou

Ningthoukhong Thangnarel	Yumnam Yumjao Lairemma
Sagolmang Ereima	Patpul Eroom Ningthou
Nungu Laimanai	Charangpat Mamang Arong- Ningthou
Pengi Arong Ningthou	Moirangpurel Pushi Lairemma
Pouribi Puthiba	Khurai Lainingthouhanba
Loktonbam Arai Leima	Naklabam Chingol Ningthou
Khurai Mamang Yangoi Ningthou	Khurai Angouba
Khurai Puthiba	Soubol Lairembi
Top Lungmai Leima	Sekta Laingthou Achangba
Khurai Ningthem Pokpa	Angom Pokpa (Leithong)
Atom Khuman Pakhangba-Ningthem Pokpa	Lamdeng Thoongong Lairemma
Lamdeng Poireiton Laikhurembi-Leima Leinaotabi	Luwang Guru Ningol
Khagi Maibi Yubham	Thinungei Loiyarakpa
Thinungei RamjiNingthou	Ethai Phouoibi
Thangtek Yangoi Ningthou	Ngairangbam Kunou Pakhanga
Kha Yumnam Khunou Pakhangba	Khurai Soubon Lairemma

Uchekkon Panthoibi	Konthoujam Lairemma
Takhel Nongpok Ningthou	Pukhao Laipham Ereima
Awang Phououibi	Pukhao Khabam Ereima
Heibongpokpi Koubru	Kangamung Tongbram Loiyarakpa Khathong Pakhangba SatpamKhongjom Ningthou
Thokchom ArongNingthou	Athokpam AwangNingthou
Keirok Sekmai Ningthou	Khurai Thareima
Khaidem Loiyarakpa	Heirok Ekop Ningthou
Wabgai Pakhangba	Lairen Kabi Koubru
Chajing Lakpa	Erengbam Nameirakpam-Khubomba
Khoijuman Yangoi Ningthou	Ningombam Sang Sang Ningthou
Nongpok Lourembam Awang-Ningthou	Heisnam Panthoibi
Oinam Souombung Ereima	Thouban Ningombam Thouban
Kongpal Uraleima Ningthou	Kongpal Puri Puraba
Bamonkampung Pureiromba	Tangkham Khuleima (Kalika)
Charangpat Maning Nongpok-Ningthou]	Khongjom Ningthou
Ahallup Marjing	Thongak Lairemma Longol
Erengbam Khoriphaba	Langol Kameng Koubru
Kongpal Langmaleima	Wakharakpa

Pangei Marjing

Keirao Lakpa

Khekman Pakhangba

Wangkheirakpam Yumjao-Lairemma

Meisnam Lairemma

Elangbam Panganba

Kyamgei Khagemba

Selungpham Nongpok Ningthou

Ningthoubung Puraba

Pangan Ṣiphai Nungthileima

Phouden Pakhangba

Heinoukhongnembi Laishram-Lairemma

Samurou Khwai Ningthou

Morok Engol Koubru Keinou

Keinou Khongthak Koubru

Karam Nongshaba

Sagoltongba Suraisam Khagemba

Khadem Nganuleima

Lammabam Erongleima

Khekman Wangbren

Khekman Leikairakpa

Sagolmang Ereima

Langmeidong Pakhangba

Meijrao Lakpa

Kyamgei Mungyamba-Pakhangba

Kabokwangching Loiyarakpa

Khangmung Siphai Loiyarakpa

Hiyanglam Panganba

Phouden Nongpok Ningthou

Nongchup Sunjenbam Koubru- Samurou Lakpa

Samurou Leitang Ningthou

Ahongsangbam-Lairemma

Ngaikhong Yangoi Ningthou

Waheng Khuman Pakhangba

Soubam Mawao Leima

Maibakhul Marjing

Maklung Nungthil Leima	Heiyen Ekop Ningthou
Hunggoan Kalika	Tera Khunou Ekop Ningthou
Tentha Khunou Ekop Ningthou	Sinam Kom Lainingthou
Kabaw Wakching Nongabi	Keibi Ereima
Langol Ningthou	Tarung Leima
Phubala Pakhangba	Pechi Arong Ningthou-Ekop Ningthou
Thangmeiband Kangkhujam-Naothingkhong	Khurai Laikhurembi
Charangpat Mayai Nongpok	Laphupat Kalika
Thamnapokpi Thangjing	Lairem Khul Koubru
Khabi Lairemma	Waroichingmalung Humoiba
Yaingang Pokpi Haoreima Sumbubi	Nongpokameng Khamlangba
Kakmayai Panthoibi	Thongam Mondum Nungang- Maharaba
Khwarokching Arang Saraba	Ningel Phouoibi Lokchao-Thanungba
Chandrakhong Nongpok Sawang- Lallam Phoriba	Koirengei Pakhangba Khumanpokpa
Kongmaru Konglouron Loukhiba	Koubru Enimung Chandeba- Khongcheba
Koudruk Koubru	Khurkhul Echum Lairemma
Sekmai Wangbren	Phayeng Sawang Soraren

Leimaram Koubru	Thongjao Mayangamba
Nung Sanathong Pan Sundong- Nungyungbi	Chothethangwai Pakhangba
Ngakchoupokpi Yangoi Ningthou	Esok Chingpu Ningthou
Kha Chingpu Ningthou	Thiyam Laikom Pakhangba
Sunsenbam Panthoibi	Pukhrambam Panthoibi
Thounaojam Panthoibi	Awang Jiri Kabokhonng-Lairemma
Kha Potsangbam Panganba	Naorem Panthoibi
Pombikhong Lo Ningthou	Kondong Lairemma
Chairen Khunbu Leima Khunmabi	Panthoibi Tangkhul-Huithok Pakhangba
Nongmaijing Nongpok Apanba-Khullang Machangba Laipham	Tera Urak Koubru
Kanto Khullel Koubru	Pukhao Naharup Ereima
Naharup Terapur Ereima	Chajing Mairelkhong-Puthiba
Lematak Pakhangba Hidel Pakhangba	Prejek Mapal Pakhangba
Upokpi Sorarel	Lamdong Makha - Mayangamba
Heikrujam Mamang Loiyarakpa	Heikrujam Mamang-Khuman Pokpi
Churachandpur Awang Makha- Maigei Ngakpa	Lairenjam Khoriphaba

Appendix-III

List of *Umanglais* in Ng. Kullachandra Singh, *Meitei Lai Haraoba*, 1953, Appendix, pp.1-10. (Note: The names listed in W. Lukhoi Singh, *Lai Haraoba*, are not repeated here).

Sugnu Lokningthou	Thangga Chingningthou
Top Chingtha Enamung	Yambem Yairi Ningthou
Awang Yumnam Khunou Puthiba	Khurai Puthiba
Chandrakhong Yenkhurakpa	Ningthoukhong Panganba
Ningthoukhong Oknarel	Haobijam Chairelakpa
Salam Sorel Sanahal	Heisnam Chingningthou
Maibram Tampak Lainingthou	Khoyangbam Ayangleima
Phairelbam Loklangleima	Kiyam Ui Ningthou
Thongam Thongnang Ningthou	Kumphi Santhong Ningthou
Sangai Santhong Ningthou	Patsoi Khunou Nongkabi
Changangei Khumombi	Wangjing Wangjing Ningthou
Tentha Ekop Ningthou	Thoudam Erongleima
Lamsang Esing Chaiba	Malem Khunjaoba
Thoubal Sabaltongba Thoubal-Ningthou	Sapam Solai Khongjom-Ningthou
Chabungkampani Wangbarel	Erum Siphai Ngangourakpa
Thangbijrou Thangba	Meitram Sebu Leima
Keinou Khuleima	Thongam Mondum Khuleima

Samram Khongjom Ningthou	Thongam Panganba
Elangbam Panganba	Mayengbam Yaoreibi
Elangbam Khanpokpi Panganba	Uchekol Moriba
Keirao Langdum Keirao Lakpa	Khurai Lai Awangba
Wangbal Ekok Ningthou	Huirem Chingbal Leima
Lamding Wangjing Ningthou	Chingtham Khongjom Ningthou
Nungu Laimanai	Khurai Lainingthouhanba
Loktonbam Arai Leima	Nakabam Chingol Ningthou
Khurai Mamang Yangoi Ningthou	Khurai Angouba
Sekta Laingthou Angouba	Thangtek Yangoi Ningthou
Kha Yumnam Khunou	Athokpam Arong Ningthou
Keirak Sekmai Ningthou	Khurai Thareima
Ningthoukhong Oknaren	Ningthoukhong Thangnaren
Ningthoubung Puraba	Hiyanglam Panganba
Samuroulakpa Khwai Ningthou	Samuroulakpa Leitang Ningthou

Appendix-IV

Genealogical table of the seven *salais* include a list of the *sagei/yumnak* (sub-clan) as given in the list prepared in connection with the *Census 1901* in T.C.Hodson, *The Meitheis*, 1989 (Reprint), pp.182-187.

Ningthouja *Salai*

Enkhom	Kaithel-lakpom	Nowrem	Ipoo-shangbom
Khoirom	Nahakpom	Le-u-shoongbom	Khoisnam
Shanglen-moum	Mairenbom	Khoomon-lambom	Shingam
Fairenbom	Eroom-hairom	Namoijam lambom	Mayang-
Khongnam	Nowkon	Nowroibom Shenbom	Kanga-
Shangbom	Ta-yumjom	Ningthoujom	Shoram
Loitam	Erom	Chong-ning-henbom	Nga-ri-yanbom
Kham-lang-Shangbom		Na-kanbom	Shingam
Laishongbom	Thingnam	Ensheubom	Thoudam
A-khom	Khoondrakpam	Hodam	Sangonsem
Kangabom	Howkhom	Senasam	Fouroongbom
Shanoujam	Lai-kangbom	Namoirakpom	(Moirang Ningthoumoum)
Wa-reppom	Lourangbom	Paobom	Sangai-senbom
Eangnoo-eaibom	Shairem	Khoonjahanbom	Sanabom
A-khongbom	Sho-yam	Waikhom	Khang-jrakpom
Mutum	Haisnam	Eng-pokpom	Feejam
Sapom	Kongbajom	Ahoibom	Wangkhei
Hairang-khongjom		Thang-gan-shabom	Falambom

Kaisam	Hooi-rongbom	Fe-lem	Lourembom
Ahanthem	Laichonbom	Laitonjom	Moichem
Erengbom	Satokpom	Houdeijom	Khoinoojom
Choribom	Loitombom	Nowtam	Lantham
Atom	Paonam	Kontha-howbam	Shorenshonbom
Eroongbom	Lookram	Khoondom	Shingkhangbom
Laimaram	Nongthonbom	Shaikhom	Khoori-eanbom
Famdom	Hemnam	Shouka-rakpom	Chanjanbom
Cherom	Khoidongbom	Nongmai-kappom	Tensoobom
Huidram	Manoi-rakpom	Wangkheir-akpom	Khooai-rakpom
Yumnam	Laipokpom	Wangkhei-moum	Sharoongbom
Kanghoojam	Langpok-lakpom	Khoomon-cha-rappom	

Angom *Salai*

Lonjam	Lairen-lakpom	Ningonbom	Laitonjom
Wang-khem	Kashuwam	Hooirem	Eumlembom
Akoijam	Hidam	Longmaithem	Kaokanbom
Longmaithem(Telongba-shangbom)		Nongthonbom	Thanjom
Sheram	Naroombom	Nakpok-hanchabom	Khoimom-tabom
Achoowam	Hai-haibom	Moirang-laishangbom	
Ngarenbom	Ongnam	Ekhoi-shangbom	Achoibom
Hongnam-shoongbom		Poshangbom	Nganglebbom
Kongbom	Chakprom	Angom-yumkhaibom	Nganoo-kappom
Mang-sha-tam	Aengbom	Khana-choubom	Kho-younthen
Wanglembom	Chingangbom	Moong-khom	Shangombom
Terem	Loitanthem	Pooton-jom	Shangdon-jom

Shairom	Khangenbom	Kiam	Mandingom

Chenglei *Salai*

Thangjom	Tongbrom		
Aekpom	Shoorai	Laoitam	Moinam
Loishangthem	Chongtham	Sharak-khaibam	Kharaijom
Kha-gokpom	Now-shekpom	Konsam	Langon-jam
Yumgoodom	Shorangthem	Moing-lambom	Maibram
Wairokpom	Chanam	Khoisnam	Haiwam
Elangbom	Chingakhom	Pot-sangbom	Konthoujom
Maiba-thiam	Shamnom	Hourokcham	Wakambom
Tourangbom	Thoom-gan-bom	Thangjom-you-pambom	
Nganthem	Loushigam	Konjengbom	Loktambom
Hooiwam	Amam	Yanggoijom	Hemoibam

Nganba *Salai*

Maihoubam	Tekchom	Thongbom	Sanjeeram
Hentakpom	Howbajom	Ahaibom	Thongam
Thinbom	Langonjom	Kaborambom	Khaidem
Wangbajom	Khoodangbom	Khoomoo-jom	Feejam
Nongjenbom	Khooroijom		

Luwang *Salai*

Asangbom	Arambom	Maisnam	Maitram
Tinbijom	Lairingjom	Yumlembom	Thounoujom
Toibijom	Aboojom	Athokpom	Hijam
Mayengbom	Oorit-khinbom	Salam	Nong-pokpom
Aroobom	Nongthonbom	E-a-ngambom	Chigan-bom
Poongraijom	Nangom	Hourongbom	Laishom

Looang-shangbom	Wanglenbom	Thangjom	Thoudoijom
Haitham	Thamang-jan	Nahakpom	Loukhom
Fam-mi-hanbom	Wakongthem	Nowroibom	Wahengbom
Khoonjao-moum	Thiam	Laikangbom	Nanbom
Kambang-moum	Faroi-jom	Lairenjom	Loija-e-ang-bom
Thangjam-shoran	Waikhom	Ngoubom	Chingjabom
Khoomook-cham	Shoubam	Ningchitpom	Shambam-tooram
Shembangjom	Khoknam	Maiboong-lakpom	Khoibom

Khuman *Salai*

Tentha-maibom	Thoidingjom	Oenam	Maibam
Eanglem	Thingoojom	Khamnam	Ahong-shangbom
Pookrem	Fairenbom	Chaboongbom	Thongram
Chandam	Pankhaijom	Ahongbom	Hekroojom
Mongjom	Langdem	Senam	Thongbom
Ngangbom	Akangjom	Eang-noo-eaibom	Hanglem
Laikhooram	Thoudem	Karam	Tonjam
Konam	Shougaijom	Pooyam	Shangkhom
Ashem-nga-kha-khoi-moum		Moijem	Langhaibom
Wa-reppom	Taipongjom	Fanjom	Paloojom
She-atpom	Houbijom	Lantham	Eam-bem
Kabo-rambom	Thangjom	Tourem	Nga-sheppon
Pookrambom	Likmabam	Shantham	Toumom
Maitan-keishangbom		Pang-nganbom	Tokpom
Maibom	Thingom	Shan-shen-bom	Kadam
Moing-lambom	Chingkhooam	Enshenbom	Chingtham
Maifuuam	Amakcham	Sha-ka-pom	Howronbom

Charoibom	Khoolem	Lantham	Thangjam
Akooam	Lamabam	Thangjam-eou-sham	Khoomonthem
Khoirishoongbom	Tourem	Ahaibom Tonbom	Wankom
Yaithingbom	Lang-gam	Eanglaibom	Polembom
Shamook-cham	Thingbaijom	Terem	Tonthrom
Khoirom	Na-maran	Howaibom	Thangang-shabom
Howbom	Mairengbom	Khoothaibom	Langkhombom
Hentakpom	Neprom	Shoram	Ha-wai-bom Im-goo-doom
Laisram	Shendam	Akham	Amom

Moirang *Salai*

Chongtham	Melem	Ley-u-jom	Namboojam
Wa-enbom	Pookrambom	Wangbijom	Kaba-jom
Narengbom	Ngangom	Noongleppom	Narengbom
Kabo-rambom	Thangajom	Kong-kham	Thangjam
Shangkhom		Ningthou-khongjom	Okrom
Moirang Nongthombom		Moiramg-khaithel-Lakpom	
Poothem	Konjengbom	Eaikhom	Polem
Chakpa-fam	Kumabom	Shoibom Pookrambom	Shoibom
Hanglen Chatpatabam		Maifooam	Laifrakpom
Moirangthem	Thongjom	Lairenmoum	
Akhoo-eaibom	Namoojom	Khoinaijom	Laimajom
Wanglembom	Fairenjom	Wangkhem	Hitom
Moirang-yumkhaibom		Shingkhangbom	Ha-wai-bom
Khoo-youm-them	Moongkhom	Kaithel-lakpom	Ngangkhom
Khoieangbom	Howrongbom	Ahaibom	Ngasep-pom
Laikhoojom	Eao-renbom	Moirang-moum	Laima-khoojam
Konjengbam	Akooram	Khooai-rakpam	Ashem
Moiang-lombam	Lisham	Thock-chom	Khondram

Glossary of Meitei Word(s)/Term(s)

Agaru/agar	tree, *aquilaria agallocha*
Ahonglon	an archaic song sung to venerate ancestors
Amaiba/Maichou	scholar, high priest
Amaiba Loisang	Department in charge of Royal Archives
Mangba	impure, unclean
Ametpa Loisang	College of Traditional Physicians
Anam Athou	ritual for driving off evil spirits
Apokpa	ancestor, progenitor
Aronba-macha	secret child
Ayaba-macha	accepted child
Ayokpa-macha	adopted child
Bor-senapati	Commander-in-Chief
Chak	cycles of great time orders; age
Chaboksang	hut erected for child delivery
Chakluk	food-share
Changsaba	personal bodyguard accompanying the crew
Chayom	food (eg., rice) tied in a bundle of leaves
Chei	stick
Cheithaba	person appointed by the king to bear all the calamities of the year; the man after whom the year is named
Chenba	elopement
Chellakpa	brought
Chengluk nungshang	basketful of rice offered to ancestral deities
Chingba	capture
Chinghi-uti	locally made solution from rice water for washing hair
Chingthrao	flower, *banhinia purpurea*

Chupsaba	rite observed for those who died in unnatural circumstances; also for the death of issueless couples
Enaphi	a type of shawl
Hainaba	engagement
Heloi	witch
Hei-lei	flowers and fruits
Heibi	medlar, tree with a small fruit resembling an apple
Heijingpot	ritual signifying formal announcement of marriage
Heikru	small edible fruit, *emblica officialis*
Heining	small edible fruit, *spondias magnifera*
Hidongba	crew leaders in the boat race *Heikru Hidongba*
Hinaosaba	coxswain
Hingchabi	monstress
Hiri	thread
Hiyang Tannaba	boat race
Hongnemse	an archaic term in hymns to venerate ancestors; literally translated as 'let us offer food'
Ibudhou	great grandfather
Iche	elder sister
Ihaifu	earthen pot joined by a thread to the *leiyom* at the *Lai Haraoba*
Ima	mother
Inkhol	compound
Ishaifu	pot used for carrying water from the place of *ikouba* at the *Lai Haraoba*
Kkabok	parched rice
Kai	coffin
Kang	an indigeneous game

Kangchei/kangjei	polo stick
Kausel	a cultic vessel used at the *Lai Haraoba*
Khainaba	divorce
Khajing	prawns
Khallong	a ritual article made of iron in the shape of a spoon
Khangpoksang	hut erected for a dying person
Khaobunai	attendant
Khao-taiba	stitched up to half the length width-wise
Kharai	a carrier made of small pieces of bamboo
Khayom	packet consisting of seven layers of plantain leaf containing rice, egg and *langthrei* buds tied with bamboo strips
Khuda	altar
Khubam-peeba	indication
Khullakpa	leader of *Ahallup* or elder village folk
Khura	uncle
Khurumba	to bow down; worship
Khoichu-laikham	local herbs used as incense
Konyai	gold and silver pieces
Koyet	headgear
Kujaba	to offer; intrinsic aspect of Meitei marriage
Kumshak phanek	dark coloured sarong used in coronation ceremonies
Kwakshang	hut erected for crows at the *Kwak Tanba*
Lai	god, deity
Lai amangba	impure gods, evil spirits
Laibungthou	divine youth
Lai Haraoba	festival of 'pleasing the gods'
Lainura	divine girls

Laining	way of worship
Lainingthou	god king, used for both gods and kings
Laiphi	garments for the deity
Lairembi/Lairemma	goddess, female *lai*
Lairup	community of gods
Laitongba	act of divination
Lakpa	divisional officer
Lallup Kaba	to attend forced labour
Lamchel	foot race
Lamlai	*lais* of the locality or area
Lannaba-macha	child begotten by another
Lang-ol-lakpa	to be reborn
Lap	a bamboo rack
Laplakpa	leader of *Naharup* or younger village folk
Laplel-ka	second room of a typical Meitei house
Langthrei	plant, *eupatorium birminiacium*
Leishabi	young unmarried girl
Leiyom	the cultic packet of flowers
Lepsoom	a mortar, cultic object used at the *Lai Haraoba*
Lonnaba-macha	child of a concubine
Loukhatpa	recognition of unsolemnized marriage
Lubak	bamboo basket
Luhongba	marriage
Lukmai	round basket with short legs
Maiba	priest; traditional physician
Maibi	priestess; midwife
Maigei Ngakpa	Guardian of Direction
Malem	earth; mother

Mani	jewel
Mapa Mashak-	
Khangdaba-macha	child of unknown father
Mayek Naiba	striped colourful sarong worn by women
Meerolakp- macha	child of pregnant bride
Mi	shadow
Mirup	community
Mityengphu	pot filled with water to which one's vision is focussed
Mongpham	cremation site
Mukna	Manipuri style of wrestling
Naheiba	purification rite
Namungba	taboo
Naomangthaba	real rowers in the boat race *Heikru Hidongba*
Naorongba	front rowers in the boat race *Heikru Hidongba*
Ngakra	*clarius batrachus*, common catfish
Ngamu	mudfish, *ophioccphalus harcourt butleri annandale*
Nganthak	a funnel shaped article made of clay
Ngaprum	eel
Ningol maral	property rights of unmarried girls
Ningsa	a breathing method
Nonglum	a divine cloud egg
Nupi maral	property rights of married women
Ougri	an archaic song sung for the prosperity of the land
Palem	mother
Pana	territorial division
Pandit Loisnag	College of Priests
Panthou	father

Paphal	symbolic diagrams;coiling serpent forms representing *Pakhangba*
Paya	a strip of bamboo
Pena	one stringed fiddle
Phamnaiba	a person honoured with a title by the king
Phanek	a kind of skirt/sarong worn by Meitei women, ankle length consisting of two pieces of material joined length-wise
Phida	a piece of cloth used for sitting on it
Phijet	costume
Phiroi	last rite held for the dead at the end of one year
Phungga	hearth
Phura	shrine
Phirel phurit	a long loose worn at the time of coronation
Piba	male head of a *sagei* or *salai*
Pokpa	to be born
Pokchaba-macha	legitimate child
Poktaba-macha	step child
Potyengba	ritual observed on the birth of a child where gifts are sent by the women's natal family through a procession of women
Pungphai	plant, *dactylotinium aegypticium*
Puya	A particular kind of old narratives in Manipuri literature
Sagei	sub-clan, group bearing the family name
Sagol Kangjei	a variant of modern polo
Saji	a species of deer
Salai	clan
Sanathong	south western direction
Sareng	fish, *wallago atu*
Sarik	brass metal bell

Saroi	evil spirit
Sel	a bell metal coin
Senkhai	an ancient coin
Senmit	act of divination
Shing	firewood; stick
Shingang	piece of reed
Siba	to die; to be on an errand
Sidaba	immortal
Tada	elder brother
Tairen	plant, *cedrela toona*
Thaban	Meitei lunar calender
Tharaochi	bugle like pipe made of copper
Thawai	soul; life-essence
Thinbi	a ritual article made of iron in the shape of an hour glass though not too constricted at the middle
U-hongba	initiation or inauguration ritual of a tree
Umanglai	literally forest deities, used of ancestral deities in wider context
Wangonsang	hut erected for the delivery of child
Wakma	poet
Waroipo-puba	ritual signifying the final agreement of marriage
Yathanghanba	official consent given for marriage
Yaong-inba	adoption of son-in-law, thereby moving in to the house of the father-in-law and assuming the responsibilities of a son for all purposes
Yangkok	winnowing fan
Yek	name of the *salai*
Yoirengshang	department in charge of *pena*
Yu	rice beer
Yumlai	household deity
Yumnak	name of the sub-clan
Yumsengba	sanctification rite after childbirth, death, etc.

Bibliography

I Primary Sources

A. Unpublished *Puyas* (in Manipuri)

Epudhou Thangjinggi Wahoudok, custodian, L. Suresh Singh.

Khumanlon, custodian, N. Khelchandra Singh.

Khumukchamlon, custodian, Oinam Bhogeswar Singh.

Khunung Lon, custodian, N. Khelchandra Singh.

Lai Khunta Lon, custodian, Y. Mohendra Singh.

Langthaballon, custodian, Y. Mohendra Singh.

Leimaren Naoyom, custodian Y. Mohendra Singh.

Leimaren Sekning, custodian, N. Khelchandra Singh.

Ningthou Naophangba Puya, custodian, Y. Mohendra Singh.

Ningthoujagi Meihoubaron, custodian, Y. Mohendra Singh.

Nongpok Haram, custodian, N. Khelchandra Singh.

Nongchup Haram, custodian, N. Khelchandra Singh.

Pakhanga Laihui (Handwritten copy), custodian, L. Suresh Singh.

Pakhangba Yangbi, custodian, N. Khelchandra Singh.

Pudin (Handwritten copy), custodian, Y. Mohendra Singh.

Sanamahi Laihui (Handwritten copy), custodian, Y. Mohendra Singh.

Sanamahi Laikan (Handwritten copy), custodian, N.Khelchandra Singh.

Sanggai Phammang, custodian, Y. Mohendra Singh.

Sangai Phambal, custodian, Kh. Mangi Maiba.

Sakok Wakok, custodian, Y.Mohendra Singh.

Thokchomlon, custodian, Oinam Bhogeswar Singh.

Yapirokne, custodian, Kh. Yaima.

Yukouron Puya, custodian, Y. Mohendra Singh.

B. Published *Puyas* (in Manipuri)

Athokpam, Yaima Langdum (ed.), *Khamlangba Erengba Puwari: Neinarol,* Nungpok Thouthi Kanglup, 1993.

Bamon Khunthoklon, (anon.), Yek Salai Press, Imphal, n.d.

Bhogeswar, O. (ed.), *Leimaren Mingkhei,* O.K. Store, Imphal, 1970.

Bhogeswar, O. (ed.), *Moirang Ningthourol Lambuba,* Imphal, Pt.I, 1982; Pt.II, 1988.

Chongtham, Meramcha (ed.), *Leishemlon Ariba,* Imphal, 1947.

Devi, Keisham Sobita (ed.), *Moirangthem Kangleirol,* Manipur State Museum, Imphal, 1982.

Ibochouba, N. (ed.), *Thiren Layat,* Imphal, 1981.

Kangbam, Chaoba (ed.), *Pakhangba Naoyom,* Imphal, 1989.

Khagemba Yumbi (Handwritten copy), custodian Y. Mohendra Singh.

Khuman Ningthourol (Handwritten copy), custodian Y. Mohendra Singh.

Kullachandra, B. (ed.), *Sanamahi Puya,* Universal Literary Association, Imphal, 1989.

Laimit M. and L. Iboyaima (ed.), *Wakoklon Hilel Thilel Amailon Pukok Puya,* Imphal, 1982

Malem Yaiphasang (ed.), *Wachet Lon Pathup,* Imphal, 1974.

Mayanglambam, Gourchandra, (ed.), *Thouwan Thaba Hiren,* Peoples Museum Kakching, 1982 (2nd Reprint).

Mayanglambam, Gourachandra (ed.), *Erat Thounirol*, Peoples Museum, Kakching, 1988.

Meitei, Hijam Ibopishak (ed.), *Bamon Khunthoklon*, Imphal, 1987.

Meitei, Y. Bhagya (ed.), *Sakok Lamlen Ahanba Amasung Meihouron*, Imphal, 1988.

Moirangcha, Kala (ed.), *Amai Laining Khuda Punshirol*, Imphal, 1988.

Moirangthem, Chandrasing (ed.), *Poireiton Khunthok*, Manipuri Sahitya Parishad, Imphal, 1979.

Naorem, Amuyaima (ed.), *Sanamahi Phankhong*, Imphal, 1981.

Nongthombam, Naran, *Hung Sidaba Nonglon Pathup Wachetlon Sanamahi*

Ningba Punshirol, Meitei Marup, 1982 (Reprint).

Pudin (Handwritten copy), custodian N. Khelchandra Singh.

Sharma, Pandit Atombapu (ed.), *Pakhangba*, Imphal, 1952.

Sharma, Pandit Atombapu (ed.), *Meiteigi Meihourol*, Imphal, 1952.

Singh, A. Mangi (ed.), *Chakparol*, Chakpa Phayeng, 1972.

Singh, Ch. Manihar (ed. and tr.), *Naothingkhong Phambal Kaba*, Manipur, University, Canchipur, 1983.

Singh, Irom Amubi (ed.), *Nunglon*, Ningthoumacha Manisana Keibung, n. d.

Singh, Irom Amubi (ed.), *Leihou Naophamlol*, Khagempalli Panthak, Imphal, 1981.

Singh, Kh. Chandrashekhar (ed.), *Loiyambc Shinyen*, All Manipur Umanglai

Haraoba Committee, Uripok Naoremthong, 1982.

Singh, Kh. Chandrashekhar (ed.), *Lai Haraoba Lairol*, Meitei Matek

Organising and Research Association, Uripok Naoremthong, 1982.

Singh, Kh. Chandrashekhar (ed.), *Erat Laisol*, Meitei Mayek Organising and Research Association, Uripok Naoremthong, Imphal, 1982.

Singh, Kh. Chandrashekhar (ed.), *Sakok Lamlen Ahanba Amasung Meihourol Sakok*, All Manipur Umanglai Haraoba Committee, Uripok, Imphal, 1992.

Singh, Kh. Yaima (ed.), *Pakhangba Phambal* , Imphal, 1964.

Singh, Kh. Yaima (ed.), *Poireiton Khunthokpa*, Imphal, 1971.

Singh, Kh. Yaima (ed.), *Kanglei Layat*, Manipuri Sahitya Parishad, Imphal, 1987.

Singh, L. Iboongohal and N. Khelchandra Singh (ed.), *Cheitharol Kumbaba*, Manipuri Sahitya Parishad, Imphal, 1989.

Singh, Laishram Nitya (ed.), *Hung Ningthou Kangparol Ponglol Puya Meihoupa*, Imphal, 1982.

Singh, M. Chandra (ed.), *Panthoibi Khongul*, Manipuri Sahitya Parishad, Imphal, 1987.

Singh, Naorem Amuyaima (ed.), *Khunung Eratlon*, D. Lila Singh Memorial Press, Kakching Bazar, 1980.

Singh, Naorem Amuyaima (ed.), *Yabirok*, M.D. Brothers' Publishing, Kakching, 1981.

Singh, Naorem Amuyaima (ed.), *Sanamahi Phankhong*, Soubon Yairen Chanu Liching Press, Kakching, 1981.

Singh, Naorem Amuyaima (ed.), *Panthoibi Naherol Amasung Aman Sikum Lon*, Kakching, 1986.

Singh, Naorem Amuyaima (ed.), *Tinthum*, Times Printers, Kakching Bazar, 1987.

Singh, N. Khelchandra (ed.), *Chada Laihui*, Imphal, 1966.

Singh, Ningthoukhongjam Khelchandra (ed.), *Thainagi Seirang*, Imphal, 1966.

Singh, N. Khelchandra (ed.), *Parishadki Ariba Manipuri Wareng Lairik*, Manipuri Sahitya Parishad, Imphal, 1972.

Singh, Ningthoukhongjam Khelchandra (ed.), *Naothingkhong Phambal Kaba*, Imphal, 1979.

Singh, Ningthoukhongjam Khelchandra (ed.), *Khuman Kangleirol*, Atombapu Research Centre, Imphal, 1979.

Singh, Ningthoukhongjam Khelchandra (ed.), *Chingoiron*, Manipur State Kala Academy, Imphal, 1982.

Singh, Ng. Kullachandra (ed.), *Leimaren Naoyom*, Pandit Loisang, Sanakonung, Imphal, 1969.

Singh, Ng. Kullachandra (ed.), *Apokpa Thounirol*, Manipur Pandit Loisang, Imphal, 1992.

Singh, Nongmaithem Manaoyaima (ed.), *Chengleiron*, Kakching, 1979.

Singh, Oinam Bhogeswar (ed.), *Ningthourol Lambuba*, Imphal, 1967.

Singh, Oinam Bhogeswar (ed.), *Loiyna Sinlon*, Imphal, 1967.

Singh, Oinam Bhogeswar (ed.), *Numit Kappa*, Imphal, 1986 (2nd Reprint).

Singh, Pebam Ibomcha(ed.), *Thiren Meiram Liba*, Lamboikhongnangkhong, 1992.

Singh, Thongam Madhob and N. Khelchandra Singh (ed.), *Khunung Leechat Sajat*, Imphal, 1970.

Singh, Y. Bhagya (ed.), *Pakhangba*, Yaiskul Policelane, Imphal, 1985.

Wakoklon Hilel Thilel Salai Amailon Pukok Puya, (author not mentioned), Tera Meetei Eeyek Sintam Sanglen, Imphal, 1972.

Yengkhoiba, Bhagya Singh (ed.), *Leithak Leikharon*, Imphal, 1988.

Yumnamcha, Buddhachandra (ed.), *Thaloi Nongkhailon*, Enat Kanba Amasung Semgatpa Lup, Imphal, 1985.

Yumnamcha, Buddhachandra (ed.), *Emoinu Ahongbigi Tungnapham*, Heirangoithong Keibung, 1963.

Yumnamcha, Buddhachandra (ed.), *Emoinu Ahongbigi Likhul Pomit*, Enat Kanba Amasung Semgatpa Lup, Imphal, 1992.

II Other Primary Sources

A Report on the State Archaeology Department, Directorate of Social Welfare and Arts and Culture, Government of Manipur, 1983.

Allen B.C., *Census of Assam, 1901*, Vol.1. Report, Manas Publications, 1984 (Reprint).

Allen, B.C. et.al., *Gazetteer of Bengal and North East India*, Mittal Publications, 1979 (Reprint).

Bahadur, Mutua and P. Gunindra Singh, *Epigraphical Records of Manipur*, Vol. 1, Mutua Museum, Imphal, 1986.

Bhattacharya, M., *Gazetteer of India: Manipur*, Anushilan Press, Calcutta, 1963.

Brown, R., *Selection from the Records of the Government of India*, Foreign Department, No. LXXVIII, Annual Report of the Munnipore Political Agency for 1868-69, Foreign Department Press, Calcutta, 1870.

Census of India, 1981(Series I), Paper (1984), India, Household Population by Religion of Head of Household (HH).

Dun, E.W., *Gazetteer of Manipur*, 1886, Manas Publications, Delhi, 1992 (Reprint).

Grierson, G.A., *Linguistic Survey of India*, Vol.III, Pt.II, 1903; Vol III, Pt.III, 1904, Motilal Banarsidas, Delhi, 1967 (Reprint).

Memoranda on Native States in India, Superintendent Government Printing, Calcutta, 1909.

The Imperial Gazetteer of India, Vol. XVII, The Clarendon Press, Oxford, 1908 (Reprint).

Parratt, Saroj Nalini Arambam (tr.), *The Court Chronicle of the Kings of Manipur:The Cheitharon Kumpapa*, Routledge, New York, 2005.

III Secondary Sources

Abraham, Francis M., *Modern Sociological Theory*, Oxford University Press, Delhi, 1988.

Ahern, Emily M., *The Cult of the Dead in a Chinese Village*, Stanford University Press, Stanford, 1973.

Amubi, L., *Sajibu Cheiraoba*, Imphal, 1980.

Anesaki, Masaharu, *History of Japanese Religion*, Charles E. Tuttle Co., Tokyo, 1928.

Angom, Sudhir, *Yek Taretki Ningthourol*, City Press, Imphal, n. d.

Aron, Raymond (tr. R. Howard and H.Weaver), *Main Currents in Sociological Thought*, Vol.2, Penguin Books Ltd., Harmondsworth, 1982 (Reprint).

Asokumar, L., "Christagi Mamangi Manipur Umanglaigi", *Seminar on Cultural History of Manipur before 33 A.D.*, International Society for Cultural Studies, Imphal, Sept. 22-23, 1990.

Banton, Michael (ed.), *Anthropological Approaches to the Study of Religion,* Tavistock Publications Ltd., London, 1969, (3rd Reprint).

Beattie, John, *Other Cultures*, The Free Press, New York, 1964.

Berger, Peter L., *The Social Reality of Religion*, Penguin Books, Harmondsworth, 1967.

Bhattacharyya, N.N., *History of the Tantric Religion*, Manohar Publications, New Delhi, 1982.

Bloch, M. and J. Parry (ed.), *Death and the Regeneration of Life*, Cambridge University Press, New York, 1986 (Reprint).

Bohannan, Paul, *Social Anthropology*, Holt, Rinehart and Winston Inc., New York, 1963.

Bokul, T., *Moirang Thangjing Haraoba*, Imphal, 1964.

Bokul, T., *Cheiraoba Ishaiphu Latpa*, Meitei Marup, 1968.

Bokul, T., *Meitei Enat*, Imphal, 1983.

Brown, R., *Statistical Account of Manipur*, Sanskaran Prakashak, Delhi, 1975 (Reprint).

Bunce, W.K., *Religion in Japan*, Charles E. Tuttle Co., Tokyo, 1955.

Chaki-Sircar, Manjusri, *Feminism in a Traditional Society: Women of the Manipur Valley*, Shakti Books, New Delhi, 1984.

Chatterji, S.K., *Kirata-Jana-Kriti : The Indo-Mongoloids and their Contribution to the History and Culture of India*, The Asiatic Society, Calcutta, 1974.

Chibb, S.S., *Castes, Tribes and Culture of India: North East India*, Vol.8, S.S. Publications, New Delhi, 1988.

Clark, L.O., *A Vocabulary Manipuri to English Dictionary,* Manipuri State Archives, 1924.

Cultural Heritage of Manipur (author not mentioned), Department of Arts and Culture, Manipur, n. d.

Devi, H. Bilasini (ed.), *Manipur University Museum Bulletin,* Vol.2, Manipur University, Canchipur, 1982.

Devi, Kh. Sarojini (ed.), *National Register of Private Records and Manuscripts,* Vol. I, Manipur State Archives, 1987.

Devi, K. Sobita, *Hiyang Hiren*, Manipur State Museum, Imphal, 1988.

Devi, L. Basanti, *A Study of Political History of Manipur from Pakhangba to Khagemba (33-1652 A.D.),* Unpublished Ph.D. Thesis, Manipur University, Canchipur, 1988.

Devi, L. Kunjeswori, *A Study of Archaeology in Manipur since Pre-historic Times*, Unpublished Ph.D. Thesis, Manipur University, Canchipur, 1989.

Devi, L. Sanajaobi, *A Study in History and Culture of Manipur (1597-1709),* M.Phil. Dissertation, Manipur University, Canchipur, 1988.

Devi, N. Ekasini, *Meitei Amaibisinggi Lai Tingi Oiba Mahei,* M.Phil. Dissertation, Manipur University, Canchipur, 1988.

Devi, N. Pramodini, *The Cultural History of Early Manipur,* Unpublished Ph.D. Thesis, Manipur University, Canchipur, 1987.

Devi, N. Pramodini, *Numit Kappa and Panthoibi Khongun: A Study of Socio-economic and Politico-religious Aspects of Early Manipur,* Times Printers Publishing House, Kakching, 1988.

Devi, P. Binodini (ed.), *Manipur University Museum Bulletin,* Vol. 3, Manipur University, 1988.

Devi, P. Parvabati, *The History of Rise and Growth of Hinduism in Manipur from the Earliest Times to the Beginning of the 19th Century A.D.*, Unpublished Ph.D. Thesis, Manipur University, Canchipur, 1987.

Dubey, S.M. (ed.), *North East India : A Sociological Study*, Concept Publishing Company, Delhi, 1978.

Durkheim, Emile (tr. J. W. Swain), *The Elementary Forms of the Religious Life*, The Free Press, New York, 1965.

Elaide, Mircea (ed.), *The Encyclopaedia of Religion*, Vol. 12, Macmillan Publishing Company, New York, 1987.

Elwin, Verrier (ed.), *India's North-East Frontier in the Nineteenth Century*, Oxford University Press, London, 1959.

Exhibition of Old Manipuri Manuscripts and Academi Publications, (author not mentioned) Manipur State Kala Academy, 1989.

Gennep, Arnold Van (tr. M. B. Vizedon and G. L. Caffee), *The Rites of Passage*, The University of Chicago Press, Chicago, 1966 (4th Edition).

Ghosh, G.K., *Environment: A Spiritual Dimension*, Ashish Publishing House, New Delhi, 1991.

Ghosh, G.K., *Tribals and their Culture : Manipur and Nagaland*, Vol. 3, Ashish Publishing House, New Delhi, 1992.

Giddens, Anthony (ed.), *Emile Durkheim: Selected Writings*, Cambridge University Press, New York, 1985 (Reprint).

Gogoi, L., *The Tai Khamtis of the North East*. Omsons Publications, New Delhi, 1990 (2nd Revised and Enlarged Edition).

Gogoi, Padmeswar, *The Tai and the Tai Kingdoms*, Department of Publications, Gauhati University, Gauhati, 1968.

Goody, Jack, *Death, Property and the Ancestors*, Tavistock Publications, London, 1962.

Gourmani, T., *Ancient Cult and Culture of Manipur*, Imphal, n. d.

Gould, Julius and W. L. Kolb (ed.), *A Dictionary of the Social Sciences*, Tavistock Publications, London, 1962.

Gunindra, P., *Manipuri Numismatics*, Mutua Museum, Imphal, 1983.

Gwinn, Robert P. et.al., (ed.), *The New Encyclopaedia Britannica: Micropaedia, Knowledge in Depth*, Vol.17, Encyclopaedia Britannica Inc., University of Chicago, (15th Edition), 1988.

Hastings, James (ed.), *Encyclopaedia of Religion and Ethics*, Vol. I, New York, 1959 (4th Impression).

Herkovits, Melville J., *Cultural Anthropology*, Oxford and IBH Publishing Company, New Delhi, 1974 (2nd Indian Reprint).

Hodson, T.C., *The Meitheis*, Low Price Publication, Delhi, 1989 (Reprint).

Hoffman, Helmut (tr. Edward Fritzerland), *The Religions of Tibet*, G.A. and Unwinn Ltd., London, 1961.

Hsu, Francis L.K., *Under the Ancestors' Shadow*, Stanford University Press, Stanford, 1971.

Ichiro, Hori (ed.), *Japanese Religion*, Kondansha International Ltd., Tokyo, 1972.

Irom, Amubi, *Sajiphu Cheiraoba Singsatpagi Maong*, Khagempalli Panthak, Imphal, 1990.

Jaiswal, Suvira, *The Origin and Development of Vaisnavism*, Munshiram Manoharlal Publishers Pvt. Ltd., New Delhi, 1981.

Jevons, F.B., *The History of Religion*, Orient Publications, Delhi, 1985 (Reprint).

Johnstone, R. L., *Religion and Society in Interaction : The Sociology of Religion*, Prentice Hall Inc., New Jersey, 1975.

Johnstone, Maj. Gen. Sir James, *Manipur and the Naga Hills*, Cultural Publishing House, 1983 (Reprint).

Jugindro, N., *Chakpa Haraoba*, Sangeet Kala Sangam, Khurai Lamlong Bazaar, 1992.

Kabui, Gangumei, *History of Manipur (Pre-Colonial Period)*, Vol. I, National Publishing House, New Delhi, 1991.

Karve, Irawati, *Kinship Organisation in India*, Asia Publishing House, Bombay, 1968.

Khare, R.S. (ed.), *The Eternal Food : Gastronomic Ideas, Experiences of Hindus and Buddhists*, State University of New York Press, Albany, 1992.

Kirk, G.S., *Myth: Its Meaning and Functions*, California University Press, London, 1970.

La Capra, E.D., *Emile Durkheim : Sociologist and Philosopher*, Cornell University Press, Ithaca, 1972.

Laininghan, Naoriya Phullo, *Ahan Yathang*, Meitei Marup, Imphal, 1972.

Lainingthou Sanamahi Laining (author not mentioned), The Laiyingthou Sanamahi Temple Board, Imphal, 1981.

Lainingthou Sanamahi Laining (author not mentioned), The Laiyingthou Sanamahi Temple Board, Imphal, 1982.

Lai Tomba, *Meitei Yek Salai*, Imphal. 1989 (2nd Reprint).

Leach, E.R., *Political Systems of Highland Burma : A Study of Kachin Social Structure*, Beacon Press, Boston, 1968 (3rd Reprint).

Leach, Maria (ed.), *Standard Dictionary of Folklore, Mythology and Legend*, Vol. 2, Funk and Wagnalls, New York, 1950.

Lessa, W.A. and Vogt, E.Z. (ed.), *Reader in Comparative Religion: An Anthropological Approach*, Row, Peterson and Company, New York, 1958.

Levy Jr., M.J., *Modernisation and the Structure of Societies : A Setting for International Affairs*, Princeton University Press, 1966.

Lightfoot, Loiuse, *Dance Rituals of Manipur, India*, Times standard Press Ltd, Hongkong, 1958.

Lowie, Robert H., *Primitive Religion*, Peter Owen Ltd., London, 1960.

Luce, G.H., *Phases of Pre-Pagan Burma*, Vol. I, Oxford University Press, 1985.

Mair, Lucy, *An Introduction to Social Anthropology*, Oxford University Press, Delhi, 1937 (Reprint).

Mangi, A., "Chakpa Haraoba", *Seminar on Lai Haraoba*, Manipur State Kala Academy, Imphal, Apr. 22-26, 1987.

Manijao, N., *Pombi- Lang*, O.K.Stores, Imphal, 1986 (Reprint).

Max Muller, F., *Anthropological Religion*, Asian Educational Services, New Delhi, 1977 (Reprint).

Moirangcham Kala, *Amai Laining Khuda Punshirol*, Imphal, 1988.

Mbiti, John S., *African Religions and Philosophy*, Heinemann Educational Books Ltd., London, 1971 (Reprint).

McCulloch, W., *An Account of the Valley of Munnipore*, Gian Publications, Delhi, 1980 (Reprint).

Mundkur, Balaji, *The Cult of the Serpent: An Interdisciplinary Survey of its Manifestations and Origins*, State University of the New York Press, Albany, 1983.

Naorem, Amuyaima, *Manipurda Phura Saba Houdokpa*, Imphal, 1989.

Naorem, A. M. and Th. S. Luwang, *Taoroinai Yangbi Lamlen*, Chingtam Yek Salai Sana Kangleipak Laining, Meitei Sana Leipak, 1971.

Naorem, Sanajaoba (ed.), *Manipur: Past and Present*, Vol. I, Mittal Publications, New Delhi, 1988.

Naorem, Sanajaoba (ed.), *Manipur: Past and Present*, Vol. II, Mittal Publications, New Delhi, 1991.

Naoriya Phulo, *Meitei Houpham Wari*, Imphal, 1980.

Naoriya Phulo, *Ahan Yathang*, Imphal, 1982.

Newell, William H., *Ancestors*, Modern Publishers, The Hague, Paris, 1976.

Nongthombam, Naran, *Angang Ipan Thaba Thouram Pareng Asuba, Meitei Marup*, Imphal, 1976 (Reprint).

Nongthombam, Naran, *Ahalna Nahada Apokpa Khurambagi Wari Liba*, Imphal, 1981.

Nongthombam, Naran, *Nonglom Pathup Wachetlon*, Lanthaban Mayai Leikai, 1982 (Reprint).

Nongthombam, Naran, *Ahalna Nahada Laining Lambigi Paotak*, Meitei Marup, Imphal, 1984.

Nongthombamcha, Mangang Mera, *Eikhoigi Thouramlon*, Kangla Sangumsang, 1989.

Norbeck, Edward, *Religion in a Primitive Society*, Harper and Brothers Publishers, New York, 1961.

Ono, Sokyo, *Shinto: The Kami Way*, Charles E. Tuttle Co., Tokyo, 1964.

Pandey, S.N. (ed.), *Sources of the History of Manipur and the Adjoining Areas,* National Publishing House, Delhi, 1985.

Parratt, S.N., *The Religion of Manipur : Beliefs, Rituals and Historical Developments,* Firma KLM Pvt. Ltd., Calcutta, 1980.

Parratt, Saroj N. Arambam and John Parratt, *The Pleasing of the Gods: Meitei Lai Haraoba,* Vikas Publishing House Pvt. Ltd., New Delhi, 1997.

Pemberton, R.B., *The Eastern Frontier of India,* Mittal Publications, Delhi, 1979 (Reprint).

Phayre, Lt. Gen. Sir A.P., *History of Burma,* London, 1967.

Radcliff- Brown, A.R., *Structure and Function in Primitive Society,* Cohen and West Ltd., London, 1956 (Reprint).

Radin, Paul, *Primitive Religion*, Dover Publications, New York, 1957.

Rajkumar, Sanahal, *Satjal*, Pt. I, Imphal, 1970 (Reprint).

Rawlenson, George, *The Religions of the Ancient world,* Award Publishing House (Indian Edition), New Delhi, 1980.

Rivers, W.H.R., *The Todas,* Vol. II, Rawat Publications, Jaipur, 1980.

Robertson, Roland (ed.), *Sociology of Religion: Selected Readings,* Penguin Books, Harmondsworth, 1971 (Reprint).

Roy, Jyotirmoy, *History of Manipur*, Eastlight Book House, Calcutta, 1973. (2nd Reprint).

Sanabam, Mangang, *Meitei Law and Hindu Law: Compared and Contrasted*, Imphal, 1991.

Sangermano, V., *The Burmese Empire*, B.R. Publishing Corporation, Delhi, 1984 (Reprint).

Scott, Sir J.G., *Burma: From the Earliest Times to the Present Day*, T. Fisher Unwin Ltd., London, 1924.

Sekho, M., "Moirang Thangjing Haraoba", *Seminar on Lai Haraoba,* Manipur State Kala Academy, Imphal, Apr.22-26, 1987.

Seligman, E.R.A and A. Johnson(ed.), *Encyclopaedia of the Social Sciences,* Vol.5, The Macmillan Co., New York, 1931.

Segei, Jokarev, *History of Religion,* Progress Publishers, Moscow, 1989.

Shakespear, J., "The Religion of Manipur", *Transactions of the Folklore Society,* Vol.24, No.4, Calcutta, Dec. 1913.

Shastri, D.R., *Origin and Development of the Rituals of Ancestor Worship in India,* Bookland Pvt. Ltd., Calcutta, 1963.

Sills, David L. (ed.), *International Encyclopaedia of the Social Sciences,* Vol. 3, The Macmillan Company and The Free Press, New York. 1968.

Sinha, Surajit (ed.), *Tribals and North Eastern India,* K.P.Bagchi and Co., Calcutta, 1987.

Singer, Milton (ed.), *Krishna: Myths, Rites and Attitudes,* East-West Centre Press, Honolulu, 1966.

Singh, Bhagya Y., *Pakhangba,* Yaiskul Policelane, Imphal, 1983.

Singh, Ch. Kaomacha, *Manipur Itibritta,* Imphal, 1940.

Singh, Ch. Manihar, "Meiteigi Ariba Laining", *Journal of Manipur Sahitya Parishad,* Sl. No. 58/59, Vol. 16, Imphal, 1985.

Singh, Ch. Manihar, "Lai Haraoba", *International Cultural Festival Conference,* Imphal, Nov.27-Dec.2, 1991.

Singh, E. Nilakanta, "Manipur- A Land of Dance", *Folklore,* Vol. 2, No. 4, Calcutta, Jul-Aug., 1961.

Singh, E. Nilakanta, *Fragments of Manipuri Culture,* Omsons Publications, New Delhi, 1993.

Singh, Irom Amubi, *Meitei Thouni Lichat,* Khagempalli Panthak, Imphal, 1990.

Singh, J.P and Gautam Sengupta (ed.), *Archaeology of North Eastern India,* Vikas Publishing House Pvt. Ltd., New Delhi, 1991.

Singh, Kalachand, *Sagei Salailon*, O.K Store , Imphal , 1965.

Singh, Kh. Chandrashekhar (ed.), *Umanglai Khunda* , No.4 (1980), No. 5/6 (1981) , No. 7/8 (1981), No. 9/10 (1982), No. 15/16 (1984), No. 19/20 (1984), No. 23/24 (1986).

Singh, Khullem Chandrashekhar, *Lai Haraoba Lairol*, Meitei Mayek Organising and Research Assn., Uripok, Imphal , 1982.

Singh, Konjengbam Dhan, *Meitei Puya Wari Machang*, Imphal, 1978.

Singh, L. Asokumar, "Meiteigi Ariba Laining Leechat", *Seminar on Meetei Religion:Laining*, Universal Literary Assn., Manipur, Oct.30, 1988.

Singh, Ksh. Brajamohon, *Yakeiron*, Peoples Museum, Kakching, Manipur, 1991.

Singh, L. Bhagyachandra, *A Critical Study of the Religious Philosophy of the Meeteis before the Advent of Vaisnavism in Manipur*, Imphal, 1991.

Singh, L. Iboongohal, *Introduction to Manipur*, Sagolband, Imphal, 1963 (2nd Edition).

Singh, M. Kirti, "Vaisnab Dharmana Changlaktringei", *Seminar on Manipurgi Samajda Dharmagi Yaol*, The Cultural Forum, Imphal, Dec. 25, 1983.

Singh, M. Kirti, *Religious Developments in Manipur in the 18th and 19th Centuries*, Manipur State Kala Academy, Imphal, 1980.

Singh, M. Kirti, *Religion and Culture of Manipur*, Manas Publications, Delhi, 1988.

Singh, M. Kirti, *Folk Culture of Manipur*. Manas Publications, Delhi, 1993.

Singh, Mutua Jhulan (tr. Y. Khoimacha Singh et.al), *Bejoy Punchalee or History of Manipur*, Part I, Imphal, 1936 (3rd Edition).

Singh, Mutua Jhulan, *Sahitya Itihas (History of Manipur Literature)*, Imphal, 1950.

Singh, Naorem Amuyaima, *Khunung Eratlon*, Kakching, 1980.

Singh, N. Birachandra, "Ancestor Worship among the Meiteis with Special Reference to Family Ancestors", *Proceedings of the North East India History Assn.*, 3rd Session, Imphal, 1982.

Singh, N. Birachandra, "Traditional Rituals of the Meiteis", *Seminar on Ancient History of Manipur*, S. R. Institute of Manipur Studies, Imphal, 1987.

Singh, N. Birachandra, *Socio-religious Life of the Meiteis in the 18th Century A.D.*, Unpublished Ph.D. Thesis, Manipur University, Canchipur, 1987.

Singh, N. Birachandra, "Kings and Emperors who Reigned in Manipur Before the Christian Era", *Seminar on Cultural History of Manipur Before 33 A.D.*, International Society for Cultural Studies, Imphal, Sept. 22-23, 1990.

Singh, N. Khelchandra, *Manipuri to Manipuri and English Dictionary,* Uripok, Imphal, 1964.

Singh, N. Khelchandra, *Ariba Manipuri Sahityagi Itihas,* Imphal, 1969.

Singh, N. Khelchandra, *Manipur Itihas,* Imphal, 1970.

Singh, N. Khelchandra, *Ariba Manipuri Lonjei*, Manipur State Kala Academy, Imphal, 1978.

Singh, N. Khelchandra (ed.), *A Catalogue of Manipuri Manuscripts*, Manipuri Sahitya Parishad, Imphal, 1984.

Singh, N. K., " Marriage by Elopement Among the Meiteis of Manipur", *Man in India*, Vol. 53, Jun, 1973.

Singh, N. Shyam, *Lois in Manipur: A Case Study of Andro*, M.Phil. Dissertation, Manipur University, Canchipur, 1988.

Singh, Ng. Kullachandra, *Meitei Lai Haraoba*, Manipuri Raj Pandit Loisang Sanakhong, 1953.

Singh, Ng. Kullachandra, *Apokpa Thounirol*, Manipuri Raj Pandit Loisang, Imphal, 1992,

Singh, O. Ibochouba, *Sculpture of Manipur*, Mutua Museum, Bulletin No.2, Imphal, December, 1982.

Singh, O. Ibochouba, *Manipur Temple Architecture*, Mutua Museum, Bulletin No. 3, Imphal, August, 1983.

Singh, O.K., *Archaeology in Manipur*, State Archaeology: Arts and Culture Department, Imphal, 1988.

Singh, P. Gunindra (ed.), *Catalogue of Manuscripts and Manuscript Paintings of Manipur*, Mutua Museum, Keishampat, Imphal, 1987.

Singh, R.K. Jhalajit, *A Short History of Manipur*, O.K. Stores Book Sellers and Publishers, Imphal, 1965.

Singh, R.K. Jhalajit, *Manipur*, Publication Divisions, New Delhi, 1975.

Singh, R.K. Jhalajit, *A History of Manipuri Literature*, Imphal, 1987.

Singh, R.K. Sanahal, *Manipur Itihas*, Imphal, 1947.

Singh, R.K. Sanahal (ed.), *Glimpses of Manipur*, Imphal, 1951.

Singh, R.K. Sanahal, *Peeps into Manipur*, Rajkumar Publications, Imphal, 1985.

Singh, W. Yumjao, *Report on the Archaeological Studies in Manipur*, No.1, Manipur State Library, 1936.

Singh, W. Yumjao, *Manipur Itihas*, Imphal, 1950.

Singh, W. Yumjao, *An Early History of Manipur*, Imphal, 1966.

Singh, W. Yumjao, *Religious Belief of Ancient Manipur*, Imphal, 1966.

Singh, W. Yumjao, *Archaic Meitei or Early Manipuri Monograph on Early Manipuri Monograph on Archaic Meitei*, Imphal, 1985

Singh, W. Lukhoi, *Lai Haraoba*, Imphal, 1989.

Singh, Y. Mahindra and N. Birachandra Singh, *Nongda Lairen Pakhangba Hourakpham Thiba*, Manipur Research Society, Imphal, 1981.

Smith, Robert J., *Ancestor Worship in Contemporary Japan*, Stanford University Press, Stanford, 1974.

Sougaijam, Iboyaima, *Lainingthou Sanamahina Haying Khongbal Tolong Yumpham Sana Sanggaida Lengsillakpa*, Lainingthou Sanamahi Temple Board, Imphal, 1991.

Spencer, Paul (ed.), *Society and the Dance: The Social Anthropology and Performance*, Cambridge University Press, 1985.

Srinivas, M.N. et al. (ed.), *A Survey Research in Sociology and Social Anthropology*, Vol. II, Popular Prakashan, Bombay, 1974.

Thokchom, Rajo Maibi, *Lang-ol*, Imphal, 1977.

Tomba, T., "Chakpa Phayengda Sidabi Thouramsing", *Seminar on Manipuri Sibagi Laihousing*, Manipur Folklore Society, Imphal, May 26, 1990.

Temple, Col. R.C., " Some Account of the Thirty Seven Nats (Royal Ghosts) of the Burmese", *Journal of Indian Art and Industry*, Vol. IX, No. 70, London, October 1992.

Uberoi, Patricia (ed.), *Family, Kinship and Marriage in India*, Oxford University Press, Delhi, 1993.

Waddell, L.A., *The Tribes of the Brahmaputra Valley*, Logos Press, New Delhi, 1986 (1st Indian Report).

Watt, George, " The Aboriginal Tribes of Manipur", *Journal of the Anthropological Institute*, Vol.16, London, 1887.

Westropp, Hodder M. and C. Staniland Wake, *Ancient Symbol Worship: Influence of the Phallic Idea in the Religions of Antiquity*, Curzon Press Ltd., London, 1972 (2nd Edition).

Yinger, Milton J., (ed.), *Religion, Society and the Individual*, The Macmillan Company, New York, 1957.

Index

A

Amaiba Loisang, 13
Ametpa Loisang, 127
Ancestor worship, 8, 14, 16, 23, 59, 66, 67, 72, 124, 131, 139, 198
Annam, 2
Apokpa Khurumba, 135, 147
Aryans, 4, 5
Assam, 2, 4, 8, 57
Atingkok, 45, 70, 97

B

Baruni hill, 187
Brahmanas, 8, 10, 22, 24, 54, 58, 59, 202
Brahmanisation, 58
Buddhism,187
Burma, 4, 13, 18

C

Caste, 57
Chada Laihui, 48
Chaks, 68
Cheitharol Kumbaba, 7, 12, 14, 20, 21, 48, 85, 98, 100, 127, 144, 164, 201
China, 107
Christianity, 187
Clan ancestors, 89-90
Cosmic significance, 33
Cremation, 145

D

Deified kings, 93
Deities,
  human beings worshipped as, 90
Divine egg, 104, 105

E

Egypt, 107
Evil spirits, 141

F

Family, 56
Father/fatherhood, 33
Festivals (of Meitei),
  Cheiraoba, 157-162
  Chinggoi Iruppa, 162-163
  Heikru Hidongba, 163
  Hiyang Tannaba, 164-165

Kwak Tanba, 166-167
Lai Keithel Kaba, 168-169
Mera Mentongba, 186
see also Lai Haraoba
Food offering, 148
Functionalist school, 31, 34

G

Garibniwaz (King), 87
Genealogies, 46, 47
Gods, 72, 73
Gotra, 57, 58
Guardians of directions, 84

H

Hangko age, 67, 68
Haya Chak, 144
Hinduism, 54, 55

I

Ima Guru, 128, 129
Imoinu worship,83
Immortal Lord, 72, 73, 96
India, 7
Inheritance, 56
Ipanthaba ritual, 141

K

Kami, 76
Kangla, 37, 39, 81, 89, 105, 109, 171
Kanglei Haraoba, 172
Khasis, 2
Khagemba, 94, 95, 109
Kinship, 199
Kokthok-Chamthokpa, 140
Kuki-Chin, 4, 6

L

Lai Haraoba (festival), 5, 50, 93, 126, 128, 134, 157, 169-172, 173, 185, 200
and other festivals, 156-190
Chakpa haraoba, 179
Kakching haraoba, 181
Kanglei haraoba, 172
Moirang haraoba, 182
see Festivals (of Meitei)
Land, 55
Lallup system, 203
Legitimation, 32, 33, 34
Lois, 57, 58
Loiyumba Shinyen, 46

M

Mahabharata, 5
Maiba, 125, 126
Maibis, 55, 126, 127, 128
Maigei Ngakpas, 84
Manipur,
antiquity of coinage in, 18
location, 1
myth of origin of, 5
names of, 1
Marriage, 50, 51, 52
Meitei(s), 2, 6, 7, 58, 59
confederacy, 35, 38, 46
kinship system among, 47, 48

language, 2, 3
mayek, 10, 20
pantheon, 66-111
salais, 36, 37, 38, 39, 40, 42, 43, 44
social organization, 31-59
Myth of Creation, 68-71

N

Ningthouja, 105
Ningthourol Lambuba, 10, 14, 21
Nongshaba, 82
Numit Kappa Puya, 18

P

Pakhangba, 43, 44, 80, 102-110
Pana system, 52
Pandit Loisang, 188, 200
Pangal Guru, 81
Paphal, 106, 107
Persia, 107
Pharyang Copper Plate, 10, 17
Phungga Apokpa Khurumba, 136, 137
Piba, 49, 52, 53
Prayer, 67
Puran Meithaba, 13
Puyas, 8, 11, 12, 13, 14, 16, 17, 19, 22, 24, 35, 41
types of, 11

R

Rebirth, 111
Religion, 31, 32, 33, 35, 188
Religious history, 78
Rituals,
and ritual specialists, 124-150
community, 189
death, 143-147
for ancestors, 125
marriage, 142-143

S

Salai Apokpas, 86
Sanamahi, 42,72, 95, 96-102
Sagei Apokpa Khurumba, 134, 135
Sati, 54
Serpent, 110
Seven Years War, 13
Shamanism, 125
Society, 31, 32
Sonship, 55
State Kala Academy, 11

T

Taibangpanba Mapu, divine family of, 79
Time orders, 67
Chak, 67
Hangko, 67
Todas, 46
Tribal religion, 23
Tripura, 8, 57

U

Ultimate Father, 77, 81, 102, 145

Umanglais, 76, 77, 78, 79, 198

V

Vaisnavism, 1, 57, 66, 202

W

West Bengal, 8, 57
West Town China, 45
Widow remarriage, 53
Women,
status of among Meiteis, 200, 201

Y

Yek clan exogamy, 50

■■■